AMERICAN DANCE

The Complete Illustrated History

MARGARET FUHRER

Foreword by Alicia Graf Mack

First published in 2014 by Voyageur Press, an imprint of Quarto Publishing Group USA Inc.,
400 First Avenue North, Suite 400, Minneapolis, MN 55401 USA

Voyageur Press titles are also available at discounts in bulk quantity for industrial or sales-promotional use.
For details write to Special Sales Manager at Quarto Publishing Group USA Inc., 400 First Avenue North,
Suite 400, Minneapolis, MN 55401 USA.

To find out more about our books, visit us online at www.voyageurpress.com.

ISBN-13: 978-0-7603-4599-3

Library of Congress Cataloging-in-Publication Data
Fuhrer, Margaret.
American dance : the complete illustrated history / Margaret Fuhrer.
        pages cm
Summary: "A lavishly illustrated history of American dance; covers more than four centuries, from Native
American ceremonial dances to the early 21st century; written by journalist and dancer Margaret Fuhrer"--
Provided by publisher.
ISBN 978-0-7603-4599-3 (hardback)
1. Dance--United States--History. 2. Modern dance--United States--History. I. Title.
GV1623.F84 2014
792.80973--dc23
                              2014022261

Editor: Grace Labatt
Design Manager: James Kegley
Cover: Carol Holtz
Page designer: Kim Winscher
Layout: Diana Boger

Cover photo: Martha Graham performing in *Letter to the World*, a ballet about the life of poet Emily
Dickinson, in 1940. Photo by Barbara Morgan. *Getty Images*

Frontis photo: Alonzo King LINES Ballet dancers Keelan Whitmore and Caroline Rocher.
Photograph by R. J. Muna, courtesy Alonzo King LINES Ballet

TOC photos: (l to r, row 1) *Jose Gil, Shutterstock; Library of Congress; Photofest; Lisa Green of Stephen
Green Photography, courtesy MOMENTA; Getty Images;* (l to r, row 2) *Laurent Paillier, photodanse.com;
Grant Halverson; © Julie Lemberger, 2014; Universal, Photofest; WireImage, Getty Images*

Printed in China
10 9 8 7 6 5 4 3 2 1

To Mom and Dad

Contents

1

2

6

7

8

Foreword

It is easy to pretend that we are original artistic creatures, sprung from our teachers and mentors with distinct thoughts and uniqueness of character. Especially for those of us who consider ourselves artists, it is our greatest virtue to be mavericks—to be the results of our own hard work and independent artistic discoveries. But that is not true. Not for me, and not for any dancer.

I am a product of the history of dance in America. As much as I would like to believe that my movement quality is entirely my own, I am the perfect embodiment of the diversity and rich legacies of the dance pioneers who shaped what American dance is today.

As a young child I dreamed of becoming a professional dancer. My bedroom walls were filled with 8x10 black-and-white photos of Cynthia Gregory, Virginia Johnson, Judith Jamison, and Gregory Hines, along with the iconic Harvey Edwards poster of a ballet dancer's legs, adorned in tattered leg warmers and shoes and poised in a tight fifth position. For me, those images symbolized what it meant to be a dancer. There were the perfect beauty, power, and grace of the performance photos, and the dedication and sacrifice of the dancer in training, always striving for perfection. The walls of my room became my vision board, providing clarity for my dreams.

I trained at a small modern dance school in Maryland, where the teachers used a syllabus based on the legacy of the post-modern masters of the American dance world. The ballet school where I received my formal classical training recognized that an American ballerina should have a knowledge of all the methods of ballet, including Royal Academy of Dance, Vaganova, and Cecchetti. Besides the hours of Olympic-like training in the studio, I lived on pop music, and studied the videos of Michael Jackson, Janet Jackson, and MC Hammer. In the 1990s, I worshipped hip hop artists like it was my religion.

And so, like my own racial make-up, I am a dance mutt. I am American ballet, modern, jazz, and commercial dance. Reading the chapters of Margaret Fuhrer's *American Dance* is like discovering my family tree. I can trace my own dance lineage through my teachers and directors, all the way back to the days of America's first social dances, the Ballets Russes, and the early evolution of modern dance.

From my work with Arthur Mitchell and the Dance Theatre of Harlem, with the technical precision and jazzy hips of the Balanchine style, to the grounded, soul-stirring repertoire of the Alvin Ailey American Dance Theater, my career has spanned the entire spectrum of American dance. Flipping from dancing the *Nutcracker* Grand Pas de Deux to performing Ailey's *Revelations* was no easy feat. But I was prepared. Being a dance mutt has its advantages.

American Dance celebrates the rich history and diversity of the way our nation communicates through movement. In the same breath, we are the product and the pioneers. If "dance is the hidden language of the soul," as Martha Graham declared, then the human capacity for developing movement systems speaks volumes to the artistry, intellect, and passions of the human spirit, made manifest through dance.

Alicia Graf Mack, 2014

Alvin Ailey American Dance Theater's Alicia Graf Mack.
Photograph by Andrew Eccles

Alicia Graf Mack dances with Alvin Ailey American Dance Theater. She has been a principal dancer with Dance Theatre of Harlem and a member of Complexions Contemporary Ballet, and has received the Columbia University Medal of Excellence and Smithsonian *magazine's Young Innovator Award.*

Introduction

What *is* "American dance"? How do American bodies move?

The United States is overwhelmingly a nation of immigrants. Waves upon waves of newcomers brought with them the traditional tarantellas, jigs, and other dance rituals of their home countries. The ceremonial dances of Native Americans, though brutally repressed by European settlers, also make up a piece of this cultural crazy quilt. But no single dance connects all Americans to their fellow countrymen and women. No one way of moving unites the people of the United States. So what is distinctly American about American dance?

In the nineteenth century, as the adolescent nation struggled to establish its identity, some artists searched for an American aesthetic—not in bodies, but in images and words. The painters of the Hudson River School looked for it in the pastoral settings of the Adirondacks and the Catskills. Their landscapes juxtaposed peaceful agricultural scenes with the untamed beauty of nearby wildernesses, locating an American ideal at the intersection of the two. Writer James Fenimore Cooper made Natty Bumppo, a courageous frontiersman who grew up among the Delaware Indians, the hero of his *Leatherstocking Tales*. In Bumppo, Cooper created a "knight of the woods"—a New World reimagining of an Old World fictional tradition. Like the Hudson River painters, Cooper saw the combination of ruggedness and nobility as quintessentially American.

But what of American dance? Nearly one hundred years later, when concert dance began to take solid root in the United States, some of its leading choreographers thought in a similarly self-conscious way about what American dance should look like and sought to impose their vision on the newly evolving form. Martha Graham channeled the American pioneer spirit in her technique, which was at once earthbound and sweepingly grand. Her choreography lionized the individual, the independent trailblazer who pushed courageously forward into new worlds, just as America's early settlers had. She was particularly drawn to the kinds of frontier stories that—thanks in part to writers like Cooper—had become part of the United States' creation myth. "We must look to America," she said, "to bring forth an art as powerful as America itself."[1]

It took a foreign-born artist to make ballet, that most courtly of the European arts, look and feel American. Choreographer George Balanchine, a product of the Russian ballet tradition, found inspiration in the hard-driving American spirit—and in the majestic landscapes of the twentieth-century United States. "There is that love of bigness that is so important a part of the ballet," he said. "The skyscrapers, vast fields, gigantic machines, all make for thrilling spectacles."[2] With dancers as his brushes, Balanchine, like a Hudson River School painter, shaped works that blended wildness and bigness with refinement. He especially loved the Wild West—he often wore bolo ties and cowboy boots in the studio—and in *Western Symphony* (1954), he created a paean to the cowboy and the dance hall girl.

Graham and Balanchine were just two of the many choreographers who thought about distinctly American ways of moving. The efforts of these artists make up much of the recorded history of American dance. Their lives and works are thought-provoking and well-documented; their theories are catnip to writers looking for overarching themes in dance's story.

But the majority of the vibrant dance traditions America can claim as its own weren't imposed from the top by avant-garde leaders. Instead, they rose up from the bottom, from the country's street corners and back alleys and jook joints, where immigrant cultures mixed and merged and mutated. Irish jigs and clogs met West African drumming rhythms and spawned tap; more than a century later, African American funk music met Brazilian *capoeira* met competitive gymnastics, and b-boying was born. (Syncopated African beats became the most common metal in the alloying process.)

These crossbreeds, adaptive and innovative, have proven to be the hardiest styles of all. They were—are—the truest reflections of America, because they came directly from its people. Incredible diversity begets tension, and in street and popular dance we can see reflections of America's political and class struggles. Yet that diversity has also made the American dance scene one of unparalleled richness and robustness. There is no single definitive "American" way of moving—and that's not a problem to be solved, but a distinction to be celebrated.

Patricia McBride (left), Jacques D'Amboise, and Suki Schorer in George Balanchine's *Stars and Stripes*, 1964. The 1958 ballet, with music by John Philip Sousa and baton-twirling dancers, is a celebration of America. *Gjon Mili/The LIFE Picture Collection/Getty Images*

Chapter One
Native American Traditions

A 1585 painting of the Secotan Indians in North Carolina, by explorer John White.

"Wee sawe [seven canoes of] wilde men . . . all of which approached neere unto our boate, dancing and making many signes of joy and mirth. . . . Some of the women who came not over, we might see stand up to their knees in water, singing and dancing." —*The first mention of dance in the New World: Jacques Cartier, 1534, near the mouth of the St. Lawrence River*[1]

Native American dances were utterly alien to the first Europeans to witness them. But they evolved over the next five centuries as a result of that encounter between foreign cultures—first through suppression, then commercialization, then cultural synthesis, and finally through a profound influence on American modern dance.

The great variation in American Indian dance makes generalizations difficult, but most dances take place in a line, circle, or procession. The style is often organic and naturalistic, reflecting a spiritual connection to the earthly environment. Steps are usually low to the ground and tend to favor bent knees and flat-footed or toe-heel steps rooted to the earth. Much of the movement occurs in the head and torso, as the dancers represent animals or mimic their daily or seasonal work—hunting, harvesting, fishing, and warfare. Even dances that look simple are often rhythmically complex. The pulsing of the body accents certain beats of the accompanying songs, creating a rhythmic unity between dancers and musicians, who sing or play instruments ranging from turtle-shell rattles to tall drums.

Ritual dancing at life-cycle ceremonies, on days of celebration, and during agricultural, religious, and medicine rites are also central to Native cultures. Because ceremonial dances are tied to theology, all of their various components—songs, steps, and costumes—are significant. These dances are not performances; they're potentially transformative acts. Even the dancers themselves are transformed. A participant in a Plains tribe Buffalo Dance isn't just imitating a buffalo, he's becoming it. When a Pueblo kachina dancer dons a mask and costume and performs a dance ritual, the kachina god he's representing enters and transfigures him. Ceremonial rites are performed in a state between consciousness and trance, and while some of the movements are quite difficult, the source of a dancer's power is his complete involvement, not his virtuosity.

But not all dances are highly serious. Many social dances, especially today, are done just for fun, and can sometimes be funny. Some Tewa Pueblo social dances, for example, are actually parodies of other tribes, or even Catholic priests.

Unfortunately a great many American Indian dances have been lost, often as a result of determined repression by European settlers. Dance was one of the first aspects of Indian culture to be attacked by white men, many of whom considered all Indian dancing "war dancing." Christian missionaries and settlers often viewed Native dance as corrupt and uncivilized pagan practices that must be extirpated.

Since dance was a fundamental part of American Indian religious ceremonies, the United States government's ban on Indian religion in the 1880s devastated Native dancing. That ban specifically targeted the Sun Dance and Ghost Dance for their perceived-to-be-dangerous blend of Indian culture, faith, and politics. Even as late as 1904, the US government was enacting laws against American Indian dance. Article No. 4 of the *Regulations of the Indian Office* from that year read:

> The "sun dance," and all other similar dances and so-called religious ceremonies, shall be considered "Indian offenses," and any Indian found guilty of being a participant in any one or more of these "offenses" shall . . . be punished by withholding him from his rations . . . or by incarceration in the agency prison. . . .[2]

(That particular law wasn't repealed until 1934, when social reformer John Collier became Commissioner of Indian Affairs.)

More than a generation of American Indians had no direct experience with dance. With such active suppression, many of the older religious and ceremonial dances disappeared, and what evidence we have of them comes mostly from Euro-American sources with Western biases. Records of several traditional dances do remain, however, and some dances are still performed today, albeit in forms that have evolved significantly over time. Here are a few representative examples.

Pueblo Eagle Dance, New Mexico. Originally published by *Southwest Arts and Crafts*, Santa Fe.

One of the most famous Native American dances was the sometimes gory and often misunderstood Sun Dance of the Plains. Also known as New Life Lodge Dance, Sacred or Mystery Dance, They Dance Staring at the Sun, Thirst Dance, and Dance for the World, this rite—performed by many Plains tribes, including the Cheyenne, Ponca, and Kiowa—reached its height in the late nineteenth century. Each summer, when the tribe's scattered hunting groups reunited, they gathered at a special Sun Dance campground where they constructed a sacred Sun Lodge. Here they held a social and political rally that lasted between eight and fifteen days and served as a "renewal of communion with the earth, sun, and the supernaturals . . . in order that the tribe might have fertility, health, and continuing abundance of buffalo herds."[3]

Much has been made of the self-mutilation that occurred during the Sun Dance, usually on the fifth day of the ceremony. Young warriors offered to participate in this part of the dance to fulfill vows made during times of danger or stress. After fasting and otherwise depriving themselves in the days leading up to the ceremony, these men were attached at the breast or back with skewers that were connected by rawhide thongs to the sacred central pole in the Sun Lodge. They moved in a slow circle around the pole until they either tore themselves loose or were released by the dance leader after collapsing. Others offered a "red blanket"—ten to one hundred tiny pieces of skin cut from the arms or shoulders. The purpose of this bloody self-mutilation was not to prove one's bravery or ability to withstand pain. The Sun Dancer's suffering was symbolic of the terrible fate that had imperiled him at the time he made his vow. He connected with higher forces through his pain and ultimately became unconscious of his body.[4] He physically and psychically conquered the threat to himself or his people. And he did not dance—and suffer—alone. During intervals in this ordeal, which could take many hours, other tribe members performed social dances, uniting their efforts to commune with the supernatural and secure tribal well-being.

In the religious belief of the Apache, who live in the mountainous Southwest, *gaan*, or mountain spirits, have the power to drive away evil. The Apache dance to summon the supernatural assistance of the *gaan* for critical moments of their early journey. In the past the Apache Mountain Spirit Dance (often

Shoshone Sun Dance, c. 1925.
National Archives

Navajo dance at Fort Defiance, 1873.
National Archives

one a sacred clown, the leader of the group, who prepares the way for the *gaan*. They wear elaborate crowns painted with sacred designs and carry painted wands made of yucca. Their dance is made up of short, jagged, angular movements to a slow, four-beat rhythm. It is repeated on each of the ceremony's four nights, ensuring the spiritual assistance of the supernatural during this rite of passage into adult tribal membership.

The Navajo also use dance to weave the supernatural and natural worlds together. Their Navajo Night Chant (*Ye Bi Chei*) is a form of therapy to aid or cure a sick person. But it also has wider implications: It's "a panoramic expression of Navajo cosmology."[7] One of the most sacred of Navajo ceremonies, it's also very difficult to learn, since it involves memorizing a large number of prayers and chants, as well as the designs used in its ritual sand paintings.

Usually held in late fall or early winter, the Night Chant begins at sundown and concludes eight and a half days later at sunrise. The first four days involve purification. At midnight on the fifth day, the gods are ceremonially invoked; they appear in the detailed sand paintings made by the medicine man leading the rite and his assistants, over the course of the fifth through eighth days. Dancing becomes central to the ceremony on the final night. At that point the Dance of the Atsalei (Thunderbirds) evokes the male thunderbird god. This danced invocation of the spirit world is repeated many times, creating a trance-like, hypnotic effect. Ultimately, under the influence of the dance, the medicine man conveys to the patient the power of the god and calls for the ailing tribesman's transformation to health.

The Dog Dance (also known as the Peace Dance) of the San Ildefonso Pueblo, in Northern New Mexico, is one of the more mysterious of the ceremonial dances. Two men, their faces and bodies painted black, step forward and backward in circles, advancing and retreating from their counterparts like dogs about to fight. They wear elaborate feather headdresses; each dancer holds a decorated rattle in his right hand, and a stick with a strip of cloth and feathers attached in his left. Sometimes the dancers have long sashes on their belts that are held by women, like leashes. At the conclusion of the dance, bread or coins are thrown on the floor for the two "dogs" to battle over. The mystery involves the meaning of the dance, which is supposed to symbolize peace. One explanation is that the dance depicts a scene from ancient days, when a conflict was sometimes settled by man-on-man combat between the two opposing chiefs.[8]

incorrectly called the Devil Dance) invoked the *gaan* primarily as a healing ritual. Today it is most frequently done during the Sunrise Ceremony, a girl's puberty rite.

John Collier called the Sunrise Ceremony the Apache's "most momentous ritual."[5] During the four-day rite,

> the girl *becomes* White Painted Woman, Mother Earth. The ceremony symbolically reproduces earth creation, man creation, and the history of earth and man, and it carries the girl symbolically through all the stages of her future life, into happy old age . . . she is being made, and is making herself from within, with the help of the gods, into the image of Mother Earth.[6]

The Mountain Spirit Dance, meant to drive away evil spirits and offer blessings to the girl and the tribe, is a central part of the proceedings. The young girl, dressed in bright yellow, and a girl friend first stand on a specially prepared ground and dance in place, stepping slowly from one foot to the other. Then five men enter—four portraying *gaan*, and

Dancers at San Ildefonso Pueblo in New Mexico. Photograph by Ansel Adams, 1942. *National Archives*

Rain dances are especially common in the arid Southwest. The Rain Dance of the Zuni Pueblo of New Mexico is a signal to their gods, or kachinas, that the corn has been planted and is in need of rain. The shaman leading the ceremony guides the dancers, who imitate plowing and the sowing of corn seeds. Their turning movements represent the corn plants following the progress of the sun across the sky; scooping hand motions depict the corn's need for water. The rattles they shake are intended to awaken the gods so they will send rain.

The Hopi Snake Dance, given every other year, is also a call for rain. The Hopi believe their people emerged from the underworld. They consider snakes their brothers, and ask them to carry their prayers to the Rainmakers, who also live below the earth. The Snake Dance, which is the beginning of ceremonies that go on for sixteen days, is spectacular: The dancers perform with live snakes, holding them in their hands, roping them around their necks, even placing them in their mouths.

Many Native dances from across the continent shared this goal of invoking the gods' assistance, their presence at rites of passage, and their communion with Indian people. In this sense, almost all had some spiritual significance. But the Ghost Dance, which spread in two waves in the late 1800s, was a religion unto itself. Ghost Dancers performed their ritual movements in exchange for a supernatural promise of a return to customary ways. The Ghost Dance provided psychic hope and strength

to an American Indian community that needed a reason to be hopeful.

By the mid-nineteenth century, the arbitrary system of reservations and the devastation of game populations—particularly buffalo—had reduced many Indians to desperation. In 1869 Wodziwob, a Paiute from Nevada, had a prophetic dream: If he could convince his fellow Indians to do a specific dance, which he called the Ghost Dance, the world would be returned within two years to the state it was in before the white man arrived. While Wodziwob's movement spread through California and may have reached Oregon and Washington, 1871 came and went with no change, and the Ghost Dance faded into obscurity.

In 1888, however, another Nevadan Paiute, Wovoka, fell into a similar prophetic trance—possibly induced by scarlet fever—in which he visited the heavens and was reunited with his dead friends and family members. During his vision, he spoke with the Great Father, who gave him another Ghost Dance, a simple set of movements and songs, and instructed him to teach it to every Indian. If all the Indians danced the Ghost Dance together, Wovoka believed, their dead ancestors would return to the earth, the world would be reborn, the game would return, and the whites would disappear.

This time the message traveled more rapidly, as communication routes had improved. The Ghost Dance made its way to the tribes of California, Wyoming, North and South Dakota—possibly as

Hopi dance, Oraibi, Arizona, 1879.
National Archives

many as sixteen states. Wovoka was seen as a mes-
siah. As the dance spread, variations in its message
began to appear, synthesizing aspects of different
tribes' belief systems, or indicating different ways in
which the white man would perish (through earthquake, cyclone, landslide, and so on).

The Lakota Tribe of the Dakotas embraced the
dance most eagerly, to the point that they believed
the outfit they wore during the ceremony—the
Ghost Shirt—could protect them from the bullets
of the whites. Their fervent Ghost Dance performances frightened United States officials. Escalating
alarm and tensions ultimately led to the Wounded
Knee Massacre in South Dakota, during which
between 150 and 300 Lakotas were murdered. That
the Lakotas believed their Ghost Shirts would protect them was perhaps one of the reasons the massacre was so terrible.[9] After Wounded Knee, interest
in the Ghost Dance dwindled, but its mystique as a
nonviolent spiritual protest movement lived on.

After the Ghost Dance, Native American dance
began to evolve to reflect native cultural interaction
with the white community. During the prohibi-
tion of Native American dances in the nineteenth
and early twentieth centuries, the only legal Indian
dance performances were theatrical events. Usually
these productions—at world's fairs, "ethnographic
village" exhibits, and Wild West shows—were organized by white businessmen, government officials,
or anthropologists, for the entertainment of white
audiences. They were exploitative, but they also presented an arena in which some semblance of Indian
dance culture could survive. Over time, they had an
effect on the way the dances themselves looked, as
dancers began to incorporate non-Indian customs.

Indians were encouraged to add show-stopping
feats to their dances to attract non-Indian audiences.
Even social dance crazes, like the Charleston, made
their way into Indian performances. Sometimes the
dancers would re-enact tragedies like the Wounded

Knee Massacre. To further heighten the drama, producers may have urged performers to wear increasingly elaborate costumes, often involving huge feather bustles, which eventually became popular among Indian dancers.[10]

Indian dance also evolved as methods of travel improved and tribes came into more frequent contact with each other. Oklahoma, where many tribes lived in close proximity, was the center for this kind of interaction. It became a melting pot from which a sort of pan-Indianism emerged.[11] As tribes discovered the overlaps between their dances—the fact that most began with an entrance in a parade-like line and were then performed in a circle, for example, or that several involved animal impersonations—many once distinctive dances began to look similar.

These hybrid dances became the basis for the modern powwow. While the word "powwow" originally referred to a curing ceremony, over time it came to describe a secular and frequently intertribal celebration, featuring dancing by men, women, and children.

Today's powwows might be sponsored by a specific tribe or by an intertribal powwow organization and are commonly attended by paying, non-Indian audiences as well as members of the various tribes. Most of the dances are from the Prairie or Plains regions, but some evolved purely within the powwow setting. They might even be set to songs with English lyrics or performed in Western clothing. Many modern powwows also include dance contests, other special performances, and arts and crafts booths.

The popular powwow War Dance (also known as the Omaha Dance, Grass Dance, Hot Dance, or Wolf Dance) derives from ceremonies held by old Indian warrior societies to invoke the heroism of war deeds. Today it has lost most of its warrior-society aspects and can be performed by women as well as men. There are two types of dress for the War Dance: "straight" and "fancy," with fancy distinguished by the large bustles of feathers at the waist and neck. Straight dancers are relatively restrained; fancy dancers weave intricate footwork, spins, knee-falls, and other impressive movements into their dances. (The first fancy dancers were Ponca Tribe members Gus McDonald, Dennis Rough Face, and Henry Snake, who developed the more elaborate

George Catlin painting of a Buffalo Dance at a Mandan Okipa ceremony.
De Agostini, Getty Images

style in the 1920s after becoming bored with the "limited" movements of traditional dances.)

Another powwow favorite, the Gourd Dance, gets its name from the rattle carried by the dancers, which was originally made from a gourd but is now usually constructed with tin cans or salt shakers. There are several variations of the Gourd Dance, but most involve "an in-place bobbing step . . . followed by a forward-moving toe-heel step."[12]

Nearly every powwow includes the Round Dance, a simple large group dance, in which the dancers link hands and side-step to the left. Round dances frequently lead into the Buffalo Dance, in which the dancers unclasp hands and imitate buffalo motions. Powwows also include modern social dances, performed in couples, such as the Forty-niner Dance. Legend has it that fifty Indians from a Wisconsin reservation fought in World War I,

and when forty-nine of them returned, the people created a dance in their honor.[13] In it, the dancers form a line with their partners, alternating men and women, and circle to the left, with left hands on left shoulders along the line. Forty-niner songs are always in English.

The Rabbit and Two-step Dances are social partner dances that imitate white dance styles. The Rabbit Dance, done in Western clothing, looks like a combination of the fox trot and the waltz (see Chapter 2); partners face each other in a fox trot position, and move in a clockwise circle. The Two-step is a variation on the white man's two-step, in which a leading couple guides the other pairs of men and women around the dance area. (At Northern Plains powwows, a similar dance is known as the Owl Dance.) The accompanying English songs often tell love stories. One typical Rabbit Dance

RIGHT: War Dance performed by the Yuchi. Illustration by German artist Philip Georg Friedrich von Reck, who came to America in 1736 hoping to depict "this strange new world."

BELOW: Iroquois dancers, 2008 New York State Fair. *Dave Pape*

When Alaska was colonized in the late eighteenth century, nearly all of its traditional dances (along with the rest of its traditional practices) were quashed by Christian missionaries and further discouraged by the colonizers' imposition of the Western education system. But beginning in the 1970s, interest in and performances of the old dances began to increase. Though Native American dance in Alaska today includes a mishmash of modern influences, it still maintains a connection to traditional culture.

In 1982 the Inupiat people, formerly of King Island, reconstructed their intricate Wolf Dance, which was later performed for an audience of thousands at the 1991 Alaska Federation of Natives Convention. Though a modern interpretation of a historic work, the dance's songs and movements remain fairly true to the original. Relatively stationary, the dance involves stomping steps with the feet and graceful gestures of the hands and arms, choreographed to each particular song. Dancers wear special boots made of caribou, wolf, and seal skins, as well as dresslike garments called *kuspuqs*.

The elders of the Yupik Tribe of Hooper Bay also recently revived the Bladder Feast, a ceremony that involves a changeable series of songs, dances, and masks telling the story of the village's past year. During the feast, to honor the spirits of the animals killed during the year, their bladders, which have been collected and specially treated, are thrown into the sea.

One of the most prominent venues for Native Alaskan dancing is the World Eskimo Indian Olympics, held annually in Anchorage. During the day, the event features games descended from traditional hunting and survival tactics, including the Eskimo Stick Pull and the *Nalukataq*, or Blanket Toss. At night, however, various Native Alaskan dance groups perform for hours. The heated competitions between these troupes have become a highlight of the event.

Wolf Dance of the Kaviagamutes in Alaska, c. 1914. *Library of Congress*

Maria Tallchief, 1954.
Cleanliness Bureau, Associated Press

world. But some early modern dancers, in particular, were inspired by the way Indian dancing expressed the inner self, rather than focusing solely on outward appearance, and they began incorporating aspects of it into their concert works.

Modern pioneer Ted Shawn (see Chapter 4) was vocal about his admiration for American Indian dance, and studied Indian dance customs during his travels across the United States. American Indian imagery became a recurring theme in his choreography in the 1920s and 1930s, inspiring works that included *The Feather of the Dawn* (1923), *Zuni Ghost Dance* (1931), and *Ponca Indian Dance* (1934).

Modern legend Martha Graham (see Chapter 4), who danced with Shawn, was also interested in "ritualizing contemporary experience."[15] She traveled to the American Southwest in 1931, and became fascinated with the religious dance rites of the Indians she encountered there. Her exploration of these rites, along with pagan and Catholic religious ceremonies, inspired her groundbreaking work *Primitive Mysteries*, which premiered the same year, as well as several other pieces during that period. More than fifty years later, Graham returned to the subject of Indian dance with *Night Chant* (1988), a theatrical dance with music by R. Carlos Nakai, an artist of Navajo and Ute descent.

Some Indians also learned Western dance forms, the most notable being sisters Maria and Marjorie Tallchief. Part Osage, they trained with renowned Russian dancer and teacher Bronislava Nijinska in California. Marjorie went on to become a star of the Paris Opéra Ballet; Maria became muse to (and, for a time, wife of) revolutionary choreographer George Balanchine, who called her the first truly American ballerina (see Chapter 5).

Other Indians became involved in the concert dance world by adapting traditional dances for the stage. The American Indian Dance Theatre, founded in 1987 in Colorado Springs, is the most prominent, having performed around the world. A professional company of highly skilled artists, it includes dancers, singers, and musicians from many tribal backgrounds. The group was featured in the PBS Great Performances special *Finding the Circle* in 1990, and in a second program, *Dances for the New Generations*, in 1993.

song says "Dearie, why don't you look at me? I know you will come back to me, so don't worry."[14]

Many powwows also have a contest dance division, in which dancers compete in newer, specialized styles. The categories often include men's and women's Traditional, men's Fancy, women's Fancy-Shawl, and women's Jingle-Dress. As the latter names suggest, the elaborate costumes for these dances are nearly as important as the dances themselves, and at intertribal powwows differences in details of the dancers' ensembles frequently indicate their tribal identities.

The evolution of American Indian dancing has on the whole occurred outside of the concert dance

Indian Hoop Dance, Molalla, Oregon, 1936. *Arthur Rothstein, Library of Congress*

Hula dancers at Pearl Harbor greet a Canadian destroyer returning from Korean waters, 1951. *Associated Press*

accented by small, flat-footed steps and gentle swaying hip movements.

In traditional hula, dancers were known as *olapa* and musicans and chanters as *hoopaa*. But some of the older chant dances were performed sitting down, in which case the dancers were frequently also the musicians, accompanying themselves with calabash drums and nose flutes. Before Christians arrived in Hawaii, *olapa* and *hoopaa* students received careful training, from as early as age three, in a special school, or *halau*. Becoming a dancer was an honor, and the *halau*, dedicated to Laka, was a sacred place.

When Calvinist missionaries from the United States arrived in the 1820s, they condemned the hula. Several converted Hawaiian chiefs prohibited the dance, and it essentially went underground until the reign of King David Kalākaua, which began in 1874. Kalākaua gathered experts in traditional practices, including the hula, at his court, and encouraged them to perform their arts. Many of the hula dances done today were created during Kalākaua's reign; they're sometimes grouped with pre-nineteenth century dances as "ancient hula," or *hula kahiko*.

Scholars believe the Polynesians who colonized the Hawaiian Islands in the third century first developed the hula. But in Hawaiian legend, the origins of the hula are shrouded in myth. The most common stories involve the goddesses Laka, Pele, and Hi'iaka. Some say Hi'aka learned the dance from Laka and taught it to her sister, Pele; others believe Pele taught the dance to Hi'aka, who gave it to Laka for safekeeping.

Whatever its provenance, the hula became a central part of Hawaiian culture. Though the dance itself wasn't a religious rite, it had deep significance when performed in conjunction with other rites, or in supplication to Laka, the goddess of hula.

Hula refers to dance, but traditional hula could not be performed without *mele*, the poetic chants that accompanied each dance. Before Hawaii had a written language, *mele* told stories of the island's history, or honored the beauty of natural wonders like mountains and waterfalls. The hula's arm gestures gracefully illustrated whatever story the *mele* told,

In the twentieth century, Hollywood discovered the hula. The hula of the movies, however, was sexualized for the cameras, with more pronounced hip movements. Chanting also faded out of popularity in the first and second decades of the twentieth century. The tourists beginning to arrive in Hawaii didn't know Hawaiian, and to accommodate them performers started setting their dances to songs and putting a larger emphasis on gesture.

The "Hawaiian renaissance" of the 1970s, however, rekindled interest in older hula forms. Today, hula practitioners divide hula into chant-accompanied *hula kahiko* (ancient hula, as mentioned above) and song-accompanied *hula 'auana* (modern hula). There are currently two annual hula competitions in Hawaii, at which performers compete in both *hula kahiko* and *hula 'auana*: the Merrie Monarch festival, held each April on the island of Hawaii, and the King Kamehameha Traditional Hula and Chant Competition, held each June on Oahu.

Chapter Two

American Social Dance

A 1921 *Vanity Fair* cover depicting dancers at a nightclub. Illustration by Anne Harriet Fish. *Library of Congress*

"People can say what they like about rag-time. The Waltz is beautiful. . . . One can sit quietly and listen with pleasure to [it]; but when a good orchestra plays a 'rag' one has simply *got* to move." —*Vernon Castle in* Modern Dancing, *1914*[1]

People _were_ "saying what they liked" about ragtime music and dances in 1914—mostly that they were vulgar, even obscene. The European waltz, on the other hand, was (relatively speaking) a polite kind of fun. Earlier American social dance trends had been even more restrained; they were opportunities to showcase beautiful posture and good breeding rather than to let loose. Nearly all of these formal dances had drifted downward from the elegant ballrooms of London, Paris, and Vienna.

But at the turn of the twentieth century, the tide reversed. Suddenly American dance fashions were no longer imported from Europe. Instead, they were bubbling upward and outward from the exuberant dance floors of places like New York City's Savoy Ballroom.

The English Dancing-Master.
Author John Playford dedicated his book to "The Gentlemen of the Innes of Court."

Not coincidentally, the shift came at about the same time that African American influences—specifically the irresistible syncopations of ragtime and jazz, and the freewheeling dances that went with them—first earned widespread acceptance in mainstream (read: white) America. There would always be someone protesting that they were indecent, but for the rest of the century, black, and, later on, Latin music and dance traditions would be the most important influences shaping America's popular dance culture.

Even the most stubbornly backward objectors couldn't help it. They _had_ to move.

Early Puritan colonists who first arrived in New England didn't disapprove of dancing. They were just too busy with the business of survival to do much of it. Occasional dance gatherings were held in Puritan homes or outside at celebrations like weddings. When they got the chance, the Puritans probably danced the simple round, square, and long dances common in British country towns and villages. Only "mixt" dancing, during which men and women danced together, was frowned upon.

In 1651 London bookseller and composer John Playford published *The English Dancing-Master: or Plaine and easie Rules for the Dancing of Country Dances, with the tune to each Dance.* The little book marked the first time English country dances, formerly learned through sight or practice, were written down. Playford's first edition of the book included 104 dances, mostly rounds, squares, and longs for four couples. It quickly became extremely popular, both in England and in the colonies. (Over the next seventy-eight years, there were sixteen subsequent editions of *The English Dancing-Master*—and the last included 918 dances.)

Many of the Puritans in the colonies liked Playford's book because it emphasized manners and decorum as much as steps, and Puritans considered good manners an important part of leading a moral life.[2] Playford's dances were also democratic: Couples frequently changed positions (moving from the head to the rear of groups in long dances, for example) and took turns leading figures. As the colonies became increasingly independent from Britain and distrustful of its absolute monarchy, that all-for-one-and-one-for-all symbolism might have added to the dances' appeal.[3]

Not all were sanguine about the popularity of dancing in the wake of the publication of *The English Dancing-Master*. Clergymen were especially alarmed by the dancing schools that tried to gain toeholds in Boston in the mid-1600s. They believed formal dance instruction led students to pride and vanity—or, worse, to temptation, especially the temptation to commit adultery.[4] Though all the schools were quickly shut down by local authorities, Boston was still home to a number of dancing masters, who earned notoriety by encouraging partnered dancing and even dancing on the Sabbath.

The incident that most outraged Boston clergy involved Francis Stepney, an especially brazen dancing master.[5] Boston clerics, including Increase Mather, went to court to denounce Stepney in November 1685. Judge Samuel Sewell's diary entry from Monday, November 9, 1685, reads:

> . . . the Ministers of the town come to the Court and complain against a Dancing Master who seeks to set up here and hath mixt dances, and his time of Meeting is Lecture Day [when the midweek religious gathering is held]; and 'tis reported he should say that by one Play he could teach more Divinity than [Puritan Reverend] Mr. Willard or the Old Testament.[6]

Stepney paid for his cheekiness: Sewell eventually ordered him to cease teaching in Boston or face contempt charges. Two months later Mather, greatly stirred, published *An Arrow Against Profane and Promiscuous Dancing Drawn Out of the Quiver of Scriptures.*

The thirty-page pamphlet condemns what Mather saw as the dangerous worldliness of the Massachusetts colony. (Boston attracted dancing masters and schools for a reason, after all; they must have had some hope of success.) "The Fruits and Effects [of mixed dancing] have been Tragical & Dismal," Mather thundered:

> No doubt but that the *Promiscuous Dances* (for at their Sacrifices the Heathen used to do so) between the *Moabites*

CULTURE CLASH IN NEW ORLEANS

After the Louisiana Purchase of 1803, New Orleans officially became a part of the United States. Easterners began to arrive in the French Creole city, and the tensions between disparate cultures came to a head on the city's dance floors. The Creoles preferred French quadrilles; the incoming Anglo-Americans preferred English country dances. Things got so heated that many a duel was fought over what the evening's next dance would be.

The situation was so bad, in fact, that on January 25, 1804, William C. Claiborne, Louisiana's first governor, enacted a set of regulations determining the sequence of dances played in public halls during assemblies. Projet d'Arrête established the ratio of two French contredanses or quadrilles for the Creoles to one English country dance for Anglo-Americans. English country dances were also limited to two sets of twelve couples, so that the Anglo-Americans couldn't swarm the dance floor.

Dance has had a long tradition of provocation. In this 1766 British print, dukes, earls, and devils dance together while a witch soars overhead. *Library of Congress*

Shakers perform a step dance, New Lebanon, New York. Etching c. 1830. *Library of Congress*

While most Christian groups had a complicated relationship with dance, the mid-eighteenth century saw the development of a sect that advocated it: the Shakers, or the United Society of Believers in Christ's Second Appearing.

The Shakers followed their leader, Mother Ann Lee, from England to America in 1774, and established several independent communities in New England and the Midwest. They danced during their religious services, believing it liberated their souls from sin. Since the Shakers were a celibate community, men and women always danced separately. Early dances were simple. Sometimes the men would form a large circle around an inner circle of women; sometimes the genders would dance on opposite ends of the room.

In 1788 Shaker leader Joseph Meacham introduced the "Square Order Shuffle," a dance supposedly patterned after his vision of angels dancing around the throne of God. Men and women, in separate groups, moved solemnly forward and backward, doing a double step, or "tip-tap," at each turn. Later, during the Great Revival of the early nineteenth century, the Shakers attempted to impress prospective converts with more animated and varied dances, incorporating cross, diamond, and double-square patterns. The elaborate wheel-within-a-wheel dance, in which three or more concentric circles of dancers moved in different directions around a central chorus of singers, served as a metaphor for the all-encompassing nature of Shaker gospel.[8]

and the *Midianitish* Woman, proved a snare to the Children of *Israel*. But how terrible a Plague followed? . . . *Salome*, the Daughter of *Herodias* was notable at *Dancing!* But what end did she come to? *Nicephorus* relates that falling under the Ice, her feet *Capered* under the water; and her Head being cut off by the Ice, it danced about water.[7]

But the tide was already beginning to turn against Mather and his allies. Following the Glorious Revolution in England in 1689, a new governor was appointed in New England, who allowed the use of the organ, long silenced due to Puritan objection, at King's Chapel in Boston—and also allowed the organ master to earn money on the side by teaching music and dance. By 1700 wealthy New Englanders were throwing balls, and dancing schools throughout the region were flourishing.

In colonial Virginia, dancing faced less stringent resistance. The colony's lucrative cash crops (especially tobacco) helped create a hierarchical class system—with wealthy plantation owners at the top and indentured servants and slaves at the bottom—that looked remarkably European. The richest

Virginians had plenty of free time, and they began to pattern their social habits after the similarly leisured European aristocracy. Dancing became an accomplishment expected of proper Virginian gentlemen. Dancing masters soon spread throughout the colony, ready to teach English country dances as well as a few more dainty, filigreed French dances, like the minuet.

Eventually dancing became one of the most effective ways to reinforce class divisions in colonial society, where class was based, rather precariously, on wealth alone. As Virginia grew more and more prosperous, each generation brought with it a wave of "new money." The upper crust of the previous generation fought hard to prevent the incursion of social climbers into their exclusive circles. Elaborate codes of etiquette were the best way to discourage and intimidate newcomers, and few pastimes were as complicated, etiquette-wise, as dancing in Virginia ballrooms.[9]

The Virginia Reel, which became popular in Virginia in the eighteenth century and remained an American favorite through much of the nineteenth century, was actually nearly identical to one of the Playford dances, the Sir Roger de Coverly. Danced

The Virginia Reel, Van Cortlandt Park, The Bronx, 1908. *Library of Congress*

to any song in 2/4 time, it required a group of three or four couples and was led by a caller who reminded the dancers of the steps with prompts like "forward and back," "swing right hands," "dos-à-dos," and "turn right hands." The reel ended with a processional march, putting the lead couple at the bottom of the set and creating a new lead couple. Early on, the Virginia Reel was a polished, elegant dance; over time it became livelier, even rowdy, and was eventually danced by lines of twelve or more couples.

Moving inland from Virginia's manicured plantations, settlers began to take root in wilder Kentucky, West Virginia, North Carolina, and Tennessee. Many of these pioneers were Scotch-Irish Presbyterians escaping the religious persecution they faced in their home countries. Their rural communities remained isolated from the more sophisticated stylistic influences that shaped dancing in Virginia and parts of New England. These hardy settlers preferred the classic dances of rural Britain, not their polished-for-the-ballroom cousins that made up later versions of Playford's book. Usually they danced in a circle, but sometimes they used a four-couple square formation, later called the Kentucky Running Set. That formation might be the link between modern square dancing and the old pagan dances of Europe.[10]

After the Revolutionary War, some dancing began to take on a political cast. George Washington, an avid dancer, knew the young United States

needed to shed its provincial image to earn respect on the world stage, and so encouraged prominent Americans to adapt European refinements, especially in the ballroom. Washington was particularly fond of the French minuet, in part because of the dance's political connotations—he was eager to stay in the good graces of America's French allies. He even danced the minuet at his inaugural ball in 1789.

The French invasion wasn't only happening in Washington's ballroom. A wave of French dancing masters descended on the United States after the American Revolution, bringing with them even more sophisticated versions of the traditional country dances. Following the French Revolution, which was cultural as well as political, a new group of French dances—those less popular with the ex-aristocracy—became fashionable in both France and America. The quadrille, a square dance for four couples in which each couple took a turn dancing while the others rested, was soon danced throughout the United States, as was its cousin, the cotillion.

The War of 1812, which did little to encourage love between Britain and America, solidified the popularity of the French dances. America's larger, politically engaged cities became hubs of anti-British sentiment. Many urban Americans went so far as to refuse to do English country dances, choosing French quadrilles and cotillions instead. Only in backwoods rural areas did the English dances survive. Eventually the cities' quadrilles became increasingly refined and complicated as successions of dancing masters added their own flourishes; urban sophisticates were eager to adapt the latest variations. In a few short decades, the quadrille transformed from a symbol of *égalité* into a symbol of elite refinement.

By the beginning of the nineteenth century, Southern plantations had already seen several generations of African slaves. Slaves had been an integral part of the economic and cultural worlds of Southern plantations from the mid-seventeenth century on. In West Africa, their ancestral home, dancing was an integral component of religious rituals and ceremonies. Like much Native American dance, it helped bind tribes together and honored important moments in the life cycle. In America, elements of African dance survived, but eventually they lost their religious meanings. Instead, as slaves

Nineteenth-century depiction of slaves dancing. *The Bridgeman Art Library, Getty Images* realized that the dances of their various tribes were more similar than their languages or other aspects of their cultures, dance became a way for them to connect when they were thrown together on American plantations. It was something familiar to hold onto in an unfamiliar place.[11]

Even a few generations out, slave dancing still looked a lot like the ceremonial dance of West Africa. Both were characterized by the isolation of various body parts and the use of complicated polyrhythms, percussive movement, and improvisation. During "Ring Shouts," which were danced on plantations throughout the South, slaves moved in a counter-clockwise circle, stamping, clapping, swinging their arms, and shimmying their shoulders and hips. Sometimes they were accompanied by a drum or stringed banja (an ancestor of the banjo); sometimes they provided their own accompaniment, humming and slapping their thighs. It was a celebration of the survival of another day. Though it was disconnected from any African religion, the Ring Shout eventually became a spiritual event, a symbol of unity within the community.[12] (Later, Ring Shouts were incorporated into black Christian worship services.)

White Americans were threatened by any slave display of solidarity, and events like Ring Shouts alarmed them. Spurred by the "Stono Insurrection" of 1739—when a group of slaves, while attempting to escape to Florida, drank too much rum on the road, stopped to have a dance party, and were captured—South Carolina enacted the harsh Slave Code of 1740, intended in part to suppress slave dancing. Section 36 of the legislation read:

> *Be it enacted* . . . That it shall be lawful for all masters, overseers and other persons whomsoever, to apprehend and take up any negro or other slave that shall be found out of the plantation of his or their master or owner . . . especially on Saturday nights, Sundays or other holidays. . . . And whatsoever master, owner or overseer shall permit or suffer his or their negro or other slave or slaves . . . to beat drums, blow horns, or use any other loud instruments, or whosoever shall suffer and countenance any public meeting or feasting of strange negroes, . . . shall forfeit ten pounds . . . for every such offense.[13]

Barred from using drums and horns, slaves instead made even more intricate use of their bodies as percussion instruments. The virtuosity of a dancer's footwork now took the place of virtuosic drumming during dance gatherings.

Frightened as they were by black dancing, however, whites were also strangely fascinated by it. Sometimes that fascination turned grotesque, as when plantation owners staged dance competitions pitting their best slave "jiggers" against each other and bet on the results. Other times it was more like enchantment. Later in the nineteenth century, Anson De Puy Van Buren described the slave dances at Christmas time in his *Jottings of a Year's Sojourn in the South*:

> [The slaves were] whirling in the giddy mazes of the dance. . . . No restraint of the ettiquettish ball-room, to fetter their actions and motions, but charged like galvanic batteries, full of music, they danced with a vigorous vim. . . . This is *dancing*. It knocks the spangles off your light fantastic tripping, and sends it whirling out of the ballroom.[14]

But it would still be some time before black dance made it into the American mainstream, because for most of the 1800s, the white world was in the grips of "closed couple" dance fever. The closed hold, which brought men and women's bodies within inches of each other—dangerously, scandalously close, many thought—was the century's biggest dance breakthrough. It was also essentially a sexual revolution.[15]

The waltz, which probably derived from the whirling folk dances of Germany, was officially introduced in America in 1834, when Boston dance master Lorenzo Papanti gave an exhibition at a ritzy mansion on Beacon Hill. From there the dance spread quickly through ballrooms across the United States. By the 1880s there was a variation called the Boston waltz, which was slower and more stately than the European original. (It wasn't until the 1910s that the hesitation waltz—the precursor of the modern waltz, which incorporated a slight hold on the standing foot on count three—developed.)

The polka, which has roots in Bohemia (modern-day Czech Republic and Slovakia), made its way to America a little later. First danced in the United States on May 10, 1844, at New York City's National Theater by dance teacher Lawrence De Garmo Brookes and Mary Ann Gammon, it was picked up by other dance instructors and soon embraced by Americans of all classes. Less formal than the waltz, the polka soon surpassed it in popularity. It moved rapidly in a counter-clockwise circle around the edge of dance floor, with the feet tripping a giddy pattern of "step, close, step, hop."

Couples whirling and twirling, clasping each other at the waist or around the neck—to conservative Americans, ballrooms were beginning to feel lewd, even dangerous. The waltz and then the polka swept away centuries of rules about what constituted appropriate public displays of physicality. They weren't just dances; they were challenges to traditional mores.

Numerous outcries denounced closed couple dancing. One of the most hyperbolic is *From the Ballroom to Hell*, penned in 1894 by Thomas A. Faulkner. A former dancing master who'd been "converted," he claimed that "two-thirds of the girls who are ruined fall through the influence of dancing." *From the Ballroom to Hell* lays out the hypothetical story of an innocent young girl who, through dancing, becomes utterly corrupted. The dramatic climax:

> She is now in the vile embrace of the Apollo of the evening. Her head rests upon his shoulder, her face is upturned to his, her bare arm is almost around his neck. . . .

She is filled with the rapture of sin in its intensity; her spirit is inflamed with passion and lust is gratified in thought. . . . [The dance ends, and they get into a carriage together.] Oh, If I could picture to you the fiendish look that comes into his eyes as he sees his helpless victim before him . . . and that beautiful girl who entered the dancing hall as pure and innocent as an angel three months ago returns to her home that night robbed of that most precious jewel of womanhood—virtue! . . . society shuns her, and she is today a brothel inmate, the toy and plaything of the libertine and drunkard.[16]

While the closed couple debate raged in Eastern cities, settlers were beginning to explore America's recently acquired western territories. Frontier farms and towns were rough-and-tumble, and so were their dance gatherings.

Scandalous waltzers, including a kissing couple, 1907.
Library of Congress

"Zoopraxiscope" illustration of a waltzing couple by Eadweard Muybridge, c. 1893. When the disc was spun, the dancers seemed to be in motion. *Library of Congress*

By the later part of the nineteenth century, the term "barn dance" applied to pretty much any community dance in a rural area—sometimes because it actually celebrated the recent completion of a barn, other times because a barn was the only space large enough to accommodate dancers. It was at barn dances that the old Kentucky running set evolved, by the addition of a caller and some aspects of the French quadrille, into American square dancing.

Square dances were usually accompanied by a fiddler. Initially he was the dance's sole leader, acting as caller in addition to musician and frequently becoming quite a showman. After the 1890s, however, separate callers emerged, and the best square dance callers became famous in the western territories. Here's a traditional square dance call as remembered by Charles Weaver, one of the most popular callers in the 1890s:

> [Allamand] left with the left hand partner
>   with a left hand round
> Right hand to your partner and right
>   and left around the ring
> [Meet] your partner and grand promenade
> Everybody swing
> First couple out to the right
> And three hands round

> Lady promenades, open the door
>   and circle the four
> Ladies do and the gents so low
> Then on to the next and then to the third
> Right on home and a grand promenade
> (Repeated until all four couples have
>   taken first couple's part)[17]

(Interestingly, this same kind of dance was also being performed in some city ballrooms. But it was still called a quadrille, and the caller had less freedom. Rather than improvising calls on the fly, he called a predetermined set of figures, reminding the dancers of what came next instead of leading them.)

The frontier mining towns, farther west, were overwhelmingly male. Eager for the company of women, miners flocked to hurdy-gurdies: bawdy, rowdy dance halls that sold alcohol and frequently offered gambling. Men would sometimes travel seventy-five miles to attend a dance. Their partners at hurdy-gurdies were Calico Queens—dance hall girls or prostitutes, sometimes both. They'd dance with miners and cowboys for a fee, or receive a commission from the dance hall owner.

Following emancipation, African Americans found themselves tossed into mainstream society, no

ABOVE: Cakewalk dancers at the 1901 Pan Am Expo in Buffalo, New York.
Getty Images

LEFT: Jook joint jitterbug dancers outside Clarksdale, Mississippi, 1939.
Library of Congress

longer confined to the plantation groups that nonetheless provided a sense of community. Black jook
joints, or honky-tonks, became important gathering
places in towns in the North and South.

Jook joints were dance and music halls that usually offered gambling and liquor. Out of these gritty
dives the beginnings of the blues emerged, as did
some of the most popular dances of the next half-
century: the Charleston, the shimmy, the twist. In
the jook joints, African American culture began
to jell. They were the first places American blacks
could do their own dances and play their own music
without looking over their shoulders.[18]

By the 1890s black dancers were making a splash
in white ballrooms, too. The cakewalk started out as
a black mockery of European dance styles. Essentially
a strutting walk, with men and women promenading
side by side, it incorporated exaggerated swoops of
the head and torso, spoofing dances like the waltz and
the polka, and was frequently set to spirited marches
by John Philip Sousa. Over time the dancers' antics
became increasingly goofy as they added flourishes
like wobbly knees and satirical hat-tipping.

White dancers, not picking up on the cakewalk's sardonic bite, found the dance extremely
funny. It became common at formal white balls
to have African Americans compete in a cakewalk
competition for the guests' amusement, with the
prize usually being a large cake (hence the phrase
"take the cake"). Soon cakewalk contests took on a

life of their own: The first official cakewalk competition was held in 1897 at Madison Square Garden in
New York City, and similar contests were later held
throughout the country.

In an ironic twist, white dancers began to imitate cakewalk movements in their ballrooms. For
the first time, white and black Americans were doing
the same dance. It was also the first time Americans
were influenced by an African American dance
trend. And it represented a moment of transition:
From this point on, most American dance crazes
would derive from either black or Latin traditions.

In the later 1890s cakewalk dancers began to
prefer ragtime, a musical genre that mixed Sousa-
style marches with African polyrhythms. Ragtime
added syncopation to the American musical vocabulary; it was an African trait that became American.
Those "ragged" syncopated rhythms were eminently
danceable. By the early twentieth century ragtime was
popular among Americans of all types and classes.

Ragtime gave rise to a number of "animal"
dances—Turkey Trot, Chicken Scratch, Monkey
Glide, Grizzly Bear, and Bunny Hug—that looked
a lot like the dancing happening in jook joints and
honky-tonks. They were all simple, usually involving little more than taking a single step on each beat
while the upper body shimmied, shook, and imitated the movements of barnyard animals. They also
tended to involve cheek-to-cheek holds, with the
dancers grasping each other's shoulders and necks.

ABOVE: "The fascinating lure of the Ragtime dance," a 1913 illustration by John T. McCutcheon, depicts the stages of ragtime acceptance—from reluctance to mania. *Library of Congress*

LEFT: Fox trot sheet music. c. 1922.

OPPOSITE: Vernon and Irene Castle, c. 1913. *Library of Congress*

(The Grizzly Bear, for example, was just a tightly squeezed bear hug that swayed from side to side.)

The fox trot, despite its name, wasn't an animal dance. Harry Fox, a lower-class vaudeville performer, created the dance during his 1914 act at the New York Theatre. He alternated a slow walk with three trotting steps, and called the result "Fox's Trot." Soon dance masters refined Fox's Trot, and it became a fun, versatile technique, the first ragtime dance to echo the music's syncopation by alternating between slow and quick steps (slow, slow, quick, quick, slow, slow).

Ragtime backlash, especially against the down-and-dirty animal dances, exploded in the early 1900s. In 1914 the Vatican denounced the turkey trot; the Dancing Teachers Association of America refused to teach any form of syncopated dancing. In New Jersey, an especially aggressive turkey trotter was sentenced to fifty days in jail.

Then the Castles stepped in to "clean up" the ragtime dances. Vernon and Irene Castle, a young couple from England and New York, respectively, had discovered dance on their honeymoon in 1910. They were stylish, graceful, and elegant—and they loved ragtime. Their smooth dance styles eliminated the bump-and-grind aspects of the animal dances, and the two of them made it respectable to dance to ragtime at dance halls and in restaurants.

In the introduction to the couple's book, *Modern Dancing* (1914), Vernon Castle lays out the Castle philosophy:

> We feel that this book will serve a double purpose. In the first place, it aims to explain in a clear and simple manner the fundamentals of modern dancing. In the second place, it shows that dancing, properly executed, is

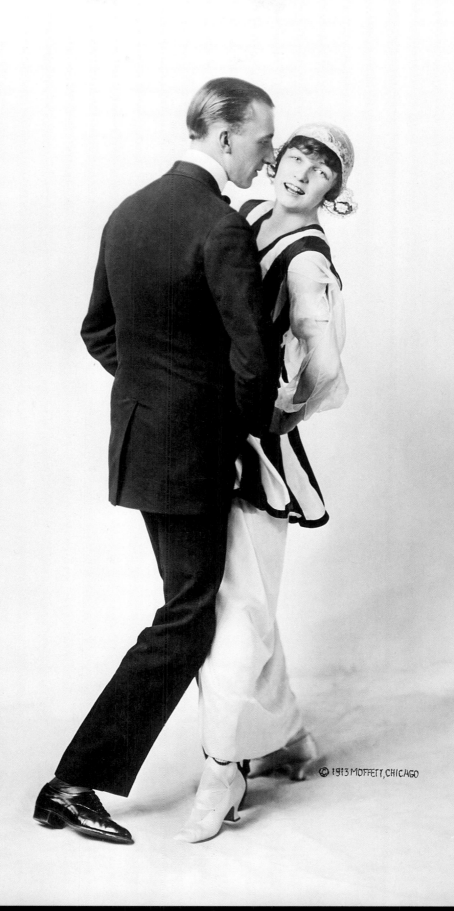

© 1913 MOFFETT, CHICAGO

neither vulgar nor immodest, but, on the contrary, the personification of refinement, grace, and modesty.[19]

One of the reasons the ragtime animal dances were considered "vulgar and immodest" was because they had roots in black culture. Objections to dancing took on a racist tint, which the Castles never addressed explicitly, but assuaged implicitly. Later in the *Modern Dancing* introduction, Vernon Castle promised to remove the shoulder shimmies and hip undulations that characterized the African American dances of the time:

> Our aim is to uplift dancing, purify it, and place it before the public in its proper light. . . . Drop the Turkey Trot, the Grizzly Bear, the Bunny Hug, etc. These dances are ugly, ungraceful and out of fashion.[20]

Just how popular were the Castles? There was a Castle House studio with its own Castle House Orchestra; a Castle Park at Coney Island, so vacationing New Yorkers could keep up their lessons; and a Castle Club (Vernon was president) and Castles-by-the-Sea dance hall in Long Beach, which was then an elegant retreat. In 1915 the couple performed *Castles in the Air* at the roof garden of the Forty-Fourth Street Theatre for a salary of $1,500 (about $33,500 today) a week. They were also a major influence on Fred and Adele Astaire, then a brother-sister ballroom act, who saw the Castles in the Broadway show *The Sunshine Girl* at least nine times. People all over the world now looked to the Castles for dance trends. (And fashion trends, too: Irene Castle became a style icon, with women everywhere copying her easy, flowing dresses, short bob and close caps.)

Despite the Castles' efforts to "refine" African American dances, the rise of jazz music in the 1910s and 1920s brought with it another wave of irresistible dance crazes that came out of black jook joints and honky-tonks. Jazz, born in New Orleans, blended black folk traditions with French Creole and old-world European styles. As blacks migrated north after emancipation, they brought jazz with them. The style picked up more influences in the Mississippi River Valley and, eventually, Chicago and Harlem. Musicians like "Jelly Roll" Morton, Louis Armstrong, and Duke Ellington sped up jazz beats, and their faster "hot jazz" became especially popular.

The Charleston was actually a short-lived dance fad, but because it covered so little space, it was easy to film,

which ensured it a lasting legacy. It probably originated in African American dance halls in Charleston, South Carolina, around 1913, and from there was featured in several all-black musicals and revues. The dance was free-flowing and fast-moving, characterized by high kicks forward and backward and the signature hands-on-knees step. In 1923 choreographer Ned Wayburn learned the Charleston from a young black dancer and added it to the Ziegfeld Follies revue, inaugurating its mainstream popularity. The line between the Broadway stage and the ballroom dance floor became very blurry: At the Charleston's high point, popular dances to do and popular dances to watch were essentially one and the same.

In the 1920s dance marathons also became a fad. The Audubon Ballroom in New York held the first official marathon, which lasted twenty-seven

The Dancing Marathon, 1923. Sketch by Johan Bull. *Library of Congress*

The non-stop baby needs new shoes.

They've just become engaged, and where there's no sense there's no feeling.

The gentleman seems to have lost the spirit of the thing.

THE DANCING MARATHON

"The first hundred hours are the hardest"

Sketches by Johan Bull

The hours I spend with thee, dear heart, are but a string of blisters.

The odds are against him.

What a difference just a few hours make! The light fantastic grows a trifle heavy.

hours. Eventually marathons became a spectator sport, with people paying to watch the competitors. Usually contestants were allowed a two-minute toilet break and ten-minute rest every hour (though sleep was forbidden) and were required to shower once every twelve hours. But audiences began to expect more and more outrageous marathons. The longest, in Pittsburgh, Pennsylvania, lasted twenty-four weeks and five days.

In the early 1930s, as America plunged into the Depression, these marathons took on a grimmer cast: They were often made up of poor couples desperate for the prize money. The physical and mental toll dance marathons took on these tragic figures was documented in the 1935 book, and later 1969 movie, *They Shoot Horses, Don't They?* In 1933 dance marathons became illegal.[21]

Not before, however, George "Shorty" Snowden had a chance to make dance history. During a 1928 marathon, the music sped up for a while, and Snowden started to do a dance the reporters covering the event had never seen before. According to legend, when they asked him what it was, Snowden said, "I'm doing the hop, just like Lindy"—i.e. Charles Lindbergh, who'd made his first transAtlantic "hop" of a flight in 1927.[22]

The Lindy hop developed at Harlem's Savoy Ballroom, a glamorous hall with a block-long dance floor that catered to a mostly black crowd. The Lindy was revolutionary in that it involved both a rocking step in a closed hold and a "break-away," or "swing-out," a designated time for improvisation that echoed the improvisatory runs in jazz music. Accordingly, the individual creativity of the dancers became important, with the best Lindy hoppers creating their own signature moves.

The northeast "Cat's Corner" of the Savoy dance floor was where Lindy stars congregated, and where rival duos tried to out-dance each other. It was a fiercely territorial place; many dancers were members of gangs, and stealing another dancer's steps could earn you a beating. (Gang members even figured out a way to do the Charleston that let them kick their enemies' shins.) The most famous of the Lindy duos were Shorty Snowden and Big Bea, and Stretch Jones and Little Bea. Between the four of them they brought the Lindy hop into its own, exhausting every possible combination of basic steps and creating many more.

For nearly a decade the Lindy belonged solely to dancers like these—the elite amateurs of New York and a few other big cities. For the rest of America, the dance didn't arrive until the mid-1930s, to accompany a new type of music: swing.[23] Bandleader Benny Goodman was the swing prophet, bringing swing music to the fore of the American mainstream. Swing was an offshoot of jazz, but swing bands had larger, more prominent drum and horn sections: the "big band" sound. The heart of swing music, the "swing" itself, is tricky to define. As Goodman said, "Those who have asked for a one-word or one-sentence definition of swing overlook the fact that it was originally a term used among musicians to identify something they all recognized. How, for example, would you describe *red* for a child, who did not know what it was?"[24] Essentially, it was a rhythm with a different flow—more of a slide than a bounce. It gave dances a new kind of momentum. And it was an even more perfect fit for the spirited showmanship of the Lindy hop.

As it traversed America, the Lindy became a dance that unified different ethnic, racial, and class groups. Malcolm X, who started out shining shoes—including Duke Ellington's—at Boston's Roseland Ballroom and eventually became an enthusiastic Lindy hopper, emphasized the importance of dance to the civil rights cause. During World War II, US soldiers spread the Lindy, by then also called the jitterbug, all over the world. Regional styles of the Lindy, like the British jive, developed.

In fact, dances were seen as a critical part of supporting the war effort during World War II. Dance served as a great diversion for both soldiers and civilians. The United Services Organization (USO), a military entertainment unit, hosted hundreds of dances during the war; they were some of its most popular events. Young women saw dancing with soldiers as a patriotic duty. The hostesses at New York's Stage Door Canteen were told never to refuse a dance with a man in uniform. In 1944 *New York Times* dance critic John Martin visited the Stage Door Canteen and wrote, "Listen, Mac, the war is nothing to dance about, and you can say that again: but what I mean, it sure is something to dance on account of."[25]

From 1920 to the Castro revolution in 1959, Latin music exerted an especially significant influence on US dance and culture. Cubans and other Hispanics immigrated to US cities in large numbers, and as air travel improved, Central American countries became popular tourist destinations for US residents. The tango of Argentina, samba of Brazil, and rumba of Cuba all had moments in the spotlight on American dance floors.

But the biggest Latin hit was actually a Latin American invention: the mambo. An exhilarating combination of Latin rhythms and American jazz, mambo music was created in the 1940s by Cuban

ABOVE: Dancers at the Stage Door Canteen, 1940. *Getty Images*

LEFT: Mambo contest at the Savoy Ballroom, Harlem, 1953 *Associated Press*

THE SWING DANCE REVIVAL

The Lindy hop had essentially disappeared by the 1980s. At that point a few clubs in New York, including Small's Paradise in Harlem, began playing swing dance music again—and they attracted some of the original Lindy hoppers, most notably legend Frankie Manning. Small's closed in 1984, but the seed had been planted, and in 1985 twelve of the old-school Lindy dancers founded the New York Swing Dance Society.

In 1992 Manning and fellow Savoy swing dancer Norma Miller choreographed and danced in the fantastic Lindy hop scene in Spike Lee's *Malcolm X*. Americans began to show a renewed interest in swing dance, spurred further by the rise of retro-swing music groups like the Royal Crown Revue and, later, the Cherry Poppin' Daddies, Squirrel Nut Zippers, Big Bad Voodoo Daddy, and the Brian Setzer Orchestra.

Before long, the swing revival became a mainstream phenomenon. The Royal Crown Revue was featured in the movie *The Mask* (1994), with Jim Carrey swing dancing with Cameron Diaz; in 1996 Jon Favreau swung with Heather Graham in *Swingers*, accompanied by Big Bad Voodoo Daddy; The Gap had a hit with its "Khakis Swing" commercial in 1998. Swing clubs opened in cities across the country, and young people flocked to studios to learn how to dance. Today "swing dancing"—a mix of the Lindy and newer styles, like East Coast Swing—remains popular at certain bars and dance clubs throughout the United States.

bandleaders. In New York, they drew from the harmonies and rhythms of Puerto Ricans, Dominicans, African Americans, and Europeans alike, creating a flashy, brassy, dance-friendly New York Latin sound.

The origins of the mambo dance are hazy. While the basic step may have been invented years earlier in Cuba or Haiti, in its modern form it was almost purely a New York creation, developed to fit that New York sound. There was some controversy as to whether the first step of the basic was off the beat (count two) or on it (count one), but everyone agreed on the relatively simple back-and-forth foot pattern—and the seductive hip action, known as "Cuban motion," that accompanied it.

Cuban bandleader Pérez Prado was the man responsible for introducing most Americans to mambo music. His instrumental mambo songs incorporated elements of the swing-y big band sound, making them more accessible to white audiences. By 1954 the mambo was a bona fide craze, especially among adults in New York City and Miami. Even non-Latin singers got into the mambo game: Rosemary Clooney had a major hit with "Mambo Italiano," Perry Como with "Papa Loves Mambo."

As mambo dancers incorporated more and fancier steps into their vocabulary, the cha-cha (sometimes called cha-cha-cha) developed as an "easier" alternative to the mambo. It slowed down the mambo basic by adding a triple-step in the middle, in place of the mambo's hold ("one, two, cha-cha-cha"). The cha-cha made its way through Cuba in 1953, and it didn't take long for Latin musicians to bring it to American cities.

The merengue also arrived in America after World War II. Its appeal was its simplicity: Merengue dancing is just one step per beat of music, alternating feet and swaying the hips. The national dance of the Dominican Republic, merengue was probably developed in the nineteenth century by the island's native tribes. Some claim the dance evolved from the movements of enslaved sugar-cane cutters as they worked, chained from foot to foot.[26]

During the 1950s, radio and television became the biggest driving forces behind dance crazes. By the early 1950s rhythm and blues songs—which were essentially simplified, intensified versions of swing, with the emphasis placed on the second and fourth beats of the measure—had already been popular among young black Americans for a few years. At that point they started to get more airtime on mainstream radio stations. In 1951 Cleveland radio DJ Alan Freed started playing R&B records by Fats Domino, Chuck Berry, and Little Richard; they quickly became hugely popular. Freed also presented live stage shows featuring R&B artists, which, notably, attracted racially mixed crowds. Many of the songs had "rock" in the title or mentioned "rocking and rolling" (a euphemism for sex). In 1952 Freed began using the term "rock and roll" on the air, and a revolutionary movement had a name.

Unsurprisingly, Freed's edgy rock and roll shows, and the wildly enthusiastic teenage responses to them, provoked indignant anger. An article about rock and roll in the *New York Times* sported the headline, "Experts Propose Study of 'Craze': Liken it to Medieval Lunacy, 'Contagious Dance Furies' and Bite of Tarantula."[27] FBI director J. Edgar Hoover called the music a "corrupting influence"; *Time* magazine compared rock concerts to "Hitler mass meetings."[28] The real problem for most objectors, however, was that the majority of rock and roll artists were black.

Elvis Presley, the rock and roll musician who came closest to bridging the cultural gap between blacks and whites, stirred up his own share of controversy. Popular as his music was, it was his dancing that caused the biggest outcry. He swiveled, gyrated, and centered all of his movement, oh-so-suggestively, in the pelvis. In 1955 authorities at two different performances warned Elvis that if he moved during the show, he would be arrested for obscenity. When he sang his version of the R&B hit "Hound Dog" on the *Milton Berle Show* in 1956, grinding and twisting, fans went crazy. On a later *Ed Sullivan Show* appearance, however, Sullivan insisted the cameras only film him from the waist up.

Controversial or not, the power of dance on television was undeniable. Philadelphia radio DJ Bob Horn began capitalizing on that power in 1952, with a televised dance party called *Bandstand*, featuring local kids dancing to popular songs. When the wholesome, clean-cut Dick Clark took over for Horn in 1956, the show's popularity skyrocketed. *American Bandstand*, as it became known in 1957, was especially appealing because it never featured professional dancers—they were all young amateurs, people whom teenagers across the country could relate to. Most of the dancers were white, but they embraced black dance trends and introduced them, in a nonthreatening way, to a mainstream audience. Thanks to television, a dance formerly known only by a few urban black teens could become a national craze overnight.

The most ferociously popular of those crazes was the twist. R&B singer Hank Ballard wrote the song "The Twist," but Clark asked nineteen-year-old Ernest Evans, a charismatic black *American*

Bandstand regular known for his impressions of famous singers, to cover it. Clark's wife, after hearing Evans' impression of Fats Domino, apparently nicknamed Evans Chubby Checker, and Chubby Checker's "The Twist" exploded onto the *Bandstand* airwaves on August 6, 1960.

The song was deliciously catchy, but what really hooked people was the dance, which Checker introduced during his performance on *Bandstand*. It was simple—just a twisting of the hips and feet—and endlessly customizable. You could twist down low to the floor. You could twist while waving your hands in the air. You could twist with a partner, or in a group. But you could also twist just as effectively by yourself.

After its initial bang, the twist would probably have died a quick death if not for the help it received from New York City's Peppermint Lounge—a tiny, unlikely club, initially catering to a gay clientele, which accidentally became the world's twist headquarters. "The Peppermint Lounge!" Tom Wolfe says in *The Kandy-Kolored Tangerine-Flake Streamline Baby*. "You know about the Peppermint Lounge."

One week in October 1961, a few socialites, riding hard under the crop of a couple

OPPOSITE: Chuck Berry, whose R&B music shaped 1950s dance crazes. *Associated Press*

BELOW: The Peppermint Lounge, 1964. *Michael Ochs Archives, Getty Images*

of New York columnists, discovered the Peppermint Lounge and by next week all of Jet Set New York was discovering the Twist, after the manner of the first 900 decorators who ever laid eyes on an African mask. Greta Garbo, Elsa Maxwell, Countess Bernadotte, Noël Coward, Tennessee Williams, and the Duke of Bedford—everybody was there, and the hindmost were laying fives, tens, and twenty-dollar bills on cops, doormen and a couple of sets of maître d's to get within sight of the bandstand and a dance floor the size of somebody's kitchen.[29]

The force of all that twisting celebrity meant that the twist became acceptable everywhere, to pretty much everybody. It was the first teenage fad to cross generations; it was the first craze to capture all of mainstream America.

Well, almost all. Critics of the twist were scandalized not only by its suggestive hip motions (which were probably the reason the White House issued a formal denial that anyone danced the twist at a party in November 1961), but also by the fact that it could be—and was most frequently—danced alone. They saw it as a sign that society had become broken and fragmented.[30] But the 1960s *were* a time of great social upheaval, and condemning the twist was a form of denial. As scholar and writer Marshall Fishwick wrote in his defense of the dance in 1962,

> . . . the Twist is a valid manifestation of the Age of Anxiety; an outward manifestation of the anguish, frustration, and uncertainty of the 1960s; an effort to release some of the tension which, if suppressed and buried, could warp and destroy.[31]

The twist almost annihilated traditional ballroom dance. In its wake, organized dances seemed to all but disappear. Even faddish trends like the twist itself eventually faded away. As a young person in the later 1960s, if you were dancing at all, you were free-form dancing, "doing your own thing"—an idea that jelled perfectly with the developing hippie culture. Hippie "be-in" gatherings (as represented in the musical *Hair*, which opened in 1967) featured dancing that was really just expressive swaying, trance-like, without touching a partner. For several years, America's social dance scene wasn't much of a scene at all.

A few years of grungy hippie culture left some Americans hungry for glamour—and disco made glamour fashionable again.

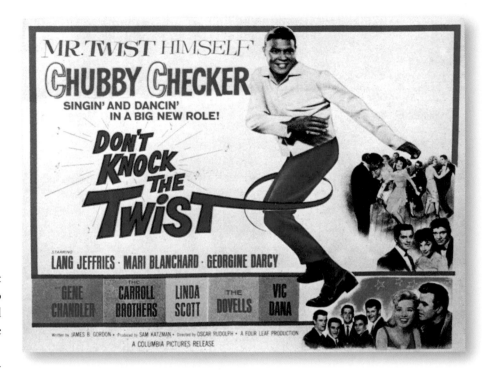

Chubby Checker. *RedFerns, Getty Images*

The *discothèque* idea originated in France during World War II. As a library full of books is a *bibliothèque* in French, so a *discothèque* was a club full of records, a venue that played songs from their collections instead of hiring a band. The idea spread to England and, eventually, to the United States, where the name was shortened to "disco." Elaborate light shows, added to make up for the visual vacuum left by the band, became a disco signature.

In the late 1960s discos began hiring DJs who would mix records by using two turntables, eliminating the breaks at the ends of songs that formerly caused awkward pauses on the dance floor. By the early 1970s the new, bass-heavy, dance-friendly music these DJs liked to play was known as disco.

It was 1975's "The Hustle," by Van McCoy and the Soul City Symphony, that started the disco dance craze in earnest. The hustle was originally an underground Latin dance style, probably created by Puerto Ricans in the South Bronx; later, it spread to the gay and black communities in both New York and San Francisco. It was a funkified version of the moves these dancers had seen their parents do, essentially a smoothed-out Lindy hop that incorporated elements of the merengue and other Latin dances, as well as the signature Latin hip action. Significantly, it was danced with a partner. The song "The Hustle" paved the dance's route to the mainstream, and it quickly became popular at discos throughout the United States. Soon all kinds of hustle variations emerged: the Latin hustle, tango hustle, New York hustle. People were re-learning how to dance with each other.

American Bandstand may have featured performances by black artists, but the dancers were almost uniformly white. Recognizing a hole in the television lineup, and hoping to feature some of the black soul musicians who received little mainstream attention, producer Don Cornelius created the television variety show Soul Train in 1970.

It was essentially a hipper, all-black version of Bandstand, but unlike Bandstand's noodlish amateurs, the Soul Train dancers were legitimate talents. (In fact, it was extremely difficult to become a Soul Train dancer—you usually had to have a recommendation from one of the show's regulars.) Their creative, stylish moves became the highlight of the show.

The Soul Train crew even sowed the seeds of larger dance movements. One of the most popular dancers, Don Campbell, introduced the "lock"—an impressive robotic movement that stopped in a freeze. He went on to form a professional dance group called the Lockers, which influenced the stage career of Michael Jackson and, eventually, the development of hip hop dance (see Chapter 10).

Dancers on Soul Train, c. 1970. Michael Ochs Archives, Getty Images

But not all disco dancing was partner dancing. A string of disco line dances—like the bus stop, which involved a series of steps, claps, foot taps and turns, repeated to each corner of the room—swept across dance floors. There was also the infamous disco point, which was sometimes "used as a means of derision or exclamation," with dancers pointing at the best or worst movers or dressers. Some dancers just pointed diagonally up and down to the ceiling and the floor, marking the song's beat.[32]

In 1977 disco dancing officially arrived with the release of *Saturday Night Fever*. Based on the *New York* magazine story "Tribal Rites of the New Saturday Night" by Nik Cohn, it starred John Travolta as Tony Manero, a floundering Brooklyn teenager whose world only makes sense on the dance floor of disco club 2001 Odyssey. Travolta, already a talented dancer, was coached by choreographer Deney Terrio for seven months, and his dance scenes in the film were electric.

By the late 1970s disco fever had a firm hold on America's kids—and its celebrities. Studio 54 opened on April 26, 1977, at 54th Street in Manhattan and quickly became a disco hot spot for a very glittery crowd. For the first time a dance club was more about the scene than the dancing. It became extremely difficult to get past Studio 54's velvet rope, and the club's exclusive door policy later became the norm at high-end dance clubs.

Disco eventually drowned in its own popularity. By the early 1980s even grandmothers were disco dancing, and the style lost its cachet. Young music fans began to view the disco scene as campy and tacky rather than posh. The "disco sucks" campaign, which began in the late 1970s, was more than just a dig at a passé trend. Disco culture was centered in black, Hispanic, and gay communities. "Disco sucks" was essentially an expression of homophobia and racism.

As disco waned, country and western dancing surged in popularity. American country-western music had been gaining momentum since the 1950s, thanks to artists like Johnny Cash; by the 1980s it was a well-developed genre. And disco had re-established the tradition of couple dancing, as well as the whole idea of learning a social dance rather than "doing your own thing." All it took was the 1980 movie *Urban Cowboy*—another John Travolta phenomenon—to provide the spark that started the country-western fire.

Country-western couple dances evolved from square dance and a smattering of other dance styles. (Most of them are based on a footwork pattern that looks a lot like the fox trot.) They include East Coast swing, West Coast swing, cowboy, and two step, as well as countrified versions of the waltz, cha-cha, and polka. Country line dances, which have roots in old English country dances, rose to prominence in the 1990s after Billy Ray Cyrus' hugely popular country song "Achy Breaky Heart" inspired an equally popular line dance.

Despite the seemingly relaxed atmosphere at most country-western dances—participants are usually dressed in jeans and cowboy boots—dancers embrace old-fashioned etiquette. The dance floor is tacitly divided into lanes, for example, allowing slower dancers to congregate in the middle, where they won't be run over by the faster dancers, who keep to the outside. And it's an unspoken rule that you should dance the first and last songs with the partner you came with. It took 150 years for dancers to re-embrace it, but on certain nights in certain country-western bars, the old tradition of ballroom gentility appears to be alive and well.

SALSA AND THE LATIN REVIVAL

As rock music flooded the radio airwaves, the mambo, cha-cha, and merengue dances that had been so popular in the 1950s went into a decline. Latin dance needed a makeover. And that's exactly what salsa was: a rebranding campaign.

The term "salsa," meaning simply "sauce," is a catch-all that applies to Cuban-derived popular dance music. It was initially promoted and marketed in New York in the late 1960s and early 1970s, in an effort to reinvigorate the Latin music and dance scene. Salsa dancing is a jumble of the major Cuban dance styles—the mambo, cha-cha, and rumba—but it owes its biggest debt to mambo, with which it shares a basic step.

The new name worked. Older dancers, in particular, embraced salsa. The style waned in the later 1970s and 1980s, but it was revived again in the 1990s, and today enjoys huge popularity in America, especially among Latinos. Salsa clubs, along with swing dance halls and country-western bars, are some of the only places where partner dancing can be found in the United States today.

Country-western dancing in Turkey, Texas. *Stephen Saks, Getty Images*

Baz Luhrmann's 1992 film *Strictly Ballroom* celebrated the vibrancy of competitive ballroom dance.
© Photos 12, Alamy

Today, "ballroom dance" isn't what people do when they go out on weekend nights. Instead, it's a codified, highly stylized series of competitive dances. Ballroom dance first began to separate from recreational dancing in the 1920s in Britain. In 1924 London's Imperial Society of Teachers of Dancing added a Ballroom Branch, marking the beginning of the standardization of ballroom dance steps. Rather than try to keep up with the latest dance trends, as most teachers had until that point, the Ballroom Branch teachers established "correct" versions of existing dances, and then emphasized excellence within each particular style.

Eventually, thanks to the strictness of their criteria, a competitive branch of ballroom emerged. In 1931 the first British Open Championships were held in Blackpool, England. (Blackpool's competition remains the world's most prestigious ballroom event today.) In the 1960s competitive ballroom dance went international, and many Americans enthusiastically adopted the form. Over the years the international competitive roster grew to incorporate Latin dances—the samba, cha-cha, rumba, paso doble, and jive—which joined the "standard" waltz, tango, fox trot, quickstep, and Viennese waltz. In the United States and Canada, dancers now compete with a slightly different collection of dances, developed by the two major American studio chains—the Arthur Murray Dance Studios and the Fred Astaire Dance Studios—as well as other independent studios. The American Smooth group includes the waltz, tango, fox trot, and Viennese waltz, while the American Rhythm group includes the cha-cha, rumba, East Coast swing, bolero, and mambo.

Today ballroom dance is essentially an elite sport. (In fact, the governing body for ballroom dance is called the International Dance Sport Federation, having dropped the word "ballroom" from its name in the 1990s.) It has enjoyed renewed popularity in America since 1981, when PBS started airing the Ohio Star Ball dance competition on a show named *Championship Ballroom Dancing*. *Dancing with the Stars* (see Chapter 10), which debuted on ABC in 2005, hooked yet another new generation of ballroom dancers.

Chapter Three
The Evolution of Tap

Even during its hibernation period, tap was still taught. Here, students at the Platt Park Recreation Center in Denver are learning the dance in 1967. *Duane Howell, Denver Post via Getty Images*

"Single shuffle, double shuffle, cut and cross-cut; snapping his fingers, rolling his eyes, turning in his knees, presenting the backs of his legs in front, spinning about on his toes and heels like nothing but the man's fingers on the tambourine; dancing with two left legs, two right legs, two wooden legs, two wire legs, two spring legs—all sorts of legs and no legs. . . ." —*Charles Dickens on a tap dancer, presumably William Henry "Master Juba" Lane, in* American Notes, *1842*[1]

Spectacular but not pretentious,

energetic but never effortful: tap dance was "made in America," and it is characteristically our own.

Tap took many years to develop a codified technique (or even to be called "tap," a name that didn't catch on until the twentieth century). Early tappers learned not in classrooms, but on street corners and in rough-and-tumble competitions. The style's evolution was charitably haphazard, picking up bits and pieces of social dance crazes and other dance styles as it shuffled—or tripped—along. Anything went in, as long as it looked and sounded good.

A dance best done by a single person—most frequently a single man, since early tap was, unlike most other performance dances, overwhelmingly male—tap emphasized the innovation of the individual, the new and novel, rather than the perfection of a particular set of steps. Amorphous, adaptable, and endlessly entertaining, the first wave of tap dance embodied the melting-pot ebullience of a changing nation.

After the Stono Insurrection laws prohibited black slaves from using drums in the mid-eighteenth century (see Chapter 2), they transferred their intricate West African drumming rhythms to their bodies, specifically their feet. At about the same time, a wave of Irish immigrants, fleeing the potato famine, arrived in the United States, bringing their jigs, reels, and clog dances with them. While several European step dances had already made their way to America, Irish dancers actually toured the South as entertainers. Once slaves caught glimpses of their performances, they began incorporating the heel-and-toe clogging steps into their traditionally flat-footed dances, changing the simple Irish downbeat to a syncopated off-beat. But black dancers didn't adapt the cloggers' rigid postures. Their arms and torsos remained loose, relaxed, free.

And so tap was born. African glides, drags, shuffles, and stamps added a distinct flavor to the evolving style; Irish and other European clog dances, with their articulated foot patterns, allowed the technique room to breathe and grow.[2]

Early tap found a home with the rise of the minstrel scene, which, by 1840, had become one of the most popular forms of American entertainment. Black performers were rare on early minstrel stages, but white imitators of black tappers, who darkened their faces with burnt cork, became a minstrelsy signature.

One of the first minstrels (perhaps the first) to do a blackface routine was Thomas Dartmouth Rice, a.k.a. Daddy "Jim Crow" Rice. He made his initial appearance as Jim Crow in 1828, allegedly appropriating a shuffling, loose-limbed dance he'd seen performed by an old, crippled black groom, and a song he'd heard sung by a black stage driver:

> Wheel about, turn about,
> Do jus' so:
> An' ebery time I turn about,
> I jump Jim Crow.[3]

Rice's routine, though essentially a grotesque caricature, was an immediate hit with white minstrel show audiences.

It was William Henry "Master Juba" Lane, a black man born free around 1825, who broke the minstrel stage color barrier. As a teenager he lived in the Five Points area of Manhattan, where the tenement houses were filled with a mix of Irish immigrants and free blacks; he became a highly skilled jig and clog dancer by watching his neighbors. Lane went on to create a compelling mixture of tricky clog steps and movements from the black dance vernacular—the high-wattage, syncopated, devil-may-care style that so impressed Charles Dickens when he visited New York City in 1842. Lane achieved a remarkable degree of fame for a black performer of the time, even earning top billing in otherwise all-white minstrel programs. One of the show's handbills read:

> Great Attraction! Master Juba! The
> Greatest Dancer in the World! and
> the Ethiopian Minstrels! Respectfully
> announce to the Citizens of this place that
> they will have the pleasure of appearing
> before them.[4]

Lane's greatest competition at the time was John Diamond, an Irish-American dancer who represented tap's folk influence. Diamond's minstrel number, which he performed in blackface, was widely respected. The pair had a series of challenge dances, beginning in 1844, and it was Juba who came away with the title "King of All Dancers."[5]

Eventually Juba's style became known as the "buck and wing"—the ancestor of modern rhythm tap.

Another influential style also developed on the minstrel circuit: the soft shoe. Performed in footwear with soft leather soles (as opposed to buck dancers' wooden ones), the soft shoe evolved out of "The Essence of Old Virginia," one of the most famous minstrel dances, in which the dancer traveled across the stage by moving his heels and toes but keeping his knees straight, so it looked as if he were skating. Black dancer Billy Kersands popularized that step in the 1870s. While the soft shoe retained the essence's smoothness, it added a new focus on elegance in the upper body. Irishman George Primrose (real name: Delaney) became the foremost soft shoe dancer. Less a technician than a stylist, Primrose created a refined style that became an inspiration for many of the "class act" tappers of the 1930s and 1940s.

The typical minstrel show involved three parts: a group of instrumental or vocal songs, accompanied by banter or funny speeches; the Olio, a series of virtuoso acts, including dances; and a Southern plantation scene capped off with a big song-and-dance finale, the "walkaround." By the 1860s, the crowd-pleasing specialty acts of the Olio made up the bulk of most minstrel performances. Over time, the other sections fell away, and the Olio became the vaudeville variety show.[6]

Various vaudeville circuits developed as producers, encouraged by enthusiastic audiences, bought up strings of theaters in towns across America. By the 1920s, the vaudeville scene included the Keith Circuit, the Orpheum Circuit, the Gus Sun Time Circuit—and Theater Owners Booking Association (T.O.B.A.), the circuit for black entertainers. Also known as "Toby" and "Tough on Black Artists" (or, less politely, "Tough on Black Asses"), T.O.B.A. was a strange scene. Audiences loved the Toby performers, but these artists were often forced to enter through the service doors of the venues that booked them, and were paid less than their counterparts on the white circuits.[7]

Nevertheless, vaudeville, and especially T.O.B.A., was where some of the world's best tap talent developed. The subtle, knotty rhythms of virtuoso tap dancers are best heard solo, or in smaller groups of two to five dancers—the average size of a vaudeville tap act. Because vaudeville circuits were so large, acts could often go for a year or more without worrying about changing their routine, which allowed them to perfect even the tiniest details. Many dancers who went on to become major stars—Bill Robinson, Eddie Rector, the Berry Brothers—polished their technique in vaudeville.

By the 1910s, tap dancers, looking for more variety, began thinking about their whole bodies rather than focusing on their feet alone. Many started experimenting with aspects of other dance styles, developing hybrid steps that eventually became tap standards.

In "jazz" steps, taps were not essential, though they were sometimes added. Most jazz steps emerged gradually on the minstrel and vaudeville circuits, and some of them—like the shimmy and the Charleston—later made it to the social dance scene. Two jazz steps in particular became part of tap's set repertory: "off to Buffalo" (a sidewinding shuffle, in which one foot crosses and re-crosses in front of the other) and "falling off a log" (a similar crossing of the feet, ending with a leaning pause that slides into the next step).

High-energy "flash," or "air," steps, designed to impress, also didn't require taps. In fact, most were designed to be performed at the end of an act, when the dancer needed a big, splashy finish, and the music was so loud the audience couldn't hear taps clearly anyway. Two

Clayton "Peg Leg" Bates, c. 1970.
Maurice Seymour, Michael Ochs Archives, Getty Images

The vaudeville circuit prized novelty, and few tap dancers were more "novel" than one-legged Clayton "Peg Leg" Bates. Bates, who lost his left leg at age twelve in a cotton gin accident, saw his handicap as an opportunity. He wore a regular tap shoe with metal taps on his right foot, but customized the end of his peg leg with a half-rubber, half-leather sole. When doing specialty steps—balancing on the peg, for instance—he'd use the rubber on the outside to avoid slipping; otherwise, he'd work the leather side for sound. Bates made his way from T.O.B.A. to white vaudeville, and by the 1930s he was dancing in top Harlem clubs. In the 1950s he appeared on *The Ed Sullivan Show* twenty-one times— more than any other tap dancer.

OPPOSITE: The Sandow
Trocadero Vaudevilles, c. 1894.
Library of Congress

"PICKANINNIES"

classic examples are "over the top" and "through the trenches," both credited to dancer Toots Davis, who polished them in the 1913 musical *Darktown Follies*. Over the top is a figure-eight jumping step in which the dancer almost appears to trip himself; through the trenches is a stationary running step, with the arms swinging vigorously as the feet scrape from front to back.

The "wing," an important tap building block, began to develop around the turn of the century. A sort of jazz-tap-flash combination, it's an air step that *does* require taps. "The Wing is a dynamic compromise," say jazz historians Marshall and Jean Stearns, "a transitional blend of vernacular body movements and taps, executed mainly in the air. . . . With its combination of taps with an upward spring, [it] holds two opposing impulses in balance, creating a dramatic fusion which can be thrilling."[8] Frank Condos and Mattie Olvera, known as King and King, astonished audiences when they introduced the five-tap wing in the mid-1920s. At the time it seemed an impossible feat.

Not a step but a routine, the "shim sham" became a show-business standard by the early 1930s. Thirty-two bars long, it includes eight bars each of four basic steps, including the double shuffle and "falling off a log." Its origins are murky—several dancers claim to have invented it—but it achieved widespread popularity thanks to the tap group The Three Little Words, who closed their show at Connie's Inn in Harlem with the shim sham every night. The whole club would join in, waiters included. Today the shim sham is a traditional way to say goodbye at the end of a tap show, with anyone who knows it invited onstage to participate.

How did a dancer gain entry into the professional tap world? In the early 1900s, a number of young black tappers started their careers as pickaninnies. Vaudeville comedian Joe Laurie Jr. described the trend:

> Many of the so-called single women [in vaudeville] carried 'insurance' in the form of pickaninnies, or 'picks,' as they were called. After singing a few songs of their own, they would bring out the picks (a group of Negro kids that really could sing and dance) for a sock finish. . . . I never saw any picks flop.[9]

Usually between the ages of six and twelve, pickaninnies (the word probably comes from the Portuguese *pequeno*, meaning "little one"[10]) weren't featured acts, but they were working in white vaudeville—a big step up from T.O.B.A. White circuits also tended to avoid the South, a desirable situation for black dancers considering the prejudiced times.

ABOVE LEFT: Drawing of Harlem jazz by Winold Reiss, c. 1915–1920. *Library of Congress*

ABOVE RIGHT: Many tappers entered the dance world when very young, as "pickaninnies"—black children between six and twelve years old, who danced in white vaudeville shows. Photo circa 1894. *Library of Congress*

Drawing in Two Colors

Winold Reiss

Willie Covan's MGM students tap dance for servicemen in Los Angeles, 1944. *Associated Press*

Since pickaninny acts were designed to impress no matter what, they recruited some of the country's most talented young tappers, many of whom went on to become tap icons. Willie Covan, for example, started out as a pick, but by 1917 had formed the renowned tap dancing quartet the Four Covans, who appeared in the historic Broadway musical *Shuffle Along*. Covan went on to develop several well-known buck and wing variations, including the "waltz clog," and to experiment with soft shoe and acrobatic tap. (He famously invented— essentially by accident—the "around the world with no hands" trick.) Later Covan served as the head dance instructor at MGM Studios, where he coached the likes of Mickey Rooney and Ann Miller.

The Whitman Sisters troupe was another tap talent incubator in vaudeville. The royalty of the T.O.B.A. circuit, where they made more money than any other act, the sisters' caravan of two dozen or so performers traveled the country from 1900 to 1943. The four sisters became known for scooping up talented kids wherever they found them, and raising and educating them in the troupe. And they were good educators—particularly the youngest Whitman sister, Alice, a clean, clear tapper known as "The Queen of Taps." It was the pickaninny model, essentially, but because the sisters, unlike the pickaninnies' frontwomen, were also black, they were able to better earn the trust of their protégés.[11]

That kind of apprenticeship aside, however, early tap didn't have a strong teaching tradition. Instead, tappers learned (and stole) from each other on street corners and rooftops, or in basements—anywhere with a space large enough to "lay down some iron." The best places to practice, and to learn by observation, were rehearsal halls, most of which were outfitted with good wood floors and maybe a piano. Renting a room at a New York City hall like Michael's, Phil Waiman's, Johnny Nit's, or Erving Plummer's in the 1920s set you back only about twenty cents an hour, and an accompanist could be had for an extra dollar. Alternatively, you could practice in a "snake pit," a large hall, usually about forty by sixty feet, portioned into several small alcoves that were rented individually. These hives of activity also hosted magicians, ballet dancers, snake charmers, and acrobats. The noise of their collective rehearsing, plus the tappers' own cacophonous contributions, was often overwhelming.[12]

And then there was the Hoofers Club. Located on 131st Street in Harlem, next to the Lafayette Theater, the space was essentially an afterthought—it was the backroom of a pool house, about fifteen square feet, with a few benches and a well-loved upright piano. But throughout the 1920s, 1930s, and early 1940s, it served as the unofficial home of tap dance. Run by proprietor Lonnie Hicks—a dance fan who never made any money off the endeavor—the Hoofers Club stayed open twenty-four hours a day. During the Depression it also became a haven for dancers in need of a few hours of shelter and warmth.

Pretty much every great tap dancer of the era came to the Hoofers Club at some point, but the venue had its own special heroes. Perhaps the most remarkable, "King" Rastus Brown, was essentially unknown outside of the Hoofers Club circle. Not a natural comedian—considered an

THE TIME STEP

The time step originated in vaudeville, but became popular in the 1920s and 1930s, when dancers began performing with big bands and needed a way to communicate tempo to the musicians. Originally every tapper had his or her own variation, but over time the most common version became the standard. A set of two measures—the basic time step is stomp, hop, step, flap, step; stomp, hop, step, flap, step—the syncopated combination, which also has double and triple variations, is both a measure of basic competence and a test of true style. As Marshall and Jean Stearns put it: "To say of a tap dancer: 'He doesn't even know the Time Step' or conversely: 'He makes even the Time Step look good,' is the worst and best that may be said."[15]

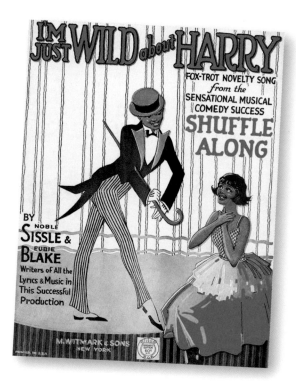

Shuffle Along sheet music, 1921.

impediment for a black performer at the time—he never made it in vaudeville or on Broadway.[13] But he was a master tapper, with a distinctive flat-footed, down-in-the-floor style. He'd regularly saunter into the Hoofers Club, ask a young tapper to "give him some stop-time"—by which he meant play the simple tune known as the "Buck Dancer's Lament"—and proceed to do six bars of the time step plus two bars of extraordinary improvisation. After this display, the younger dancers would dissect his performance, reconstructing it piece by piece.[14] And Brown was happy to share. He became an informal mentor to many of the talented tappers at the Hoofers Club.

Early in her career, Josephine Baker—shown in 1927 in her famous banana skirt—was in the chorus of *Shuffle Along*. Baker became the first black woman to star in a major motion picture, and a civil rights icon. *Popperfoto/Getty Images*

May 21, 1921, at the Sixty-Third Street Theater. Featuring songs like "I'm Just Wild About Harry" and "In Honeysuckle Time," the show told the story of an election race, with Flournoy Miller and Aubrey Lyles playing the two would-be mayors. Their histrionic tap-dancing fight became the show's hit number—and a favorite of Fiorello La Guardia, who often came to see *Shuffle* three nights a week.[17] The production also featured the Four Covans and talented tappers Charlie Davis and Tommy Woods. (Then-sixteen-year-old Josephine Baker was an end-girl on the chorus.)

Shuffle Along introduced steps and styles already well-known in vaudeville to Broadway audiences, who for the most part had never seen them. A massive success, the show resulted in a hot market for both black musicals and tap dancing.

By the 1920s no Broadway show was complete without a tap number—or four. But while the dancing in black musicals was better than anything happening in the watered-down tap chorus lines of white productions, the most important tap innovators rarely appeared on the Broadway stage. Vaudeville, still alive and kicking (or tapping), paid its stars much better money than Broadway did, and most big-name tappers found it hard to justify leaving the circuit.

The exception to that rule was Bill "Bojangles" Robinson, who, though he started out in vaudeville in the 1890s, was "discovered" in the Broadway show *Blackbirds of 1928*. At that point he was already fifty and had been honing his trademark "stair dance"—a fifteen-minute routine consisting of a series of light, elegant taps that skipped gracefully up and down a set of stairs—for years. But *Blackbirds* introduced the stair dance to New Yorkers and cemented Robinson's reputation. Bojangles' success was so great that the show's weekly gross jumped from $9,000 to $27,000.[18]

Langston Hughes described Robinson's style as:

> *. . . human percussion.* No dancer ever developed the art of tap dancing to a more delicate perfection, creating little running trills of rippling softness or terrific syncopated rolls of mounting sound, rollicking little nuances of tap-tap-toe, or staccato runs like a series of gun-shots. Bojangles, dancing alone on a stage with the orchestra quiet, could make tantalizing, teasing offbeats, sometimes merging into a series of restful continuous bars of sound that would build up in tempo and volume to a climax like a burst of firecrackers.[19]

In the 1920s and 1930s, the unsystematic development of tap continued in Broadway musicals and revues. The musical *Darktown Follies*, which opened at Harlem's Lafayette Theater in 1913—just after the venue was integrated, welcoming both black and white patrons—began the trend of whites flocking to Harlem nightly for entertainment.[16] The show's chorus boys included both Toots Davis, creator of "over the top" and "through the trenches," and his partner Eddie Rector. Rector began to develop his own take on the soft shoe in the show and eventually became one of tap's greats.

The real black Broadway breakthrough, however, came eight years later. *Shuffle Along* opened

JIMMY SLYDE

During the swing era, tapper Jimmy Slyde developed a graceful, lyrical style known as slides. Giving the impression that the floor has suddenly turned to ice, slides make a dancer appear weightless as he or she slips across the stage. Slyde began experimenting with slides thanks to the influence of an early teacher, but his elaborate riffs on the step were unlike anything else in tap. He paired up with another slide dancer, Jimmy "Sir Slyde" Mitchell, to make the duo the Slyde Brothers, and the two danced with many of the big swing bands, including those of Count Basie and Duke Ellington.

OPPOSITE: Bill "Bojangles" Robinson. © Pictorial Press Ltd, Alamy

RIGHT: John W. Bubbles and Ford Lee "Buck" Washington, a.k.a. Buck and Bubbles, 1946. © Everett Collection Inc., Alamy

the number of taps possible within a given measure. An incredible improviser who could ad-lib endlessly, Bubbles also eschewed the classic eight-bar phrase plus a two-bar improvisation break. He "ran" the bars, chaining strings of nonrepetitive phrases together. In order to cram in even more steps, he started counting four beats a bar rather than two, effectively cutting the tempo in half—and giving himself more room to experiment. Bubbles' style became known as rhythm tap. It was the beginning of tap technique as we know it today.

By the 1930s tap dance was having an identity crisis. Suffering from massive overexposure, it couldn't carry a musical anymore, and tap's vaudeville acts were in a similar decline (as was all of vaudeville). *New Yorker* critic Robert Benchley summed up the problem in a 1931 article:

> Up until three or four years ago, I was the Peer of Tap-Dance-Enjoyers. . . . [I]t didn't seem as if I could get enough tap-dancing. But I did. More than enough. With every revue and musical comedy offering a complicated tap routine every seven minutes throughout the program, and each dancer vying with the rest to upset the easy rhythm of the original dance form, tap-dancing has lost its tang.[21]

Some tap dancers found more successful homes traveling with the big swing ensembles that were beginning to come into vogue. The bands' "presentation" shows focused on the music, rather than a lineup of variety acts. They placed their musicians onstage, not in the pit, and those musicians weren't vaudeville's ragtag combos but top-notch ensembles—the bands of Tommy Dorsey, Duke Ellington, Benny Goodman, and Cab Calloway. Each band traveled with a "unit" made up of a chorus line of girls, a singer, maybe a comic, and a tap dance act. Because presentation shows brought great tappers and great musicians together, they sparked new creativity in the tap world.

Tap's presentation-style "class acts" had their heyday from the 1920s through the 1940s. They were a departure from the high-octane, big-finish bravura of most Broadway tap. In some ways "an expression of [black tappers'] drive toward equality and respectability," they generally consisted of two or more elegant-mannered dancers, nattily attired, doing identical steps in unison—with an emphasis on refined, sophisticated soft shoe and light, bright taps.[22] The sweep of ballroom dancing, the precision of the Radio City Rockettes, the aural appeal of tap: Class acts blended them all.

Robinson was a natural performer with a magnetic onstage personality. "In a sense," said dancer Charles "Honi" Coles, "Bo's face was about forty percent of his appeal."[20] He also made a specific contribution to tap technique: He brought tap up to the toes, moving away from the earthy, flat-footed style of dancers like King Rastus Brown. The effect was preternaturally light and twinkly.

John "Bubber" Sublett, a.k.a. John W. Bubbles, took the style even further. A vaudeville star (along with his partner, Ford Lee "Buck" Washington), and the original Sportin' Life in the Gershwins' *Porgy and Bess*, Bubbles introduced heel taps to Robinson's formula. These were not the flat shufflings of earlier tappers. Instead, he articulated sounds with both his heels and his toes, increasing

Eddie Rector was a defining influence on these class act teams. His soft-shoe "stage dancing" fit steps together like so many interlocking puzzle pieces, creating a seamless flow of movement. Class act Peaches and Duke (Irving "Peaches" Beaman and Duke Miller), famous for their ultra-clean taps, put a new focus on the use of the entire stage and the graceful handling of the upper body.

The class act reached its pinnacle with Coles and Atkins. Charles "Honi" (a nickname from his mother) Coles and Charles "Cholly" Atkins were one of the last acts of the type—they didn't start working together until the 1940s—but their unique

combination of lightning-fast rhythm tap and impossibly slow soft shoe revolutionized the style. The soft shoe in particular bewitched viewers with its limpid lyricism. "We had three things in mind when we put together the Soft Shoe," Atkins said:

> It had to be slower than anybody else's; at the same time, it had to be really interesting; and finally, it had to be so lyrical that it could stand by itself, that is it had to *sound* just as good with or without accompaniment, so we could do it without music.[23]

and splits looked like acts of defiance. *How could something this fabulous*, they seemed to ask, *be on its way out?*

The Berry Brothers—Ananias, Jimmy, and Warren—perfected the form. Ananias was the master of the "strut," a later version of the cakewalk; Jimmy was the singer and comedian; and Warren was perhaps the strongest dancer and definitely the most impressive acrobat.[24] Together they pioneered the "freeze and melt," which contrasted showy action with total motionlessness. The brothers frequently performed at Harlem's elite Cotton Club, were on the bill at Radio City Music Hall's opening performance in 1932, and appeared in the films *Lady Be Good* (1941), *Panama Hattie* (1942), *Boarding House Blues* (1948), and *You're My Everything* (1949).

Though often called a flash act, the Nicholas Brothers didn't fit neatly into any category. Fayard and Harold Nicholas did a routine in top hat and tails, and they were known for their beautiful hand and upper body movements, like class act dancers. But their routines also incorporated fantastic leaps ending in their signature move: the full split, as opposed to the "jazz split" most other tappers were doing, with the back leg bent. The duo appeared at the Cotton Club for years. (A legendary 1938 Cotton Club showdown with the Berry Brothers didn't produce a clear winner.) They also danced in Hollywood, appearing in more than fifty movies together. Fred Astaire called their electric routine in *Stormy Weather* (1943) "the greatest dance number ever filmed."[25]

The brothers Berry and Nicholas weren't the only tappers making names for themselves in films. By the 1930s Hollywood had begun importing Broadway's dance directors. The semi-military tap chorus parades designed by maestros like Busby Berkeley—a remarkable innovation in their own right (see Chapter 9)—looked fantastic on camera. But because they required little tap technique, some saw them as a step backward for the art form.[26] Thankfully, many films also recorded some of the era's best tap dancers.

Bill Robinson made fourteen films and helped break down some of Hollywood's stubborn racial barriers. His talent commanded respect from white and black producers (and audiences) alike. Unfortunately he was frequently forced to play old-fashioned stereotypes; in his four much-loved movies with Shirley Temple, for example, he was most often the friendly antebellum butler. By the same token, he and Temple were the first interracial pair shown together in film, and when Robinson

In New York's Hotel Edison (built in 1931), there's an Art Deco mural of Cab Calloway in front of the Cotton Club. *© Randy Duchaine / Alamy*

From 1945–1949, Coles and Atkins danced with many of the big bands, including Cab Calloway, Louis Armstrong, Charlie Barnet, and Count Basie. In 1949 they were featured in the musical *Gentlemen Prefer Blondes* on Broadway, dancing in the second act's "Mamie Is Mimi." But because they arrived on the scene a few years too late, they never achieved the stardom they deserved.

On the other end of the spectrum were the dancers of "flash acts," who competed for audiences' waning tap attention spans by incorporating ever more spectacular steps and acrobatics into their routines. Their thrilling precision-timed flips

was accused of being an ingratiating "Uncle Tom," he was deeply upset. Controversy aside, Robinson's film work made him a nationwide icon. One and a half million fans flooded the streets of Harlem and Brooklyn when he died in 1949.[27]

Jeni LeGon, like Bill Robinson, was an exception to a general rule: She was the rare female black solo dancer to eventually make it in Hollywood. (She was also the only black woman who ever danced with Robinson on film, in 1935's *Hooray for Love*.) LeGon, who trained with the Whitman Sisters troupe, was one of the few women to master all the men's flash steps—high jumps, splits with a controlled recovery—which is also why she chose to wear pants and shorts rather than skirts and dresses when performing.[28] She had a relatively successful film career, appearing in some twenty movies, although she, too, struggled in Hollywood because of her race. "I played every kind of maid, that's all I ever did," she said. "I was an East Indian, West Indian, African, Arabic, Caribbean, and black American. Eventually there weren't that many roles. They were too few and far between."[29]

There were many more options in Hollywood for white dancers, who could play substantial leading roles—women included.

Massachusetts-born Eleanor Powell was dancing professionally by age twelve but didn't start tapping until after her Broadway debut in 1928, realizing the hole in her skill set. Though she initially found tap difficult, she eventually became a talented technician, maintaining a feminine grace and elegance in spite of her earthbound dancing style. Her most successful films—including *The Great Ziegfeld* (1936), *Rosalie* (1937), and *Ship Ahoy* (1942)—featured huge, expensive numbers built around Powell as the star, which meant that she ultimately made fewer movies than some of her colleagues. Nevertheless, she performed opposite some of Hollywood's top leading men. In *Broadway Melody of 1940*, she even had a (not entirely successful, but worthy) partnership with Fred Astaire.[30]

Powell's successor was Texan Ann Miller, who was the opposite of Powell in many ways. Frank and brassy, she was better suited to less romantic supporting roles, which allowed her to leave the swooning to others and focus on high-spirited tap numbers. Miller made her film debut in *New Faces of 1937* at age fourteen; even that early on, she had mastered her signature rapid-fire "machine-gun" tap style. She was eventually listed in *Ripley's Believe It or Not* as the world's fastest tap dancer—a speedometer attached to her feet recorded 500 taps per minute—and her legs were rumored to be insured for a million dollars.[31] Some of her best-known numbers were from the 1953 film *Kiss Me Kate*, including "Too Darn Hot." But her greatest routine was "I've Gotta Hear That Beat," from *Small Town Girl* (1953). Directed by Busby Berkeley and choreographed by Willie Covan, it presented a visual and aural feast.

Of all of Hollywood's tappers, Fred Astaire had the greatest impact on how people thought about dance. A magpie, Astaire studied ballet, tap, and ballroom, but never identified himself as any one type of dancer. ("I don't know how it all started," he once wrote, "and *I don't want to know*.")[32] By doing away with boundaries and embracing aspects of every technique he admired, Astaire created a fluid, full-body dancing style that, as seen by millions in his many films, was an invaluable contribution to American dance.

Astaire developed his signature look during his years playing second fiddle to his older sister Adele on the vaudeville circuit, learning "the fine art of understatement."[33] By 1928, at age twenty-nine, he was well on his way to success: He tied for third in a buck-dancing contest for Broadway performers. (Bill Robinson took first place.) Adele retired to get married in the early 1930s, but Fred kept dancing, and in 1933 he headed to Hollywood. The next year he partnered with choreographer Hermes Pan to create the dances for *Flying Down to Rio*, and the two, finding that their styles suited each other perfectly, began a lifelong friendship and collaboration. As Agnes de Mille said, Pan's "splendid craftsmanship and dazzling technique, rather like that of a goldsmith's, set off the Astaire numbers for the jewels they were."[34] Both were inspired by the footwork of great rhythm dancers like John Bubbles, but felt that the percussiveness of the feet should be offset by a graceful upper body. They also insisted on full-frame dance shots, with no "cutaways" to audience members or the dancers' faces, and made sure that every routine was filmed in its entirety. It was not only a new style of tap, but also the first time movie audiences were really *seeing* tap.

Astaire's easy, debonair charm also contributed to his success. He was the definition of "class," a chivalrous aristocrat in a top hat and tails—squiring the likes of Ginger Rogers, who molded her dance style to his in the ten films they starred in together—but he managed to remain eminently likeable, avoiding hoity-toity upper-crust stereotypes.

Like Astaire, Gene Kelly also came from a dancing family: He was one of five Kelly siblings, all of whom were dancers. His parents took over a

Pittsburgh-area dance studio in the early 1930s, and Gene and siblings Fred and Louise became the primary instructors, teaching musical comedy, ballet, acrobatics, and tap. For a while Gene and Fred performed together on local stages, but eventually Gene struck out on his own, heading to Broadway, where he appeared in *Leave It to Me* (1938), *One for the Money* (1939), and *The Time of Your Life* (1939). (When he left the latter to take the lead in *Pal Joey* in 1940, Fred stepped into Gene's *Life* role, and ended up winning several awards. Later, Fred choreographed and danced all over Broadway.) In 1941, Gene decided to make the move to Hollywood, where he went on to make such legendary films as *An American in Paris* (1951) and *Singin' in the Rain* (1952). Energetic, athletic, and good-looking, Gene was a strong tapper and an appealing presence onscreen. Like Astaire (whom he greatly admired), he helped bridge the gap between tap and other dance forms, especially ballet.

Through film, tap dance became one of America's great exports. In the 1930s and 1940s, the worldwide popularity of tap skyrocketed. "It is hard to exaggerate the enthusiasm for it that seized people," Agnes de Mille said. "The explorer William Beebe (1877–1962) said that though he sometimes used to barter beads with savages, his ability to tap dance for them was much more efficacious."[35]

But by the early 1950s, American tastes had shifted. Jazz music was exploring a new sphere—it was difficult to tap to the opaque rhythms of bebop—and pop music was entering the equally untappable zone of rock and rhythm and blues. On Broadway and in films, classical dance was beginning to take over. Immensely appealing works like *On Your Toes* (1936), choreographed by George Balanchine, and *Oklahoma!* (1943), choreographed by de Mille, skewed toward ballet, spelling the beginning of the end for tap on the stage and, eventually, the screen. The seemingly irrepressible tap world suddenly fell silent.

Tap entered a hibernation phase. During the lull, its former stars struggled. (Honi Coles ended up as the production stage manager at the Apollo Theater.)[36] But within a generation, tap, in typical American fashion, was reborn. Though bebop and rock and roll initially baffled tappers, over time these musical styles would spur a revolution. Both

ABOVE: Ann Miller performing "Too Darn Hot" in *Kiss Me Kate* (1953). © *Moviestore Collection Ltd., Alamy*

OPPOSITE: Fred Astaire dances while Hermes Pan attempts to diagram his steps, 1936. *Museum of the City of New York, Getty Images*

rejected old-timey, let-us-entertain-you ingratiation. As tappers began to explore them in earnest, tap underwent its own transformation: "from an exhibition form," as tap scholar Constance Valis Hill wrote, "to an expressive form."[37]

Gregory Hines was one of the rare tappers whose career spanned the downturn. Hines came from a showbiz family—his grandmother danced in the Cotton Club chorus line, and his father was a musician. Hines was three and his brother, Maurice, was five when they took their first tap lessons. Their instructor, Henry LeTang, taught them not only the basics of tap technique but also several show-stopping routines, which featured rapid-fire sequences embellished with spins and flips. Later, LeTang shaped these numbers into a twelve-minute set; by 1952, Gregory (then six) and Maurice (eight) were on the road with their act. While on the variety circuit, they saw nearly every star in the business—including the Nicholas Brothers, Honi Coles, and Jimmy Slyde—and from them absorbed much of the rich history of tap. By the time the brothers came of age, however, traditional tap was out of vogue, and in the early 1970s they broke up the act. Gregory abandoned dance and formed a jazz-rock band, Severance.

OPPOSITE: Fred Astaire and Ginger Rogers in *Swing Time* (1936), choreographed by Hermes Pan. *John Kobal Foundation, Getty Images*

RIGHT: Gene Kelly, 1943. *Time and Life Pictures, Getty Images*

The 1978 musical *Eubie!*, choreographed by Hines's mentor LeTang, brought Hines back into the tap fold. *Eubie!*, which celebrated the life of Eubie Blake, one of the masterminds behind the seminal 1920s musical *Shuffle Along*, was steeped in tap history. Hines's tour de force performance earned him a Tony nomination and made him a bona fide Broadway star. Three years later he appeared in the Duke Ellington tribute *Sophisticated Ladies*, to equal acclaim.

Hines was beginning to create his own tap technique. Though an appealing performer, he never charmed for charm's sake, avoiding the "happy minstrel" persona. Offstage, he experimented with the driving rhythms of the funk and rock music he'd explored with his band. Abandoning the upright posture that had defined so much of show tap, he let his upper body relax, even as his feet hit harder and faster. The look was cool, effortless, and casually dashing.

Hines was also a charismatic actor, which made his eventual move to film feel natural. Sometimes he took straight acting parts, but occasionally a role would allow him to use all his talents. Francis Ford Coppola's *The Cotton Club* (1984) was set in the cabaret where Hines's grandmother had danced; Hines played Sandman Williams, the tap-dancing toast of Harlem. The following year he starred opposite Mikhail Baryshnikov in *White Nights*, a film best remembered for the scene in which the two dancers faced off in a high-octane ballet-tap challenge that showcased their remarkable versatility. *Tap* (1989) made even better use of Hines's diverse skills. The first movie musical to merge tap dancing with rock and funk music, *Tap* featured full-scale production numbers, filmed on location in New York City and Hollywood. It also allowed Hines to act and dance alongside tap legends Harold Nicholas and Sammy Davis Jr.—and a young up-and-comer named Savion Glover.

Eleanor Powell in *Born to Dance*, 1936, from the Golden Age of tap on film. © *Moviestore Collection Ltd., Alamy*

Eubie!, with Maurice Hines, Gregory Hines, and Lonnie McNeil, 1978. *Photofest*

Tap represented the first phase of the tap revival, as led by Hines: a reimagined style rooted in the form's older traditions, but also embracing contemporary music and dance culture. Hines would promote this new style for the rest of his life. Many saw him as his generation's Bill Robinson—a universally beloved, gracious performer, and a powerful advocate for the form.

Brenda Bufalino's career also bridged traditional and innovative tap forms. Growing up in Massachusetts, she began taking tap classes at six, and a year later she became a member of the Strickland Sisters, a traditional tap ensemble. At thirteen, however, she started commuting to Boston to study with

Stanley Brown, a teacher of rhythm tap. Around the same time, she discovered the sharp, angular bebop of Dizzy Gillespie and Charlie Parker. She became determined to add their rhythms to her dancing.

As a white woman, Bufalino was an oddity in the world of rhythm tap. Nevertheless, by sixteen she was performing in interracial revues in nightclubs. Eventually she moved to New York and began training with Honi Coles, who became a mentor. Some black tappers frowned upon colleagues who trained white dancers, but Coles shrugged off such criticism. "No blacks want it, and *she* does," he said. "Nobody else can do it, and *she* can."[38] Bufalino had immense respect for Coles's art. "He sang his steps

Gregory Hines in *Tap*, 1989.
© Moviestore Collection Ltd., Alamy

and he sang tunes as he danced," she said. "He didn't need any music; he was a one-man band. . . . His feet took on a personality. You could almost see them smile."[39] Bufalino also diversified her dance portfolio by studying modern jazz with some of Jack Cole's disciples (see Chapter 9) and Afro-Cuban forms with members of Katherine Dunham's company (see Chapter 6).

In the early 1960s, as tap's popularity began to wane, Bufalino left the dance world, and spent several years writing plays and poetry. She continued to listen to bebop jazz, however, and to think critically about the future of tap. When Bufalino returned to the form in the early 1970s, she had a new mission: to preserve the legacy of the past and integrate tap into the concert dance world, where she felt it deserved representation. In 1977 she released the documentary *Great Feats of Feet*, one of the first works to honor the achievements of the founders of black rhythm tap. She also helped coax legends like Coles and Jimmy Slyde back into teaching, so that a new generation of tappers could begin to learn the skills of the past.

To prove tap's artistic worthiness, and to explore her own choreographic ideas, she began coordinating full evenings of concert tap around New York City. *Singing, Swinging, and Winging* (1978), performed in the tiny Pilgrim Theatre on the Bowery, marked the first major showcase of her tap choreography. Critics—especially music critics—respected her efforts, applauding the way she had tappers riff and trade phrases with the show's jazz musicians.

Bufalino's concert work led to the establishment of the American Tap Dance Orchestra, which she co-founded in 1986. The group remade the tap chorus as a musical ensemble, dressed in black tie and arranged onstage like a symphony. "I was interested in the layering of sound and also in texture, tone, and the use of different points of the foot for various notes," Bufalino said. "When I arrange, sometimes it's contrapuntal, with dancers doing the same steps at different times. And sometimes it's an arrangement, with dancers taking the bass line, drum line, or different melodic lines, so that you're building."[40]

Until the late 1970s, solo performers had dominated tap. Bufalino's concerts and her work for the ATDO pioneered group tap choreography. Soon other tap troupes emerged, including the Jazz Tap

Ensemble in Los Angeles (founded in 1979) and the Chicago Human Rhythm Project (1990).

Savion Glover crowned tap's revival by becoming the first definitive master of the post-lull generation. Gregory Hines called him "possibly the best tap dancer that ever lived."[41] By the time Glover turned twenty, he was acknowledged to be the heir to Hines's mantle, the leader of the next wave of innovative tap artists.

A rhythm fiend from the beginning, Glover started playing drums in a Suzuki class at age three, and joined a band at seven. When his group was invited to play at Broadway Dance Center, one of the most prestigious studios in New York, Glover encountered tap for the first time. He began studying at BDC, and quickly demonstrated a natural talent for the form. At eleven he earned the title role in the Broadway musical *The Tap Dance Kid*, and three years later he joined the Paris production of the all-black musical revue *Black and Blue*. The impressive *Black and Blue* cast introduced him to hard-hitting rhythm tap. Glover, just fourteen,

Brenda Bufalino performs in *Tap City* in New York, c. 2010. *Debi Field*

began to formulate his own distinctive style, rooted in rhythm tap but emphasizing self-expression over entertainment.

In 1992 Glover reunited with Hines (whom he had first met on the set of *Tap*) in the Broadway musical *Jelly's Last Jam*, based on the life of jazz legend Ferdinand "Jelly Roll" Morton. Hines played the grown-up Jelly, Glover the young one. The show marked a turning point for Glover, who found in Hines a powerful mentor. "For me, knowing Gregory is like knowing you have a pops, but not meeting him until you're twenty years old," he said, "and it turns out he's been very cool all this time."[42] The two had nightly tap challenges during the run of the show, playful, experimental showdowns that let Glover explore his tap persona.

Glover hoped to get more young dancers interested in tap in its purest form: simply rhythm, wild and expressive, free of cheap tricks. "My mission is . . . to funktify everybody," he said, "just to let them know that tap isn't this corny, washed-up art form. . . . [I]t's new, and it's raw. It's today."[43] George C. Wolfe, the director of *Jelly's Last Jam*, embraced the idea. Together he, Glover, and poet Reg E. Gaines created *Bring in 'Da Noise, Bring in 'Da Funk*, which opened in 1995 at New York's Public Theater. The show, with a book by Gaines and choreography by Glover, honored the African American legacy, chronicling the story of a people as told through their feet. It used tap to describe social history, channeling the form's percussive power in a profoundly artistic way.

Bring in 'Da Noise made Glover a star and helped popularize his rough, urgent style, which he called "hitting." Hitting featured "flat-footed, piston-driven, heavily emphatic paddle-and-roll tapping," wrote historian Constance Valis Hill; it "reclaimed all areas of the . . . men's oxford tap shoe—the outside rim, inside rim, ball of the sole, and tip of the toe—as fair territory for driving the sound."[44] The arms and torso were just along for the ride. Glover funneled the energy of his entire body into his singularly expressive feet.

This was tap for the hip hop generation, and young urban dancers embraced it eagerly. Foremost among Glover's followers was Jason Samuels Smith, who performed in the Broadway cast of *Bring in 'Da Noise*, then joined Glover's company, Not Your Ordinary Tappers (NYOT). Despite his Glover-esque dreads and baggy pants, Smith wasn't a Savion clone. Hines, noting Smith's unique abilities, anointed him as "possibly the next 'Greatest.'"[45]

Smith grew up steeped in jazz. His mother was a jazz dancer and teacher, his father a jazz dancer and choreographer. The Smiths ran Jo Jo's Dance Factory, the precursor to Broadway Dance Center, and Smith spent his childhood in and around the studio. He trained in ballet, jazz, and tap before all but giving up dance in favor of sports. When Smith was a teenager, however, Glover started teaching master classes at BDC, and through Glover's instruction he rediscovered the possibilities of tap. "In my other classes I learned technique and style and more visible dancing," he said. "Savion's classes were more rhythmic and I was more in tune with the heavier hoofing style than with the lighter visible style."[46] In 1995, at age fifteen, Smith was given a *Bring in 'Da Noise* understudy contract, and by 1997 he'd earned a principal spot in the show.

Glover had a profound influence on Smith, but Smith enriched and expanded Glover's style, too.

OPPOSITE: Jason Samuels Smith. *Photograph by Matthew Murphy, courtesy Divine Rhythm Productions*

BELOW: Savion Glover performs *Bare Soundz* at the Apollo Theater in New York, 2008. *Donna Ward, Getty Images*

In his twenties Smith started collecting old film clips of black tappers, which he watched obsessively. He also began listening to the jazz of Dizzy Gillespie and Charlie Parker. These connections to the past inspired Smith to develop a style that looked backward as well as forward, creating a multicultural, musically acute blend of old and new. A charismatic figure and a gifted teacher, Smith has become a leader in the tap community; he encourages young dancers to embrace traditional as well as innovative styles.

Accompanying the development of the new rhythm tap, with its aggressively unpretty style, was another movement with an aesthetic seemingly diametrically opposed to Glover's. Yet its leaders were members of the Glover diaspora.

Young women tappers proved early on that they could master "hitting," that they understood the force of raw, gritty tap. Eventually some began to wonder why they couldn't remake the style in a way that allowed them to express their femininity, too. Leading the way were Dormeshia Sumbry-Edwards, the only woman in the touring production of *Bring in 'Da Noise*, and Chloé Arnold, who was just ten when she joined Glover's "crew" in Washington, D.C. Sumbry-Edwards and Arnold began performing new tap in high-heeled tap shoes—demonstrating that they could be womanly, if not exactly ladylike, and still hit as hard as the best of the men. Their performances emphasized more than just sound, even though sound was still their primary concern; they held their upper bodies gracefully and wore flattering, leggy costumes. (The Rockettes, they understood, got some things right.) In a way, this style of dancing issued a challenge to the guys. These women could do everything the men could do, in three-inch heels.

Michelle Dorrance presented another version of modern femininity in tap. Her mother had been a ballet dancer and her father a soccer player; as a child in North Carolina, she discovered that she felt an affinity for both pursuits. But tap was what stuck. An extraordinary tap technician, Dorrance was discovered by Glover at a tap jam while she was studying at New York University. Tall, slender, a little gawky, she had a more tomboyish look than dancers

like Sumbry-Edwards and Arnold, and she wore shoes with heavier soles. "She has a quirky, funny view of the world," said dancer Josh Hilberman, a longtime collaborator. "She falls between the young killer women in high heels and the guys."[47] Dorrance eventually began experimenting with choreography, earning the Princess Grace Award in 2012 for her innovative choreographic work.

Institutionally speaking, tap today is in a precarious place. While Glover may continue to perform to sold-out houses at New York's prestigious Joyce Theater, lesser-known tap artists struggle to find performance venues and achieve financial stability. A small but influential network of tap festivals, however, provides a home for the tap community. And tap will survive because it *is* a true community, a close-knit web of mutually supportive artists. The members of America's tap family, with the stars of the past as their common ancestors, are united today by the belief that fleet feet will always be forces for innovation—that they will continue to shape and re-shape the American dance landscape.

Chapter Four

Modern Pioneers

Loie Fuller, c. 1902. *Library of Congress*

"As I see it, the deepest lack of Western cultures is any true workable system for teaching a process of integration between soul and body." —*Ruth St. Denis*[1]

Ruth St. Denis and Ted Shawn.
Library of Congress

At the beginning of the twentieth century, dance in America, both on- and offstage, was for entertainment purposes only. A little fun at the vaudeville house, a little fun on the ballroom floor: It served as a lightweight distraction.

Then came two generations of artists who wanted to *think* about dance. The first group—Loie Fuller, Isadora Duncan, Ruth St. Denis, and Ted Shawn—explored the relationship between the body and the soul. Fascinated by the exotic mysticism of ancient Greece and Asia, they asked: How could the outer self express the inner self? How could bodily movements stir deep, primeval feelings in viewers?

The second generation—Martha Graham, Doris Humphrey, Charles Weidman, and Hanya Holm—took that question a step further. They wanted to capture the essence of the *American* psyche. How could dance portray the American experience?

While their styles eventually earned widespread acceptance in the concert and academic worlds, these modern-dance pioneers were revolutionaries in their times, challenging hard-set social and artistic norms. Together, they convinced America to take dance seriously.

Loie Fuller was not, in today's sense of the word, a dancer. She took only a few formal lessons over the course of her career. Instead, she was an illusionist, bewitching audiences with "dance" performances that involved clever manipulations of light, shadow, and drapery. She was an international sensation, the first movement artist to be esteemed by artistic intellectuals, and an inspiration to many aspiring expressive dancers.

Fuller's story is uncertain; she liked to give different versions of it to different journalists.[2] But it appears that she was born outside of Chicago in the 1860s. She became a professional actress by the time she was fifteen, working various vaudeville circuits. Her dancing appeared natural and easy: swirling turns, flourishes of her arms and torso, walks and skips. As her career progressed, and as electric lights became increasingly common in theaters, she began to experiment with dramatic colored lighting and, especially, the play of light on fabric. Though electric theatrical lights were a big step up from gaslights, they were still difficult to operate; technicians had to insert the colored gelatins by hand. At her peak, Fuller claimed to employ up to thirty-four lights, operated by fourteen to twenty electricians.[3]

Together they created fantastical effects. In Fuller's signature *Serpentine Dance*, first presented in New York in 1892, she wore a voluminous silk skirt that flew as she swirled and twirled, and lit the fabric with saturated colors, transforming herself into a supernatural creature. She toured Europe, where she became a huge success. The French christened her "La Fée Lumineuse" (the Fairy of Light),[4] or called her simply "La Loie."[5] She was so popular, in fact, that before long Loie skirts, Loie scarves, and even a Loie Fuller stove were available for sale.[6]

Fuller didn't luck into her successes. She was ambitious and high-minded. "I wanted," she said in 1914,

> to create a new form of an art completely
> irrelevant to the usual theories, an art
> giving to the soul and to the sense at the
> same time complete delight, where reality
> and dream, light and sound, movement and
> rhythm form an exciting unity.[7]

The intellectual community took note. Fuller counted Alexandre Dumas, Anatole France, and Pierre and Marie Curie, in whose home she performed, among her fans. Auguste Rodin was fascinated with her, though he was never actually able to sculpt her. Henri de Toulouse-Lautrec did a hand-colored, gold-dusted lithograph that captured the essence of her *Fire Dance*, in which she performed on glass illuminated from below.

In 1900 twenty-three-year-old Isadora Duncan saw Fuller perform a spectacular show during the Paris Exposition—at the Palais de Danse, which was crowned by a statue of Fuller. "Before our eyes," Duncan remembered,

> she turned to many coloured, shining
> orchids, to a wavering, flowing sea flower,
> and at length to a spiral-like lily, all the
> magic of Merlin, the sorcery of light, colour,
> flowing form. What an extraordinary genius.[8]

Isadora Duncan didn't invent any steps or a definite technique. She was never as popular in America as she was in Europe. (In fact, she performed in the United States only during a few short visits between 1908 and 1922.) Yet she had a profound influence on

American dance and American life. Her progressive ideas about movement, beauty, education, and women's freedom not only established the foundation for modern dance, but also contributed to an evolution in social mores that would transform the twentieth-century world. Agnes de Mille exaggerated only slightly when she said that "no one except Chaucer or Dante worked single-handedly such an astonishing change in the popular reception of an art."[9]

Duncan was born in 1877 to a troubled San Francisco family. Her parents eventually divorced, but her artistic mother, seeing Duncan's complete confidence in her own invented movements, encouraged her to pursue dance. Before Duncan was ten, she was teaching dance classes to the children in her neighborhood.

As a teen, Duncan got jobs in musical revues. But her distinctive performance style was already beginning to crystallize, and she felt that the theater

Portrait of Loie Fuller by Henri de Toulouse-Lautrec, 1893. Oil on cardboard. © *Masterprints, Alamy*

Students at the London School of Dalcroze Eurhythmics, 1934. *Arthur Tanner, Hulton Archive, Getty Images*

Modern dance evolved as part of a new, more general appreciation for movement that occurred during the nineteenth century. François Delsarte (1811–1871) and Émile Jaques-Dalcroze (1865–1950), non-dancers who nevertheless conducted groundbreaking investigations into the communication between brain and body, paved the way.

A French musician and teacher, Delsarte studied how people express emotions in their faces and bodies. By observing interactions between people in various public places, he discovered certain patterns of expression that he developed into what he called the Science of Applied Aesthetics. Though his (uncodified) method involved expression only through voice and gesture, in America his followers extrapolated outward, creating a system of "Delsartian gymnastics" that emphasized the importance of physical activity and education. American Delsartism reconsidered traditional attitudes toward the body—particularly the female body—and introduced the idea that movement might express the inner self. Delsarte's protégé, the actor Steele MacKaye, taught performer Genevieve Stebbins, whose style of "interpretive" dance incorporated Delsartian principles and in turn influenced some of America's early modern dancers.

Dalcroze, a Swiss musician and composer, provided the other component of the modern dance equation: He explored the profound experience of music through movement. Dalcroze developed eurhythmics, a system that teaches basic musical concepts by creating a movement analogue for each. He believed this made for a more complete musician. Dalcroze's relationship to dance was more explicit than Delsarte's: He taught Marie Rambert, who would go on to found the first ballet company in Great Britain, and influential German dancer and choreographer Mary Wigman.

world was untrue to her vision. She began performing sober, contemplative solos that were politely applauded by her audiences at society ladies' salons. Looking for a more enthusiastic reception, Duncan (and her family) eventually moved to Europe, settling, like Fuller, in Paris. There she honed her creative voice—and found real fame, quickly making her way into elite artistic circles. (At her Paris debut, Maurice Ravel was her pianist.)[10]

Duncan's technique was unspectacular because it wasn't about steps. She disliked virtuosic ballet, which she described as

> vainly striving against the natural laws
> of gravitation or the natural will of the
> individual, and working in discord in its
> form and movement with the form and
> movement of nature, produc[ing] a sterile
> movement which gives no birth to future
> movements, but dies as it is made.[11]

Instead, she believed that dance should be natural and, in Delsartian fashion, spring from emotion. Though she moved with great fluidity, her dances were rooted in simple walking and running. She was inspired in part by classical Greece, seeing it as a historic beacon of truth in art.[12] Eschewing the restrictive corset, she usually performed in loose tunics or Grecian-style robes. She danced barefoot—"the first naked foot seen on the Western stage in sixteen hundred years."[13] And she was one of the first dancers to perform to major works of classical music, particularly pieces by Beethoven and Wagner.

Duncan's revolution had a distinctly feminist cast. In a 1903 essay that would become a manifesto for both progressive dancers and feminists, she avowed:

> . . . the dancer of the future will be one
> whose body and soul have grown so
> harmoniously together that the natural
> language of that soul will have become
> the movement of the body. . . . She will
> dance not in the form of a nymph, nor fairy,
> nor coquette, but in the form of woman in
> its greatest and purest expression. She
> will dance the changing life of nature,
> showing how each part is transformed into
> the other. . . . She will dance the freedom
> of women; . . . she will dance the body
> emerging again from centuries of civilized
> forgetfulness, . . . no longer at war with
> spirituality and intelligence, but joining
> them in a glorious harmony.[14]

She practiced the feminist views she preached, too, particularly after watching her mother struggle with the lingering shame of divorce. Duncan chose not to marry either actor Gordon Craig, who fathered her daughter, Deirdre, or sewing-machine-fortune heir Paris Singer, father to her son, Patrick.

Despite her professional triumphs, Duncan's personal life was turbulent and unhappy. Both her children drowned in a freak accident in 1913, which left her devastated. In 1922 she surprised everyone by marrying the young Russian poet Sergey Yesenin, but he committed suicide two years later. Duncan's enthusiasm for Russian communism tarnished her reputation in the United States. In 1927 she died in a bizarre and now infamous accident, when her long scarf caught in the wheel of the Bugatti sports car she was riding in, snapping her neck.

Though Duncan was eager to establish a school, none of her attempts to do so were successful. But her legacy was never to be a technique or teaching style. Instead, she brought greater spiritual substance and artistic rigor to dance, opening doors for other expressive artists.

There are many parallels between the lives of Isadora Duncan and Ruth St. Denis. They were born just two years apart. Both were, to some degree, products of Delsartism. Both traveled to Europe and admired the work of Loie Fuller. Rodin even tried to seduce each—unsuccessfully.[15] But it would be difficult to imagine two more different artists, and women.

ABOVE: Isadora Duncan, ca. 1915–1923. *Library of Congress. Photograph by Arnold Genthe*

OPPOSITE: Isadora Duncan. *UIG, Getty Images*

St. Denis was born Ruth Dennis in 1879 in New Jersey. (She changed her name later in her career, after producer David Belasco, teasing her about her straight-laced ways and spiritual approach to dance, nicknamed her "Saint Dennis.")[16] When St. Denis was a young child, her forward-thinking mother, who had been a practicing doctor before her marriage, drilled her in Delsartian exercises and enrolled her at a local dance school. Noting St. Denis's natural gifts, her teacher encouraged her to study with ballet master Carl Marwig in New York City. Marwig also admired the young girl—enough to offer her free lessons—but because her family was too poor to afford the train fare regularly, she trained with him only intermittently.

From the beginning St. Denis loved lavish, over-the-top spectacles. Barnum and Bailey's outsized *The Burning of Rome* made a particular impression on her as a child. "Nothing had ever been seen before," she remembered in her memoir,

> like these houses going up in flames, with
> the Coliseum a black silhouette at one side.
> As a grand finale a ballet of a hundred
> angels floated about on the stage, dressed
> in costumes made of ribbons. . . . All the
> way home I sat in a corner of the carriage,
> my face tense and pale, and would not
> speak to anyone. The first thing I did when
> I got to the farm was to go into the garret
> and slash up a pair of Mother's old curtains
> to create my first dancing costume.[17]

In the late 1890s St. Denis worked wherever she could in vaudeville, primarily as an actress. She performed professionally for eleven years before mounting her first solo show. During that time, she apparently mastered all the standard vaudeville tricks, such as kicks, splits, and cartwheels. (Thomas Edison made a two-minute kinetoscope of "Ruth Dennis, Skirt Dancer" in 1894.)[18]

While performing in musical theater in 1904, she had a transformative experience thanks to an unlikely inspiration: a cigarette ad. The poster, which she saw in a drugstore in Buffalo, New York, advertised the Egyptian Deities cigarette brand, depicting the goddess Isis seated on a throne with her feet in the Nile River. "In this figure before me," she remembered,

> was the symbol of the entire nation,
> culture, and destiny of Egypt . . . the figure,
> its repose, its suggestion of latent power
> and beauty, constituting to my sharply

> awakened sensitivity a strange symbol of
> the complete inner being of man.[19]

The poster's romanticized view of Eastern culture captured her imagination. She decided to create a dance that inhabited that world.

As she researched her Egyptian dance, she discovered *devi-dassi*—the temple dancers of Indian religion—and made friends with some Indian émigrés. Fascinated by Indian spirituality, she created *Radha*, the solo that would make her name, in 1906. An "art dance" set in a Hindu temple, it depicted the Indian goddess Radha performing surrounded by symbols representing the five senses (such as bells for hearing). Though the work was far from culturally authentic—it was set to music from French composer Delibes' *Lakmé*, and included a mixture of ballet and acrobatics—the beautiful St. Denis was mesmerizing in it.

She traveled to Europe, along the way creating the four other dances that, with *Radha*, would form her Indian suite: *Incense*, *Cobras*, *Yogi*, and *Nautch*. St. Denis was very popular with European audiences, but after a year she returned to America, where she mounted a nationwide tour. She performed on the vaudeville circuit, caring far less than Duncan or Fuller about the venues in which she danced. As a result, many more Americans were able to see her works and become interested in her mystical, expressive style of dance.

In 1911, while performing in Denver, Colorado, St. Denis did for Ted Shawn what the cigarette poster had done for St. Denis. The young Shawn had been a student of theology, with plans to enter the Methodist ministry, before contracting diphtheria and becoming paralyzed by an overdose of an antitoxin. As part of his recovery, his physician advised that he study dance. He began taking ballet classes, which he compared to his theological studies as "not really a change of base at all . . . only a change of form."[20] The spiritual possibilities of dance intrigued him—but not until he saw St. Denis perform *Incense* was he truly moved by a dance performance. "I wept," he says, "not caring that it was in a crowded theatre—and never before or since, have I known so true a religious experience or so poignant a revelation of perfect beauty. I date my own artistic birth from that night."[21]

Around that time St. Denis, in dire financial straits, made an effort to cash in on the Vernon and Irene Castle-inspired ballroom craze (see Chapter 2); she hired Shawn to do a few ballroom numbers in her vaudeville program. St. Denis was drawn to him—he was young, handsome, and an admirer of

her work—and soon the two discovered that they also shared the goal of establishing a dance school and company based on utopian ideals. In 1914, they married.

A year later they opened their first dancing school, in Los Angeles. The school and the partnership were eventually known as Denishawn. "Miss Ruth" and "Papa," as St. Denis and Shawn's students knew them, made a good pair. Shawn's ambition made the school a reality; St. Denis set it on a course of high spiritual purpose, emphasizing the quest for truth through movement.[22] Eventually their pupils would fill out the ranks of the new Denishawn Company.

The Denishawn School was one of the first dance organizations to attract students from "good families." In the late nineteenth and early twentieth centuries, being a dancer was, to the middle classes, a less-than-honorable career, and stories about Duncan's gypsy lifestyle only reinforced the stereotype. St. Denis and Shawn proved the respectability of their endeavor by living respectably themselves—they did not cohabit before their marriage—and demanding that their students adhere to a strict moral code. They may have been less courageous than Duncan, who made a stand for sexual freedom, but they proved to the American middle class that dance could be an upright pursuit. No mother need worry, they promised, about sending her daughter to Denishawn.

The Denishawn Company also flourished, and its productions became more and more lavish. In 1916 at the University of California, Berkeley, St. Denis mounted a massive spectacle that used not only her own dancers but also nearly one hundred students from Berkeley's summer session. The pageant portrayed the daily lives and spiritual pursuits of ancient Egyptian, Greek, and Indian civilizations. A real river at the front of the stage became in turn the Nile, the Styx, and the Ganges. One of St. Denis and Shawn's most famous duets, *Toilers of the Soil*, came out of the Egyptian section; they moved in profile, like hieroglyphics. The production was a fabulous success, and it toured several cities in California. But its cost was enormous, leaving Denishawn deeply in debt.

While both St. Denis and Shawn dreamed of presenting "pure art" alone, they were realists. "One should *think* of dance as an art," St. Denis said, "although one may have to *do* it as a business."[23] To make ends meet, they entered two less-than-ideal arenas. The first was the film industry, which was just beginning to take root in Los Angeles. Cecil B. de Mille and D. W. Griffith wanted dancers for their epic films, and many Denishawn members were funneled into their productions. (Film icon Louise Brooks started out as a Denishawn dancer.) St. Denis also choreographed for the screen, including a Babylonian dance for Griffith's *Birth of a Nation* follow-up *Intolerance* (1916).

Denishawn's real savior, however, was vaudeville. The troupe toured crowd-pleasing acts on the Orpheum Circuit, where they earned an almost unprecedented $3,500 a week. Though St. Denis and Shawn were willing to compromise their dance ideals for a good cause—keeping their school and company afloat—their vaudeville tours were hardly creatively stale. Vaudeville was where Shawn first began to flex his choreographic muscles, exploring his enthusiasm for American Indian dance in

particular. His 1921 work *Xochitl* starred young Denishawn student Martha Graham.

While Denishawn's vaudeville appearances were popular—the company even toured in Japan, China, and India from 1925 to 1926—they were also exhausting. (In 1927, at the dedication of the new Denishawn House in New York City, St. Denis apparently cried, "And every brick a one-night stand!")[24] The Denishawn dancers grew weary of the backbreaking work and disappointed that they weren't performing high-minded artistic dance. St. Denis and Shawn's relationship was also increasingly strained. Shawn wanted more artistic control, St. Denis didn't want to play the obedient wife, and both were flirting with other men.[25]

Denishawn folded in the early 1930s. St. Denis essentially retired, but Shawn, hoping to combat the country's prejudice against male dancers, began to create dances designed to showcase the male physique and temperament. His work attracted the attention of physical education teachers, and he was invited to participate in an experimental program at Massachusetts' Springfield College, which at the time graduated more than half the athletic coaches in the country.[26] Shawn translated the distinctive movements of various sports into dance forms for the college's five hundred young physical education students, eventually overcoming the hesitations many of them had about studying dance.

By 1930 Shawn had bought a farm in the small town of Becket, Massachusetts, that he intended to use as a retreat. Named Jacob's Pillow after the large, pillow-shaped boulder behind the farmhouse, it became home to Shawn's new all-male company in 1933. He found inspiration in the success of the Springfield College program. Shawn kept his dancers in shape by having them build the group of structures we know today as Jacob's Pillow—including the Ted Shawn Theatre, the first structure in America designed specifically for dance.[27] Ted Shawn and His Men Dancers toured the world for seven years, returning to the Pillow each summer to perform and give public lectures. Eventually, after the differences between St. Denis and Shawn cooled, the two reconciled, and Miss Ruth settled in as first lady of the Pillow.

When America entered World War II, most of Shawn's dancers joined the army. He leased the empty Jacob's Pillow to ballet stars Alicia Markova and Anton Dolin. The pair staged a highly successful

Denishawn dancers. *Library of Congress*

dance festival at the site—so successful, in fact, that a local organization bought the Pillow to ensure its annual continuation. Today Jacob's Pillow has become a renowned dance institution, a summer school for students, and an off-season destination for companies from around the world.

St. Denis and Shawn were cultivators of talent, careful never to crush the distinctive voices of their students. Three of those students—Martha Graham, Doris Humphrey, and Ted Weidman—along with the German émigré Hanya Holm, would become the founders of American modern dance. The Big Four, as they were eventually known, looked not to the East but to the rich, robust American scene for inspiration.

Born in 1893 near Pittsburgh, Pennsylvania, Martha Graham was not, unlike Duncan or St. Denis, a pretty, charming child. Neither did she have a carefree or idyllic childhood. Her strict father, a neurologist, told Graham and her sister, Jeordie, that he knew when they were lying because the muscles in their faces betrayed their emotions.[28] It was an idea Graham never forgot: Later, she described her dance as "a graph of the heart."[29]

From the beginning Graham was a performer, dancing at her church and for patients in her father's waiting room as a child. In 1915, after her father's death, she came to Denishawn to study under St. Denis. Since Graham was a late starter with no innate dance gifts, Miss Ruth didn't see potential in her. Instead, it was Shawn, an admirer of Graham's remarkable work ethic, who took her under his wing. Graham danced with Denishawn for several seasons, but eventually grew restless and left the company.

After performing for two years with the Greenwich Village Follies—where her solos reportedly stopped the show—she was invited to codirect the new dance department at the Eastman School of Music in Rochester, New York.[30] Though Graham was too independent-minded to succeed in an academic institution and left Eastman after a year, it was there that she began to experiment more with movement. She explored a new way for dancers to breathe, exaggerating the sharp inhalation of air and its forceful exhalation. The breath pattern created a natural "contraction" (on the exhalation) of the torso, coupled with a "release" (on the inhalation). That simple opposition became the foundation of Graham's distinctive technique.

Unlike most dancers of the time, Graham embraced the weightiness of the body and the sweaty, unpretty effort of movement. Wiry and strong, she projected an electric energy onstage— a force that started deep in the nervous system, she believed, and coursed outward.[31] The purpose of Graham's dance was to communicate deep feeling.

An informal session with dancer, choreographer, and ethnologist La Meri at Jacob's Pillow, 1960. *Associated Press*

Dance Observer magazine, founded by Louis Horst.

Missouri-born Louis Horst was playing piano in a vaudeville house when the Denishawn Company scooped him up in 1915. Though he ended up staying with the troupe for a decade, it was Graham who would become his closest companion and, eventually, lover. As musician, composer, and dance-composition teacher, Horst had a profound effect on Graham's career.

When Graham decided to leave Denishawn in 1925, Horst opted out as well. He traveled to Europe, where he studied music composition and encountered the works of forward-thinking expressionist dancer Mary Wigman. Horst introduced Graham to Wigman's work, and Wigman's quest to honor an internal sense of momentum and rhythm informed the development of Graham's technique.

Together, Horst and Graham pioneered a new relationship between dance and music. As Graham's music director from 1926 to 1948, Horst composed many scores for her works—but only after she completed the choreography, freeing Graham to explore alternative ways to structure and shape her dances. Horst also played a key role in Graham's awareness of indigenous music, which in part inspired her exploration of American Indian material (see Chapter 1). And his rigorous sense of discipline and unsparing critical eye gave the mercurial Graham the direction she needed to create some of her greatest masterpieces.

In 1934 Horst founded *Dance Observer* magazine, one of the first literary publications focused on dance criticism and theory. He later wrote two books, *Pre-Classic Dance Forms* and *Modern Dance Forms*, both valuable resources for dancers and choreographers. He was a notoriously tough but respected teacher of dance composition, notably at the Juilliard School.

By the time Horst and Graham parted ways in 1948, he had made an indelible mark on her work. His influence would in turn help shape the perspectives of the next generation of modern choreographers, including Merce Cunningham, Paul Taylor, and Trisha Brown.

OPPOSITE: Martha Graham, c. 1940s. *Photofest*

Rooted in the earth and in the breath, it was a primordial language that transcended words.

It took some years for Graham's technique to fully mature, but all its elements were in place by the late 1920s. In 1926 she established the Martha Graham Center of Contemporary Dance in New York City as a home for her company and school. Three years later she presented *Heretic*, her first concert dance for a company of performers. Dressed in white jersey, Graham faced a chorus of twelve women in identical black dresses—they formed "a wall of defiance," she said, "that I could not break."[32] It was a symbolic moment: She was the heretic not only onstage, but also in the world of dance, challenging ideas about what dance was and could be. The following year she created *Lamentation*, one of her greatest works. Sitting alone on a low bench, she rocked and writhed in anguish within a tube of white jersey. Graham said she wanted to show "the

tragedy that obsesses the body, the ability to stretch inside your own skin, to witness and test the perimeter and boundaries of grief."[33]

By this point Graham's radical pieces were beginning to divide the dance world. *New York Times* dance critic John Martin, one of her most stalwart advocates, said that she had "embarrassingly partisan devotees on the one hand and bitterly denunciatory enemies on the other, but she has won the victory of never having left anybody indifferent."[34] A victory, indeed: "I'd rather they disliked me than be apathetic," Graham said, "because that is the kiss of death."[35]

Graham's prolific body of work is tremendously diverse, but in the early years of her long career she devoted her choreography to American themes. "We must look to America to bring forth an art as powerful as America itself," she said, and she fulfilled that promise with works that included

Night Journey, with Graham as Jocasta and Bertram Ross as Oedipus, 1947. *Photofest*

Martha Graham Dance Company performs *Every Soul is a Circus,* 2012. *Timothy A. Clary / AFP / Getty Images*

Martha Graham Dance Company in
Appalachian Spring, 2007. *Bill O'Leary /
The Washington Post / Getty Images*

American Document (1938), *Appalachian Spring* (1944, set to music by Aaron Copeland), *Letter to the World* (1940), and *Salem Shore* (1943).[36] She was also inspired by the poetic drama of classical Greek theater, particularly the stories that centered on powerful female figures; her Greek heroines seem to be the cousins of her American pioneer women. Graham's Greek canon includes *Cave of the Heart*, the story of Medea and Jason (1946); *Errand into the Maze*, the Minotaur legend (1947); *Night Journey*, the Oedipus myth, told from Queen Jocasta's perspective (1947); and her 1958 masterpiece *Clytemnestra.*

Graham was sixty-five when she made *Clytemnestra.* Many of her principal dancers choreographed their own sections under her direction. It wasn't the first time this kind of collaboration, which Graham acknowledged in conversation but never in playbills, had occurred. She was simply unwilling to confront her own physical and, some thought, artistic decline. In later years Graham also proved so possessive of her own roles that she began removing works from her company's repertoire as she became unable to dance them (a practice she finally put to an end to in the 1960s, when she realized she was harming her own legacy). Graham withdrew from the limelight in the late 1960s, only to return in 1973 at the age of seventy-nine, to again head her company and school. A powerful presence even in old age, she continued to tour with her

dancers, appearing at curtain calls until just before her death in 1991, at age ninety-six.

In 1928 two other members of the Denishawn Company struck out on their own: Doris Humphrey and Charles Weidman. Though both were strong soloists, their pieces focused on group work, as opposed to Graham's explorations of the heroic individual. The pair lacked Graham's commanding personality but developed an equally devoted, albeit smaller, following.

Doris Humphrey, born in 1895, was of old New England stock, a descendant of both Ralph Waldo Emerson and Puritan elder William Brewster. Her devout but artistically inclined parents sent her to dancing school at age eight, where she trained in ballet, ballroom dance, folk forms, "expressional" (Duncan-style) dance, and clog dancing.

She came to Denishawn in 1917, and soon became a member of the company. Unlike Graham, the graceful, well-proportioned Humphrey fit the Denishawn mold exactly. St. Denis was taken with her and soon became her mentor, encouraging her to choreograph. The two collaborated on *Tragica,* the first contemporary dance performed without music, in 1925.

After spending more than ten years with Denishawn, Humphrey, disillusioned with the workaday demands of the company's touring schedule and eager to investigate her own dance instincts, ventured out on her own. To discover her "innate

TOP: Doris Humphrey in *Concerto in A Minor* (also known as *Grieg*), c. 1928. *Soichi Sunami, courtesy Doris Humphrey Society*

ABOVE: Doris Humphrey and Charles Weidman. *Courtesy Doris Humphrey Society*

LEFT: Charles Weidman, 1934. *© Everett Collection Inc., Alamy*

rhythms," as she called them, she spent long periods standing in front of a mirror. She realized that if she allowed herself to relax, she would begin to fall before involuntarily recovering her balance. Eventually she came to believe that all movement fell somewhere within that spectrum of fall and recovery, "the arc between two deaths." She dramatized that fundamental tension: there was danger and risk in the fall, peace and stability in the recovery.[37]

In 1935 Humphrey created *New Dance*, a work that explored human conflict—power struggles, corrosive ambition, crippling possessiveness—in "symphonic" group movement. As in most Humphrey pieces, however, there were also serene, harmonious passages, expressing her fundamental faith in the goodness of human nature.[38] The following year she completed the *New Dance Trilogy*, considered her greatest work. Its middle section, *With My Red Fires*, was one of the first modern dances to explore romantic love and its place in society. In it a couple emerges gradually from a group, only to be accosted by a bitter, straitlaced Victorian matriarch, played by Humphrey, who eventually turns the crowd against them. *With My Red Fires* would become one of Humphrey's signature pieces, frequently performed in excerpt.

Humphrey also explored pure movement. Her 1928 *Water Study*, performed in silence, channeled the non-musical rhythms of waves and human breath patterns. *Passacaglia*, made two years after *New Dance Trilogy*, arrived at abstraction through music: It was Humphrey's visualization of Bach's *Passacaglia and Fugue in C Minor*.

Though a gifted choreographer, Humphrey was an even greater teacher, attracting many devoted students—most significantly José Limón (see Chapter 6), who became her protégé. Humphrey wanted to develop a dance language that facilitated choreography, and was one of the few choreographers of her time to establish specific principles for creating dances. In 1949 she received a Guggenheim fellowship to write *The Art of Making Dances*, a masterpiece codifying those principles that was published after her death in 1958.

Charles Weidman, Humphrey's partner, became interested in dance after seeing Ruth St. Denis and Ted Shawn perform. He received a scholarship to the Denishawn School at age nineteen and set out for Denishawn's California headquarters from his hometown of Lincoln, Nebraska. After arriving in Los Angeles, Weidman had only a whirlwind few weeks of training before going on the road with

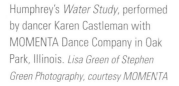

Humphrey's *Water Study*, performed by dancer Karen Castleman with MOMENTA Dance Company in Oak Park, Illinois. *Lisa Green of Stephen Green Photography, courtesy MOMENTA*

the company. But from the beginning his brilliant comic gifts were apparent. His long, gangly body and expressive face seemed designed for mime and character work.

Weidman left Denishawn with Humphrey, and the two co-founded the Humphrey-Weidman Company in 1927. He assisted Humphrey in the development of what would become known as the Humphrey-Weidman technique, based on the principles of fall and recovery. They were a well-balanced pair: Where Humphrey was purposeful and logical, Weidman was whimsical and eclectic. Something of a magpie, he liked picking up every-day movements and using them out of context, dubbing the result "kinetic pantomime."

Weidman also choreographed. He created several works that showcased his unique gifts, including *The Happy Hypocrite* (1931), *On My Mother's Side* (1940), *Daddy Was a Fireman* (1943), and *David and Goliath* (1945). Because they were so closely tailored to his particular skills, however, most of his dances have not survived.[39]

The fourth member of America's Big Four wasn't American. Hanya Holm was born Hanya Eckert in Worms, Germany, in 1893. As a child she fell in love with the dancing of Anna Pavlova, but Holm's father disapproved of dance. Not until later in life, after she had been married and divorced, did Holm begin to study the art form seriously.

Holm trained under Mary Wigman, the leader of Germany's modern dance movement. Wigman's form of expressionist dance—that distant inspiration to Graham—displayed no fear of ugliness, or of ugly subjects. Frequently compared to German expressionist art, her choreography was characterized by high drama and extravagant displays of emotion.[40]

While a member of Wigman's company, Holm became interested in teaching. She showed such promise that Wigman eventually made her director and chief instructor at her Central Institute in Germany. In 1931 Wigman sent Holm to the United States to set up a Mary Wigman school. But when Holm arrived in New York City, she discovered that Wigman's systematic, theatrical style didn't suit her freer, more adventurous American pupils. Holm also recognized that American modern dance had become fragmented, driven by several very

Hanya Holm (right) and dancers in her company perform *They Too Are Exiles*, choreographed by Holm, c. 1939.
University of Denver Special Collections and Archives

HELEN TAMIRIS AND DANCE REPERTORY THEATER

Helen Tamiris, born Helen Becker in 1905, was one of the rare early modern dancers who did not come from either the Humphrey-Weidman or the Wigman-Holm school of thought. Her poor but artistically inclined family, who lived in a rough New York neighborhood, sent her to the progressive Henry Street Settlement to keep her out of trouble. It was through the Settlement's arts program that she discovered dance. She later became a student of Russian choreographer Michel Fokine and a professional ballet dancer, touring with the Bracale Opera Company.

Dissatisfied with ballet, Becker spent some time performing jazz numbers in musical revues. When that, too, didn't feel like enough, she took a year and a half to work on her own dances, exploring her personal movement style. During this time she adapted her new name, Tamiris, from a poem about a mighty Persian queen.[41]

Tamiris felt strongly that the solution to dance's persistent financial problems was for the various modern companies to pool their resources and engage a single theater for a run of performances, with a shared advertising budget. In 1929, at Tamiris's suggestion, she, Graham, Humphrey, and Weidman formed the Dance Repertory Theater. It was a doomed effort. None of the others thought Tamiris was on their level; Humphrey thought Graham was "a snake"; Graham disliked collaborating with anyone.[42] But though DRT lasted only two seasons, the dance it generated did not go unnoticed. The first season saw the premiere of Graham's *Lamentation*. The second included a work by up-and-comer Agnes de Mille, as well as Humphrey's *Dance of the Chosen* (later known as *The Shakers*), a remarkable study of the Shakers' rapturous religious zeal.

Helen Tamiris in *Salut au Monde* from the *Walt Whitman Suite*, 1936. *Photofest*

In 1933 Bennington College was founded in southern Vermont with an avant-garde goal: to put the arts on an equal footing with academics. At Martha Graham's recommendation, the school asked Martha Hill, an alumna of the Graham company and a teacher at New York University, to organize a summer dance program.

One hundred and three students came to the first Bennington School of the Dance summer session in 1934. All the members of modern dance's Big Four taught and performed. It wasn't until the second summer, however, that Hill introduced a workshop program for the creation of new choreography. The school had already earned a reputation as a modern dance hot spot; now it became a creative home for the art form's most influential players.

Graham, Humphrey, Weidman, and Holm benefited greatly from the stability Bennington's program provided. It was the Great Depression, yet they had complementary access to theaters and studios, and talented, enthusiastic students to work with. Suddenly, they were free to simply make art. And make art they did. The summer of 1936, for example, saw the creation of Humphrey's New Dance Trilogy. In 1937 Hill also added a choreographic fellowship program, giving a few members of the next generation of modern choreographers—Anna Sokolow, José Limón, and Esther Junger (see Chapter 6)—a jumpstart.

Wartime cutbacks spelled the end for the Bennington program in 1942. But in 1948, a summer session based on the Bennington model was founded at Connecticut College. Renamed the American Dance Festival in 1969, and relocated to Duke University in 1978, that program continues to attract prominent dance companies and choreographers.

Bennington School dancers, 1956.
© Bettmann, Corbis, AP Images

different personalities, and that it needed a sounder base in instruction. With Wigman's approval, Holm adapted the Wigman technique for her American students, bringing a new energy and discipline to American modern dance.

Holm's training changed the way American dancers used space. She asked them to think about movement in terms of planes and floor patterns, in verticals and horizontals. Emotionalism was pushed to the side; the appeal of Holm's technique was the sweep of the movement alone. It came closer to "pure" dance than any of Graham or Humphrey's experiments.[43]

Although Holm is probably best known for her later work on Broadway—she choreographed

Kiss Me Kate (1948), *My Fair Lady* (1956), and *Camelot* (1960)—her greatest legacy is her teaching. Wigman ultimately faced persecution by the Nazis and was forced to close her schools, but because of Holm's hybrid style, Wigman's technique lives on in the story of American modern dance.

By the early 1940s, modern dance was no longer an experiment. It was a recognized art form worthy of intellectual consideration. Its first group of rebels had become well-established, well-respected mainstream figures. But in a few short years modern dance would see a new generation of revolutionaries, who would continue to stretch the American perception of what dance could be.

Kinetic Molpai, choreographed by Ted Shawn, 1937. *Associated Press*

Chapter Five
Ballet's Ascendancy

New York City Ballet dancers perform
Serenade, 2003. *Yevgeny Asmolov, AFP,
Getty Images*

"Transplanting ballet in this country is like trying to raise
a palm tree in Dakota." —*Lincoln Kirstein*[1]

"Superficial Europeans are accustomed to say that American artists have no 'soul.'
This is wrong. America has its own spirit—cold, crystalline, luminous, hard as light. . . .
Good American dancers can express clean emotion in a manner that might almost be
termed angelic. By angelic I mean the quality supposedly enjoyed by the angels who,
when they relate a tragic situation, do not themselves suffer." —*George Balanchine*[2]

At the turn of the twentieth century, Americans had few opportunities to study or even see classical ballet. In a way, ballet challenged everything America stood for. It was a patrician art, created in the opulent court of France's Louis XIV during the seventeenth century and later adopted by Imperial Russia. There was nothing democratic in ballet's rigid hierarchies, or in its sense of grandeur and sumptuousness. Ballets were ostentatious displays of riches for the rich.[3]

"The Four Elements" costume, designed for one of Louis XIV's ballets. *De Agostini, Getty Images*

Yet by the 1950s ballet companies had begun blooming all over the United States. The idea of ballet as spectacle persisted but was countered by the development of ballets that felt distinctly American, either in style or in substance. George Balanchine developed a new approach to ballet technique, an athletic rendering that both amplified and streamlined the classical vocabulary. Other choreographers—among them Jerome Robbins and Agnes de Mille—found inspiration in pointedly American subject matter. By the time of the "ballet boom" of the 1960s and 1970s, ballet was no longer an exotic fascination. It had become an influential part of the country's mainstream culture—something vitally, persuasively American.

America's first real exposure to ballet came in 1866, when *The Black Crook*, a lavish theatrical production starring more than seventy foreign ballet dancers, debuted at New York City's Niblo's Garden Theater. Though not the most artful work, it was immensely successful, running on and off for the next thirty years. As European cast members dropped out, it became a ballet training ground for the American dancers who stepped into their parts. The star of the original production, Marie Bonfanti, originally of Milan's La Scala opera house, stayed in New York, where she opened a studio. Many other *Black Crook* alumni did the same. These dancers' schools, which offered relatively

The opulent *The Black Crook*, c. 1882. *Library of Congress*

Anna Pawlowa

6061

rigorous ballet technique classes, were an alternative to the existing dance schools, where vaudeville hopefuls trained in adulterated "eccentric" or "acrobatic" ballet.

Most Americans, however, didn't develop a taste for ballet until the beginning of the twentieth century, when dancers from the Imperial Russian theater began touring the United States. Their undisputed queen was Anna Pavlova. A sublimely poetic dancer, she first performed in America in 1910 and returned nearly every year for the next decade and a half.

Glamorous though she was, Pavlova wasn't a snob. She proved perfectly willing to perform in small-town theaters on the vaudeville circuit, usually as part of a standard vaudeville lineup—after, say, the trained animals or the juggling act. Savvy about publicity, she granted interviews to popular magazines "on subjects ranging from pets to galoshes."[4] As a result she introduced thousands of Americans, most of whom were powerless to resist her singular magic, to ballet. "She half-hypnotized audiences," remembered de Mille, "partaking almost of the nature of a divinity. My life was wholly altered by her."[5]

In Paris, meanwhile, a ballet revolution was under way. There, Sergei Diaghilev, a colorful Russian impresario, was presenting a company of dancers from the Russian Imperial theaters. But Diaghilev's Ballets Russes wasn't a showcase for courtly Russian classics like *Swan Lake* and *Sleeping Beauty*. Instead,

Diaghilev championed the "new ballet" of Russian choreographer Michel Fokine, who believed traditional ballet had become too decadent. "Dancing should be interpretive," Fokine said. "It should not degenerate into mere gymnastics."[6] Like America's modern dancers, Fokine sought a more natural, direct style, true to human motives and feelings, which he explored in several works for the Ballets Russes—including the 1910 *Les Sylphides*, a plotless pure-dance ballet that quickly became part of the ballet canon. Some noted a rapport between his work and Isadora Duncan's.[7]

Attempts to bring Diaghilev's company to America began soon after the troupe's first Paris success in 1909. But the Ballets Russes didn't make it to New York until January 17, 1916. The following winter the company mounted an extensive American tour, playing in more than fifty cities. Diaghilev didn't pander to US audiences: He presented avant-garde works by Fokine and the equally forward-thinking Léonide Massine and Vaslav Nijinsky (also the company's brilliant star dancer). The American tour gave the Ballets Russes a way to survive during World War I and exposed a generation of Americans to Fokine's "revolutionary" ballets. Interestingly, the United States would not experience the glossy Imperial full-lengths Fokine was rebelling against for several more decades.

After the Ballets Russes returned to Europe, there was little substantial ballet activity in America

OPPOSITE: Anna Pavlova, c. 1910–1915. *Library of Congress*

RIGHT: Ballet Russe dancers rehearsing in New York, 1916. *Library of Congress*

until 1933, four years after Diaghilev's death. At that point Sol Hurok—a flamboyant Russian-born producer who had moved to the United States in 1906—brought the Ballet Russe de Monte Carlo to the United States. Established by René Blum and Colonel W. de Basil in 1932 as a successor to the original Ballets Russes, the company was on the brink of bankruptcy when Hurok took over its management and booked it for a run in New York.

Hurok believed ballet—specifically, Russian ballet—deserved a prominent place in American culture. For the next thirty years, he would present American seasons of de Basil's Ballet Russe and, later, Sergei Denham's competing Ballet Russe de Monte Carlo, established in 1938 after Blum and de Basil split. (The nomenclature is notoriously confusing; de Basil's Ballet Russe eventually became known as "The Original Ballet Russe.") The companies boasted rosters of talented Russian dancers, including the vivacious, leggy Alexandra Danilova. They were sometimes homes to choreographers like Fokine, Massine, and a young up-and-comer,

George Balanchine. And they established a new standard international repertory, which included not only Russian works but also, for example, Agnes de Mille's rollicking *Rodeo*, commissioned by Denham's Ballet Russe in 1942.[8]

With the outbreak of World War II, once again, European companies sought refuge in the United States. Denham's troupe in particular toured chiefly in America during the war and continued to do so until it disbanded in 1968. Scores of young Americans, including Alvin Ailey, Robert Joffrey, and Allegra Kent, fell under the spell of the Ballet Russe de Monte Carlo. In the 1940s and 1950s, several American dancers—among them Maria Tallchief, daughter of an Osage Indian—joined the Denham company. For years de Basil and Denham's companies had led Americans to define "ballet" as "Russian," but now the Ballet Russe was developing an American accent.

At this moment a choreographer from the Russian tradition stepped in to transform American ballet. George Balanchine, born Georgi

ABOVE: Agnes de Mille's *Rodeo*, 1942. *Photofest*

OPPOSITE: George Balanchine, 1935. © *Everett Collection Historical, Alamy. Courtesy CSU Archives, Everett Collection*

Melitonovitch Balanchivadze in 1904, was the son of a respected Georgian composer. He entered the Imperial Ballet Academy in St. Petersburg at age ten; by the time he graduated in 1921, thanks to the Russian Revolution, it was no longer an Imperial but a State school. A talented musician, he went on to study for three years at the St. Petersburg Conservatory, while also dancing with the State Academic Theater for Opera and Ballet (formerly the Mariinsky Ballet).

But Balanchine devoted most of his energy during this period to choreography. Fascinated by what little he knew of Fokine's "new ballet," he tried to work in that style, concocting choreographic experiments daring enough to upset the theater authorities, who forbade the company's dancers from taking part in Balanchine's work. Nevertheless, he was able to form a small company, the Soviet State Dancers, with soloists from the State Academic Theater. His troupe included Danilova and Tamara Geva, then just sixteen years old (and Balanchine's wife).

In 1924 the group toured Berlin. From there Balanchine, Geva, and Danilova fled to Paris, where they joined a large Russian émigré community. Diaghilev took Balanchine under his wing, inviting him to join the Ballets Russes as a choreographer.

Balanchine made ten ballets for Diaghilev, including the groundbreaking *Apollon Musagète* (1928, later rechristened *Apollo*). The work marked "the turning point of my life," Balanchine said. It was his return to pure classicism, inspired by Igor Stravinsky's perfectly balanced neoclassical score. "In its discipline and restraint," Balanchine said, "in its sustained oneness of tone and feeling, the score was a revelation. It seemed to tell me that I could, for the first time, dare not use all my ideas; that I, too, could eliminate."[9]

After Diaghilev's death in 1929, Balanchine joined the de Basil-Blum company, but, finding himself artistically at odds with de Basil, he left after one season to form his own company, Les Ballets 1933. Though not a great success, Les Ballets marked the first time a young Harvard graduate, Lincoln Kirstein, saw Balanchine's work. Kirstein, a dance connoisseur from Rochester, New York, who had been in love with ballet since first seeing Diaghilev's company in 1924, dreamed of

Alexandra Danilova and Serge Lifar in *Apollon Musagète*, 1928.
Sasha/Getty Images

Class at the School of Amerian Ballet, 1936. *Alfred Eisenstaedt/Time and Life Pictures, Getty Images*

creating a permanent home for ballet in America. In Balanchine he believed he'd found the man for the job. "Everything [Balanchine] did," said Kirstein, after seeing Les Ballets,

> spoke for the present, of immediacy, by surprise, with brilliance. . . . Everything was intensified through the physicality of the dancing itself, through the power, athletics, and lyricism of ballet's language. This was where I wanted to live. This was what I wanted to do; here I was learning how it should be done.[10]

Against many odds, Kirstein succeeded in bringing Balanchine to America in 1933. Kirstein had a grand vision for the future of ballet in the country, to which Balanchine is said to have responded, "But first, a school." The School of American Ballet (SAB) opened New Year's Day, 1934, on the fourth floor of an old building at Madison and 59th Street. The walls of the studio, which was rumored to have once belonged to Isadora Duncan, got a coat of paint in a gray-blue Balanchine remembered from the Imperial School.[11]

America inspired Balanchine. "There is that love of bigness that is so important a part of the ballet," he said. "The skyscrapers, vast fields, gigantic machines, all make for thrilling spectacles."[12] As the critic Deborah Jowitt later remarked, "He saw and liked something full-throttle and brisk and no-nonsense about the American character that he wanted to bring out."[13] At SAB Balanchine set about fashioning a new kind of dancer, his perfect ballet instrument. The school's training was rooted in the technique of the Imperial School—most of SAB's teachers were Russians—but Balanchine demanded greater athleticism, a sharper attack, and higher clarity at a higher speed.

For his new students, Balanchine created his first work in America: *Serenade*, to Tchaikovsky's "Serenade for Strings." The 1934 ballet was a learning exercise, made for a workshop performance, and Balanchine tailored it to the abilities and needs of his pupils. It used simple steps. No men were available at the beginning of the rehearsal period, so no men appeared until later in the ballet. When one dancer fell during a run-through, Balanchine incorporated her fall into the choreography.

Serenade showed the principles that guided much of Balanchine's future work. There were no star dancers. The corps de ballet was given real dancing to do. The focus was on the plotless choreography, which was a striking visual complement to an outstanding piece of music.

Out of the School of American Ballet came, later in 1934, the American Ballet Company. In 1935 the group, composed entirely of SAB students, got what was to be their big break: They became the resident ballet company of the Metropolitan Opera. But Balanchine's modern tastes upset the conservative organization. His decision to stage Gluck's *Orfeo ed Euridice* as a ballet onstage, with all the singers in the pit, ruffled feathers in the audience and backstage. Balanchine and the Metropolitan parted ways in 1938.

Meanwhile, Kirstein had founded another ballet company, Ballet Caravan, which also featured SAB students. The group performed not only Balanchine works but also new pieces by Americans, including Lew Christensen, Eugene Loring, Erick Hawkins, and William Dollar. The most ambitious of these works, Loring's *Billy the Kid* (1938, with music by Aaron Copland), remains in the repertoire of several ballet companies. In 1941 Balanchine's American Ballet Company and Kirstein's Ballet Caravan merged, under the latter's name, for a state-sponsored Latin American tour. Though there were some logistical snafus—all company women under the age of eighteen were arrested in Buenos Aires, for example, and the troupe was charged with importing dancers for prostitution—Balanchine produced two brilliant ballets for the tour, *Concerto Barocco* and *Ballet Imperial* (later *Tschaikovsky Piano Concerto No. 2*).[14] *Barocco*, set to Bach's double violin concerto, is classical technique distilled to its essence, with choreography that reflects and refracts Bach's many musical voices. *Ballet Imperial* is grander, a full-length story ballet stripped of plot and frippery and condensed into thirty-six minutes of dancing.

Following the tour, as America geared up for World War II, Ballet Caravan disbanded. Kirstein and many of the company's dancers enlisted in the army, while Balanchine took jobs on Broadway and in Hollywood and briefly worked with Denham's Ballet Russe. It had been a decade since Balanchine's arrival in America, and he and Kirstein had yet to get an American ballet company to "stick."

Balanchine and Kirstein's struggles made the 1940 debut of another new company, Ballet Theatre—later known as American Ballet Theatre—all the more impressive. The troupe arrived on the scene seemingly fully formed, mounting a glittering New York program featuring eighty-five dancers, three classical revivals, and fifteen ballets by living choreographers, including six world premieres. It was a stunning accomplishment.

Ballet Theatre's financial reality was far less encouraging. Still, the company began with an interesting and, at the time, unusual philosophy: Rather than cultivate a single form of dance, the broad-minded troupe embraced the old repertory of Diaghilev and Russian classics and, more important, encouraged emerging choreographers to create new experimental works.

Ballet Theatre was the offspring of an odd couple: Mikhail Mordkin and Lucia Chase. Mordkin, a product of Moscow's Bolshoi Ballet

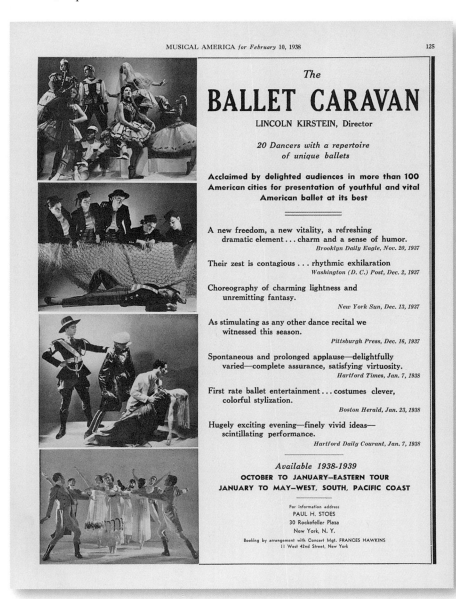

School and a former partner of Anna Pavlova, had established a company and a very successful group of ballet schools in the United States. Chase, a wealthy Bryn Mawr graduate from New England, initially danced in Mordkin's company—and served as its primary financial backer, a fact she kept secret for fear that it would discourage other potential patrons and preclude objective reviews of her own dancing. Chase also underwrote Ballet Theatre, and many of Mordkin's former dancers, as well as much of his company's costumes and scenery, formed the new company's foundation. But while Mordkin was supposed to join Ballet Theatre as principal choreographer and artistic director, through a scandalous bit of chicanery, the company's first season was actually organized by Richard Pleasant, a young man who had been running Mordkin's schools.

Pleasant saw himself as something of an American Diaghilev. He wanted to show Americans the full spectrum of ballet, from the warhorse classics to the latest choreography. In preparation for the company's first season, he reached out to numerous dancers and choreographers worldwide—from Frederick Ashton, Antony Tudor, and Margot Fonteyn of Great Britain to Russian star Michel Fokine, and even Balanchine—but had little success. Pleasant's luck changed when Hitler invaded Poland in the fall of 1939. Suddenly his offer seemed very appealing to artists hoping to escape Europe. Fokine and Bronislava Nijinska, sister of Vaslav Nijinsky, signed on; two days after Britain declared war with Germany, so did the English Tudor, who would stay in America for the rest of his life.

The result was that blockbuster first season, a huge critical success and an even huger financial disaster. Ballet Theatre ended up $200,000 in the hole. After a shrunken second season, Pleasant left the company in 1941.

Salvation came in the form of Sol Hurok, who agreed to tour the company. But ever the Russophile, he insisted that it be billed as "the best in Russian ballet," a compromise that some found upsetting. The company renewed its relationships with Fokine, Nijinska, and even Mordkin. There were guest appearances by Russian sensations Tamara

Toumanova and Vera Zorina. The period later known as the "Russian occupation" was underway.

But non-Russian choreographers also continued to forge ahead at Ballet Theatre. In 1942 the company premiered Tudor's *Pillar of Fire*. Set to Arnold Schoenberg's *Verklärte Nacht*, the psychological drama tells the story of Hagar, a lonely woman who makes a rash conquest, then suffers the punishment of her town, her family, and her own conscience. Rather than choosing one of the company's foreign stars, Tudor selected the American Nora Kaye to play the lead. Kaye understood Tudor's highly restrained, intricately nuanced style and his realistic approach to the portrayal of human emotions. She, and *Pillar of Fire*, were overnight successes.

A young man named Jerome Robbins was also making waves at Ballet Theatre. Robbins, the son of a deli owner, grew up Jerome Rabinowitz in New York City and Weehawken, New Jersey, studying all kinds of dance forms. As a choreographer, he developed a style completely his own. In 1940 Robbins joined Ballet Theatre, and in 1944 he choreographed *Fancy Free*, a portrait of four sailors on leave in the big city. He chose composer Leonard Bernstein—a man almost exactly his age, with an urban background and a sensibility that mirrored his own—as his collaborator. Robbins requested a score that would be alternately "bang-away, hot boogie-woogie, dreamy, torchy . . . not sentimental or romantic at all."[15] For his cast, he selected a group of young American kids who could not only dash off virtuosic ballet steps but could also turn somersaults and shimmy: John Kriza, Harold Lang, Janet Reed, Muriel Bentley, and Robbins himself. It was an all-American display of all-American versatility, youthful energy, and power—and it was another big hit for Ballet Theatre.

Immediately after, Robbins made *Interplay*, which followed another group of American teenagers; this time, however, there was no set, and no story. He was becoming, as critic Arlene Croce described,

> the New York play-school referee, the maestro of the slum kindergarten, the Peter Pan of arts and crafts. When Robbins speaks with a specifically local accent, when his boyhood origins and his eternal boy-genius Bronx High School

of Science sensibility are allowed to resonate with their natural color and size, his art seems universal.[16]

In 1945 scenic designer Oliver Smith, a man of good sense who had worked with Ballet Theatre for a little more than a year, assumed co-directorship of the company with Chase. His arrival signaled the end of the "Russian occupation." Quickly, Smith and Chase broke ties with Hurok and went back to the company's original many-cooks, varied-repertoire model.

Under their direction, choreographer Agnes de Mille found a satisfying home at Ballet Theatre. The New York native—daughter of playwright William Churchill de Mille and niece of Hollywood director Cecil B. de Mille—had a long and turbulent path to success. Though not a brilliant ballet dancer, she was a spirited performer, and when she was unable to find professional dance employment she began making dances for herself. Eventually the dance world recognized her gift for narrative choreography. Though de Mille was a charter member of the Ballet Theatre, she made her name outside of it with *Rodeo*, created for the Ballet Russe de Monte Carlo in 1942, and Broadway's *Oklahoma* in 1943—both skillful blends of classical dance and the American vernacular. In 1948 she choreographed *Fall River*

Legend for Ballet Theatre. The story of alleged axe murderess Lizzie Borden was another showcase for Nora Kaye, who was now ballet's foremost dramatic actress.

In 1947 Balanchine—though at work on yet another ballet company with Kirstein—gave Ballet Theatre a true masterpiece. *Theme and Variations*, to Tchaikovsky, is often described as an abstract, compressed version of *The Sleeping Beauty*. In its sweep and grandeur, in the crisp formality of its hierarchical arrangements, it pays tribute to the nineteenth-century Imperial Russian style; in its dazzling speed and sophisticated musicality, it incorporates Balanchine's "American" way of moving. Balanchine made *Theme and Variations* for two dancers who could meet its extreme demands: Igor Youskevitch, a dashing and assured partner, and the vivacious, forthright Alicia Alonso, one of several impressive American ballerinas who were beginning to earn more leading roles than Ballet Theatre's Russians.

In 1946 Ballet Theatre became the first American company to visit England after World War II. The tour marked an artistic high point. But all was not well with the company. Strapped for money, it was forced to disband for a period in 1948, and as it headed into its second decade, it seemed to be in a state of continuous decline. Ballet Theatre suffered for the lack of a New York home, with attempts

to establish a base at the Metropolitan Opera ulti- mately proving unsuccessful. Financial troubles led to artistic compromise, and the company's creative energy diminished when Robbins left in 1949, fol- lowed by Tudor and Kaye soon after.

The company's seemingly endless touring exac- erbated the situation. Chase "had a fondness for the kind of achievements that might earn Ballet Theatre entries in the *Guinness Book of Records*," according to former company manager Charles Payne, and the record she coveted most was that of becoming the first ballet troupe to perform in all forty-eight states of the union.[17] Though the company achieved that record in 1955, the constant traveling wore down the dancers. In 1958 American Ballet Theatre, as the group was known after 1957, disbanded once again. Chase was able to pull everything back together in 1960, but not until later in the decade would the company find itself on solid footing.

Ballet Theatre's deterioration coincided with the improvement of Balanchine and Kirstein's for- tunes. In 1946 the pair reunited to establish Ballet

Society, a membership group designed for the cul- tural upper crust of New York. Members were to be presented with poetry readings, art lectures, and musical concerts, in addition to the performances of a resident ballet company. Most of those goals were never realized. But the ballet's opening performance on November 20, 1946—at a less-than-auspicious venue, the Central High School of Needle Trades— was a landmark event: It featured the premiere of Balanchine's *The Four Temperaments*. Set to a com- missioned score by Paul Hindemith, the work was ballet deconstructed, reassembled, and pushed to its breaking point. Angularity replaced rounded sym- metries, the vertical line of the body broken by jazz- ily protruding hips. It was unlike anything balleto- manes had ever seen. Critic Edwin Denby, one of the first dance writers to support Balanchine's work, described it as "a long fantasy of incredible violence and amplitude, savage speed, and packed weight."[18]

A year later Ballet Society, still a fragile ven- ture, presented another Balanchine masterwork: *Orpheus*, with a commissioned score from Igor

New York City Ballet in *The Four Temperaments*, 1967. *Gjon Mili/ Time and Life Pictures, Getty Images*

Stravinsky. The choreography, reflecting the music's subdued tones, was subtle. But Japanese designer Isamu Noguchi (a favorite of Martha Graham) created striking and starkly evocative costumes and sets, and the grand scale of the production impressed critics. The response prompted Morton Baum, chairman of the executive committee of New York's new City Center of Music and Drama, to ask Ballet Society to become the theater's resident ballet troupe, the New York City Ballet. Finally, after fifteen years, Balanchine and Kirstein had found a stable home in the United States. Noguchi's abstract rendition of Orpheus's lyre was adopted as New York City Ballet's official symbol.

The new company's first major success came a year later, when Balanchine choreographed Stravinsky's *Firebird*. The work featured lavish painted sets by Marc Chagall (originally commissioned for a Ballet Theatre production) and anointed Maria Tallchief, who danced the title role, New York City Ballet's first star. Tallchief, who married Balanchine in 1946, had been studying at the School of American Ballet for several years, and Balanchine's teaching gave her already formidable technique more dimension and polish. As the Firebird, she was electrifying, almost inhuman.

Tallchief became known as a "Balanchine ballerina," but it was Tanaquil Le Clercq who pioneered

what would become Balanchine's signature look: long, lean, and breezily elegant. Le Clercq was one of the first New York City Ballet dancers to train at the School of American Ballet from an early age, and she eventually became Balanchine's ideal muse, molded to his specifications. (She became his next wife, too, in 1952.) Le Clercq also inspired Jerome Robbins, who left American Ballet Theatre in 1948 to work with Balanchine's company. For her, Robbins created *Afternoon of a Faun* (1953), a dreamy reimagining of Vaslav Nijinsky's groundbreaking 1912 ballet to the same Debussy score. In 1956, while on tour with New York City Ballet in Copenhagen, Le Clercq contracted polio, which left her paralyzed from the waist down. Balanchine, deeply upset, spent a year by her bedside.

But soon after Balanchine returned to the company, he created one of the greatest ballets of the twentieth century: *Agon*. In a sense a descendent of *The Four Temperaments*, *Agon* stripped ballet down to its bones, revealing the mechanics of the body in new and astonishing ways. It presented an eerily canny reflection of the commissioned score by Stravinsky, which filtered seventeenth-century court dances through the cracked prism of the twelve-tone technique. Balanchine called *Agon* "the IBM ballet, more tight and precise than usual, as if controlled by an electronic brain."[19] It climaxed

Orpheus, 1952. *Roger Viollet, Getty Images*

ABOVE: Arthur Mitchell in *Agon*. Mitchell founded Dance Theatre of Harlem in 1969. *Anthony Crickmay/ © V and A Images, Alamy*

OPPOSITE: Tanaquil Le Clercq in *Bourrée Fantasque*, a 1949 Balanchine ballet. *Getty Images*

in a devastatingly erotic pas de deux, in which the woman was stretched, manipulated, and turned inside-out by her partner. In a boldly political move, Balanchine cast the black Arthur Mitchell with the alabaster-white Diana Adams in the duet.

This new approach to ballet—as an art designed to showcase the expressive qualities of the human body rather than the dramatic projections of particular performers—not only became Balanchine's standard mode of working, but also shaped the larger American dance scene. Balanchine's look, by the early 1960s, *was* the "American" look. It suited American audiences, too. Gone were the trimmings and trappings of Russian spectacles. Even as he elevated ballet to a rarefied plane, Balanchine made it accessible to common people. "He's not an intellectual," said W. H. Auden of the choreographer.

"He's something deeper, a man who understands everything."[20] And Balanchine developed a stable of dancers who embodied his philosophies brilliantly, including Jacques d'Amboise, Edward Villella, Melissa Hayden, Allegra Kent, and Violette Verdy.

Whatever artistic strides New York City Ballet and American Ballet Theatre had made, both were still plagued with financial ups and downs. Help came in 1963, when the Ford Foundation gave a staggering $7,756,000 to New York City Ballet, the School of American Ballet, and five smaller American ballet companies. Some of the funds went toward developing a national program linking New York City Ballet and the School of American Ballet to schools and communities across America. Balanchine was asked to tour the country to evaluate the overall state of dance. (Roberta Sue Ficker—later known as

Suzanne Farrell—earned one of the program's first scholarships.) It was not coincidental that the grant came shortly after the Bolshoi Ballet's first tour to New York. Cold War competition proved a boon to America's ballet companies.[21]

On September 29, 1965, President Lyndon Johnson signed legislation creating the National Foundation for the Arts and Humanities. Its subsection, the National Endowment for the Arts (NEA), quickly gave American Ballet Theatre a cash grant of $100,000, saving the struggling company. Over the next thirty years, the NEA budget increased astronomically, reaching a high of $171.2 million in 1990. The swell corresponded with a major American dance boom. Between 1958 and 1969 the number of ballet companies with more than twenty members almost tripled.[22] Whether or not the dramatic increase was a result of government funding, the NEA certainly made dance more accessible to millions of Americans.

In 1953, with ballet finally taking firm root in America, a twenty-three-year-old dancer and teacher named Robert Joffrey founded a company of his own. Three years later the ramshackle troupe, just six members strong, mounted a five-week tour to twenty-three cities—twenty-three one-night stands. They made the trip in a borrowed station wagon. Joffrey's company, hardy even in less-than-perfect circumstances, was off and running.

Joffrey grew up in Seattle, where he met lifelong friend Gerald Arpino in ballet class. A gifted dancer, Joffrey joined Roland Petit's Ballets de Paris as a soloist in 1949, but soon left the company—he was short, and as a result rarely cast in leading roles. Four years later he retired from performing altogether. By that time he had begun teaching at the American Ballet Theatre School and the High School of Performing Arts. He decided to found a school of his own, the American Ballet Center, in New York with Arpino.

Joffrey was a natural teacher. Rather than relying on endless repetitions and encouraging students to imitate him, as many Russian-style teachers did, he took a more analytical and democratic approach to ballet, customizing it to fit individuals' bodies. He was especially good with dancers whose frames were not considered ideal for dance; he helped them work around their physical shortcomings.[23] American Ballet Center's classes were quickly full—and profitable.

The Joffrey company, on the other hand, had a hard time achieving financial stability. (Joffrey himself didn't travel with the dancers on that 1956 tour; he needed his teaching revenue.) But that didn't diminish the scope of Joffrey's plans for the troupe, which skewed to the contemporary side of ballet. He commissioned works from several emerging choreographers and added pieces by Balanchine, Tudor, and Ashton to the repertoire. Arpino eventually became the group's associate director and chief choreographer, creating provocative, if frequently lightweight, ballets. By 1960 the Joffrey Ballet had twenty dancers and an orchestra, and it was mounting regular tours.

Money remained tight. When philanthropist Rebekah Harkness offered to take the company under the wing of her foundation in 1962, many saw the proposal as a godsend. For a while, it was. The Rebekah Harkness Foundation's deep pockets allowed the group to perform in New York for only the second time, and meant that Joffrey could finally pay his dancers to rehearse. But two years later, the capricious Harkness decided she wanted the company to take her name. Joffrey, unsure of what his artistic role would be in the new venture, refused, and Harkness left with most of his dancers, sets, and costumes. It was a blow that would ultimately be a blessing (see Chapter 8).

Throughout the 1960s and 1970s, ballet was becoming an increasingly important part of the American mainstream. The Cold War rivalry with Russia and its well-established ballet scene generated part of that energy. Americans crowed at the seemingly symbolic defections of three electrifying Russian dancers: Rudolf Nureyev, Natalia Makarova, and Mikhail Baryshnikov.

Nureyev, who defected in 1961 at age twenty-three, danced primarily in London and Paris after leaving the Soviet Union. But Makarova, who left nine years later, and Baryshnikov, who defected in 1974, found new homes in America. All three gave the Western world a different idea of classicism. Their purity of line and dramatically vivid performances were best suited to the full-length classical ballets they had been raised on, and they brought new attention to that form, formerly underrepresented (or poorly represented) in the American ballet scene.

American Ballet Theatre became a home base for both Makarova and Baryshnikov, and in fact the company began to forge a new identity as a troupe of remarkable—and box-office friendly—star dancers. In 1968 it presented a three-week season at the new Metropolitan Opera House at Lincoln Center, which until that point had been reserved for blockbuster performances by visiting foreign companies.

Makarova was an invaluable asset to the company. Audiences flocked to see her interpretations

Rudolf Nureyev and Natalia Makarova in *Swan Lake*, 1970. *Leonard Burt, Central Press, Getty Images*

THE HARKNESS BALLET

Rebekah Harkness's company, which ran from 1964 to 1975, was one of the best-funded dance organizations in America, and one of the most turbulent. After breaking ties with Robert Joffrey, Harkness appointed a string of artistic directors before finally assuming artistic control herself in 1970.

One of the group's greatest assets was its dancers, many of whom—including Lawrence Rhodes, Helgi Tómasson, Brunilda Ruiz, and Finis Jhung—came from Joffrey's company. The troupe had an aggressively modern repertory. Its essentially unlimited resources meant that every season saw several new works, with commissioned scores and stylish sets and costumes. When, in 1965, Harkness opened Harkness House, a luxurious home for the Harkness Ballet and its school on East 75th Street, its lavish decor—which included a $250,000 chalice by Salvador Dalí—was greeted with much snarky commentary.

Though all Harkness Ballet productions looked sleek and sophisticated, the company rarely made much of an impact artistically. Harkness was a good fairy godmother, but a poor artistic leader, a role she seemed determined to fill. "What the Harkness money buys," said famously acerbic critic Arlene Croce, "is simulated art and the incompetence of good intentions."[24]

George Skibine and his wife, Marjorie Tallchief (sister of Maria), dance at the Harkness House, 1965.
Associated Press

ELIOT FELD

In 1967 Eliot Feld, a twenty-five-year-old American Ballet Theatre dancer, made two remarkable ballets for the company: *Harbinger*, to Prokofiev's "Fifth Piano Concerto," and *At Midnight*, to pieces by Mahler. Feld's witty, innovative choreography crackled with fresh energy, and its surprising naturalness earned him comparisons to Jerome Robbins. (Feld had actually performed the role of Baby John in the film version of Robbins's *West Side Story* six years earlier, and Robbins was one of the young dancer's mentors at American Ballet Theatre.) Within a year, Feld had left American Ballet Theatre and formed his own group, American Ballet Company.

Feld began creating an impressively diverse roster of ballets. His chameleon-like qualities as a choreographer probably stemmed from his early training: He started out in modern classes, studied at the School of American Ballet, and worked with several choreographers before graduating from New York's High School of the Performing Arts.[25] Critics applauded his early works for American Ballet Company. "There is so much that is new in Eliot Feld's work that one forgets how classical he is," critic Marcia B. Siegel said in 1970. "On the other hand, his company is so natural and honest, one doesn't notice how revolutionary he is either. . . . This type of aesthetic confusion accompanies every significant advance in art."[26]

ABC disbanded in 1970, but in 1974 Feld created the Feld Ballet, later renamed Feld Ballets/NY. Six years later the company was reimagined as Feld Ballet Tech, with dancers from the free school Feld founded in 1978 for students from New York City's public schools. Eventually he redubbed that troupe Ballet Tech.

In the middle part of his career Feld seemed to stumble. Many of his ballets drew heavily from the works of others, or from his own older pieces. He appeared preoccupied, in a cynical way, with style rather than substance, and kept imposing strange limitations on himself. By the early 1980s, however, he had returned to form—a rebound inspired in part by his connection to the minimalist music of Steve Reich. Feld made several notable works to Reich's music, including *Grand Canyon* (1984), *Medium: Rare* (1986), *Clave* (1991), and *Tongue and Groove* (1995).

of the classics—and to compare her Giselle to that of American Ballet Theatre's other stars, including Italian guest artist Carla Fracci and the homegrown favorite, Cynthia Gregory. In 1974 Makarova made arguably her greatest contribution to the company, staging the "Kingdom of the Shades" scene from *La Bayadère*. The ballet was an important part of the Russian ballet canon, but a full production had never been danced in the West. The Shades section featured twenty-four corps de ballet dancers moving in perfect, dreamy unison; Makarova made the American Ballet corps, which rose admirably to the formidable challenge, a star in its own right.

Baryshnikov arrived at ABT just in time to perform at the company's gala on January 11, 1975. His powerful charisma and astonishingly precise technique made him a natural prince, and he partnered especially well with Gelsey Kirkland, a tiny, ethereal, exquisite ballerina. But Baryshnikov also wanted to, and did, work with living choreographers—including choreographers outside the ballet world, among them Twyla Tharp, Mark Morris, and Alvin Ailey.

Nureyev, Makarova, and Baryshnikov all discussed their desire to work with Balanchine, but only Baryshnikov actually did so. He left ABT in 1978 and joined New York City Ballet, where he immersed

Mikhail Baryshnikov, 1981.
Associated Press

himself in the Balanchine style, learning twenty new roles over the course of just fifteen months. The experiment was ultimately unsuccessful. Though he greatly admired Baryshnikov, Balanchine made no new roles for the ballet star, in part because at age seventy-four the great choreographer's health was declining. Baryshnikov did give intelligent performances of several Balanchine classics, however, including *Apollo* and *Prodigal Son* (which Balanchine revived for him). In 1980 he returned to ABT with a fresh perspective and a new title: artistic director (see Chapter 8).

In 1964 New York City Ballet moved to the newly completed New York State Theater at Lincoln Center, designed to Balanchine's specifications. Two years later the Saratoga Performing Arts Center, with its beautiful amphitheater, opened, and New York City Ballet took up residency there every July. It was a new era of stability—and, in turn, productivity—for the company.

During his later years, Balanchine focused much of his attention on a single extraordinary ballerina: Suzanne Farrell. Long-limbed, acutely musical, and casually daring, Farrell became his ideal muse, willing and able to master any devilishly complex invention he devised. He staged a full-length *Don Quixote* for her in 1965. It was an intensely personal experience for Balanchine, who was smitten with the nineteen-year-old dancer and cast himself as the Don to her Dulcinea in several performances. In his 1966 *Jewels*, the first full-length abstract ballet, Farrell was his most precious gem, the principal ballerina of the concluding "Diamonds" section.

Frustrated by Balanchine's personal attachment to her, which was increasingly smothering, Farrell left the company in 1969 after marrying a fellow dancer, Paul Mejia. Balanchine staggered. But the loss eventually allowed him to turn his attention to the company's other promising ballerinas, among them Patricia McBride, Kay Mazzo, and

Suzanne Farrell and George Balanchine in *Don Quixote,* 1965.
Library of Congress

Les Ballets Trockadero de Monte Carlo, 2013. *Horst Ossinger, AFP, Getty Images*

Les Ballets Trockadero de Monte Carlo, a parodic drag company that takes deadly, hilarious swipes at classical ballet's traditions, galumphed onto the New York scene in 1974 and was an immediate hit with audiences and critics. Dreamed up by Peter Anastos (stage name: Olga Tchikaboumskaya), Natch Taylor (Alexis Ivanovitch Lermontov), and Antony Bassae (Tamara Karpova), the Trocks' success was a product of their intimate familiarity with the world's greatest ballets. "The Monte Carlo is the creation of ballet fanatics," said Arlene Croce. "They've seen the performances, memorized the steps, read the books (this shows in the program notes), listened to the music (this shows in the editing of the taped scores), and turned the whole scorching experience inside out."[27]

Many of the company's early pieces became instant classics, especially *Go for Barocco*, a loving jab at Balanchine, and *Yes, Virginia, Another Piano Ballet*, a go at Robbins. Later the troupe found male dancers strong enough on pointe to make it through classical Petipa choreography, including the fiendish "Black Swan" pas de deux—thirty-two fouettés and all. The Trocks may initially have been seen as a product of the Gay Liberation movement, but their smart, durable sense of humor has allowed them to outlast it. As Croce prophetically remarked after their debut: "[Their style] is so damned all-seeing that I don't think anything in ballet can be safe from it for long."[28]

Merrill Ashley. By 1972, when his wildly ambitious Stravinsky Festival resulted in three masterpieces—*Violin Concerto*, *Symphony in Three Movements*, and *Duo Concertant*—it appeared Balanchine had fully recovered. And after several years working overseas with flamboyant choreographer Maurice Béjart, Farrell reconciled with her former mentor. She returned to New York City Ballet in 1975.

In 1969 Robbins also found his way back to the company, and he stayed for the next twenty years. During his time away from New York City Ballet, Robbins had huge success on Broadway with musicals like *West Side Story* and *Fiddler on the Roof* (see Chapter 9), and he also founded his own company, Ballets USA, which toured much of the world. In 1966 he created the American Theater Lab, an experimental workshop funded by the National Endowment for the Arts that explored new ways to meld dance, drama, and music.

One outcome of that intensive, analytical work was *Dances at a Gathering*, made for New York City

Ballet the year Robbins returned.[29] Running a full hour and set to a string of eighteen piano pieces by Chopin, it was an abstract ballet that also celebrated human relationships. "[*Dances at a Gathering*] stays and exists in the time of the music and its work," Robbins wrote. "Nothing is out of it, I believe; all gestures and moods, steps, etc., are part of the fabric of the music's time and its meaning to me."[30]

The years in which both Balanchine and Robbins were premiering ballets at the New York State Theater were happy ones for ballet-goers, and for New York City Ballet's dancers. Robbins's character studies served as good foils to Balanchine's more astringent ballets. As ballerina Violette Verdy put it, "Balanchine approaches you as dancing material, Robbins as a dancing person."[31]

In the midst of the dance boom, Arthur Mitchell, New York City Ballet's black principal, founded the Dance Theatre of Harlem. Mitchell shattered ballet's color barrier when he joined New York City Ballet in 1955, but a decade and a half later there was still

ABOVE: *Dances at a Gathering*, 1969. *Time and Life Pictures, Gjon Mili/ Getty Images*

OPPOSITE: Dance Theatre of Harlem, 1965. *Afro American Newspapers, Gado/ Getty Images*

a widespread perception that black bodies weren't built for ballet. The very existence of the Dance Theatre of Harlem, a home for black classical dancers, disproved that idea.

Mitchell had dreamed for some time of opening a ballet school in Harlem, his birthplace. The assassination of Dr. Martin Luther King Jr. spurred him to realize that goal. In 1969 a Ford Foundation grant gave him just enough to rent out a garage for his school; later he moved to a church basement, and finally to a proper studio. From the beginning the school had a small performing group of high-level dancers, but Dance Theatre of Harlem made its official debut at the Guggenheim Museum in 1971. Eventually the company toured the United States, and it mounted major New York City seasons in 1974, 1975, and 1976.

Some of the group's dancers had rough-hewn technique, but Dance Theatre of Harlem was also home to superb artists, particularly Virginia Johnson, Lydia Abarca, Ronald Perry, Paul Russell, and Mel Tomlinson. Unsurprisingly, given Mitchell's background, works by Balanchine and Robbins formed the backbone of the company's repertory. But Mitchell did not want to build a black New York City Ballet. He commissioned ballets inspired either overtly or implicitly by the African Diaspora and revived a number of works associated with Diaghilev's Ballets Russes, including Fokine's *Schéhérazade*.

Dance Theatre of Harlem faced a moment of reckoning when many of the company's dancers left for Broadway or Hollywood in 1977. But Mitchell soldiered on. The group performed its first nineteenth-century ballet, *Swan Lake Act II*, in 1980. Four years later Dance Theatre of Harlem mounted a Creole revision of *Giselle*, which moved the 1841 original to 1940s Louisiana; the unorthodox work was later telecast on NBC. In 1985 the company celebrated its fifteenth anniversary in grand style, at New York's Metropolitan Opera House.

Plagued for years by financial problems, Dance Theatre of Harlem disbanded in 2004, though its school continued to train young dancers of color. And less than a decade after its closing, Dance Theatre of Harlem would rise again—under the direction of one of its former ballerinas, Virginia Johnson (see Chapter 8).

After parting ways with Rebekah Harkness, the Joffrey Ballet was forced to rethink its identity. But the daunting process of starting from scratch also energized the company. During the late 1960s, the era of Andy Warhol and be-ins, the Joffrey evolved into a youthful, iconoclastic group, unusually (for a ballet company) engaged with pop culture. It became the "bad boy" of the ballet scene, though Robert Joffrey still had serious artistic goals.

The works of Gerald Arpino, which frequently involved political and social commentary, best encapsulated the Joffrey's new ethos. *The Clowns* (1968) included references to the Vietnam War, and *The Relativity of Icarus* (1974) featured an erotically charged pas de deux for two men. But it was a ballet by Joffrey that solidified the Joffrey Ballet's reputation as "America's great swinging company," as Arlene Croce put it.[32]

Astarte, named for an ancient goddess of fertility, premiered September 20, 1967, at City Center in New York. Mystical and sensual, it was one of ballet's first multimedia works, incorporating high-decibel rock music by Crome Syrcus and film projections that gave the happenings onstage a hallucinatory quality. One particularly suggestive pas de deux featured a background film of the performers dancing the same choreography, so that the world onstage had a celluloid double. Critics had mixed reactions to *Astarte*, but the work bewitched audiences; some saw the ballet as a spiritual embodiment of the times. In 1968 *Astarte* was featured on the cover of *Time* magazine, and a *Playboy* spread inspired by the ballet's themes followed soon afterward.

Astarte represented only one part of the Joffrey formula. Robert Joffrey was also interested in reviving lost classics. His company was the first American group to mount, in 1967, German choreographer Kurt Jooss's 1933 political masterpiece *The Green Table*. Joffrey acquired works by choreographers with roots in the modern dance world, among them Mark Morris, Anna Sokolow, and Laura Dean (see Chapters 6 and 7), as well as ballets by Robbins, de Mille, and Balanchine. Though critics found many of Arpino's works inconsequential, he, too, continued to turn out premieres nearly every year. Despite lingering financial problems, during the ballet boom the Joffrey was a hive of lively, diverse activity.

Not everyone loved George Balanchine. Some thought that his no-nonsense presentation of the body diminished the magic of classical ballet. Others disliked his vision of the dancer as instrument rather than artist, his constant admonition of "Don't think, dear, do." Pragmatic to the core, Balanchine also simply produced ballets as

ABOVE: *The Green Table*, performed by Joffrey Ballet. *Photograph by Herbert Migdoll, courtesy Joffrey Ballet*

OPPOSITE: Fabrice Calmels of Joffrey Ballet in *The Green Table*. *Photograph by Herbert Migdoll, courtesy Joffrey Ballet*

needed, with no great sensitivity to failure. "My muse comes to me on union time," he famously quipped—and sometimes it didn't, which meant that a lot of less-than-brilliant Balanchine ballets made it to the stage.

Still, he was undeniably the formative influence on American ballet. "Balanchine's vision of dancers has pervaded the American ballet scene and influenced many companies abroad," critic Deborah Jowitt said.

> Now people in the United States proudly proclaim that the look of the New York City Ballet dancers is "American." We appropriate their lean, racy, long-legged look as an American ideal; we like to think of their boldness, their frankness, their speed, their cool absorption in music and dancing, their unself-conscious dignity and courtesy as attributes of American character at its best.[33]

Of all the visions of what "American ballet" might mean, Balanchine's was the most profound, and the most successful. When he died in 1983, the dance world reeled. Without Mr. B.'s clear sense of purpose, things suddenly seemed strange and uncertain. It would take American ballet a while to find its way out of the great man's shadow.

Chapter Six

Modern's Next Generations

Alvin Ailey with Alvin Ailey American
Dance Theater in Ailey's masterpiece,
*Revelations. Jack Mitchell (1961),
courtesy Alvin Ailey Dance Foundation,
Inc. © AADF*

"It is hard for many people to accept that dancing has
nothing in common with music other than the element of
time and division of time." —*Merce Cunningham*[1]

As revolutionary as their ideas initially seemed, the Big Four's choreography and teachings became "tradition" surprisingly quickly. By the 1940s Martha Graham, Doris Humphrey, Charles Weidman, and Hanya Holm were considered dance icons in both the concert and the academic worlds.

The first wave of choreographers to emerge from these artists' schools of thought stayed close to their teachers' ideals. While the Big Four had searched for a way to make dance a serious art—and an American art—most of their pupils, seeing that path already cleared, focused on creating distinctive techniques of their own, devising new ways of moving and making movement.

But some second-generation choreographers, particularly Merce Cunningham and Paul Taylor, took steps toward radicalism. These transitional artists, while honoring the heritage of the Big Four, created works of extraordinary logic and poetry that set the stage for the extreme radicals of the 1960s. They played with the dynamite that would eventually blow modern dance wide open.

Graham Disciples

Anna Sokolow, Pearl Lang, and Erick Hawkins

ANNA SOKOLOW

One of the first Graham dancers to step out on her own, Anna Sokolow saw dance as a way to change the world's social and political makeup. Like many dancers of the time, she was a Marxist. As dance critic Margaret Lloyd said, "Her left wing was always showing. It was indeed protuberant. Everything she did was riffled with caustic wit and satiric jab, not in plea for the proletariat alone, but for people (provided they were underdogs) everywhere."[2]

Born to Russian immigrants, Sokolow grew up on the Lower East Side of New York City. She started experimenting with choreography as a teenager at the Henry Street Settlement, taking Louis Horst's choreographic composition class at the Settlement's Neighborhood Playhouse. (For a few years, she acted as Horst's assistant during his classes, earning her the nickname "Louis' Whip.") Sokolow

ABOVE: Anna Sokolow.
Courtesy Sokolow Theatre Dance Ensemble

LEFT: Sokolow performs *Kaddish,* which she choreographed in 1945. *Courtesy Sokolow Theatre Dance Ensemble*

joined the Martha Graham Dance Company in 1930 and formed her own group, Dance Unit, shortly after. Because she believed in the power of dance to deliver transformative social messages, her company began performing for labor unions and workers' organizations as part of the Worker's Dance League.

Sokolow's style was rooted in Graham technique, but, as Sokolow herself said, she didn't really "have the temperament of a disciple," and she quickly distanced herself from Graham's Americana themes.[3] Instead, she showed a distinctive interest in the problems of Depression-era America, and in the increasingly unsettling political situation in Europe. Her 1935 work *Strange American Funeral* examined the plight of the industrial worker, and the 1937 *War Is Beautiful* burlesqued Fascist Italy's war obsession. In the summer of 1937, as one of the first choreographic fellows at Bennington College, she created *Façade*, a biting critique of Mussolini's regime. Though sometimes difficult for audiences to wade through, these earnest works reflected the intensity of Sokolow's beliefs.

In 1939 the Fine Arts Department of the Mexican government asked Sokolow and her dancers to give a series of concerts. At the invitation of the Ministry of Public Education, she stayed for several months, developing a school and company in Mexico City. For the next decade Sokolow spent nearly half of each year in Mexico, fostering the growth of its fledgling modern dance scene. She became known as *la fundadora de la danza moderna*

Mexico ("the founder of Mexican modern dance"), and Mexico in turn had a marked influence on her artistic evolution. Deeply inspired by the Mexican people's reverence for art, and by the work of politically active artists, including José Clemente Orozco, she created several dances on Mexican themes.

Sokolow's work, while still preoccupied with social concerns, softened slightly as she matured, becoming less strident though no less forceful. In 1955 she created her masterpiece, *Rooms*, set to jazzy music by Kenyon Hopkins. Dancers on widely spaced chairs represented, perhaps, residents of tenement apartments. Their convulsive movements expressed the intense, quiet loneliness of isolation within a sea of people. "Its ultimate aim," said critic John Martin, "seems to be to induce you to jump as inconspicuously as possible into the nearest river."[4]

Thanks in part to the diverse training in theater and dance she'd received at the Playhouse, Sokolow choreographed successfully for Broadway as well, creating movement for Kurt Weill's *Street Scene* (1947) and Tennessee Williams's *Camino Real* (1953). (She was also the original choreographer for 1968's *Hair*, but she withdrew amid logistical turmoil before the musical opened.) In 1968 she formed a company of dancer/actors and began to explore the idea of combining dance, theater, literature, and music to create a new form of artistic expression. Sokolow's groundbreaking work in this idiom inspired many later leaders of the dance and theater movement, including the brilliant choreographer Pina Bausch.

Pearl Lang, left, rehearses with Paul Sanasardo and Ellen Tittler, 1964.
Sam Falk/Getty Images

PEARL LANG

Pearl Lang was one of the Graham Company's most eloquent dancers, and the first to be entrusted with some of the parts Graham herself had danced. After a decade as a soloist with the group, Lang left to form her own company, Pearl Lang Dance Theater, in 1952, though she would continue to guest with Graham through the 1970s.

A rapturous, lyrical dancer, Lang never strayed too far from Graham's movement vocabulary. But rather than explore American folklore and Greek epics, as Graham did, Lang's works frequently probed Biblical stories and Jewish themes. "People dance for many reasons," she said. "I think mine [is] an ecstatic religious one."[5] *Shira* (1960), inspired by a Hasidic legend of rebirth, had the feel of a mysterious ritual. *The Possessed* (1975), based on the 1914 play *The Dybbuk* by Solomon Ansky, incorporated Hasidic dance steps.

Lang was a gifted teacher, serving on the faculties of Yale University, Juilliard, the Neighborhood Playhouse, and the Martha Graham School of Contemporary Dance; her students included Madonna and Pina Bausch.

ERICK HAWKINS

Erick Hawkins was studying Greek at Harvard when he first discovered Isadora Duncan's book *The Art of the Dance*. Intrigued, he began studying various types of movement. He worked in Salzburg with modern dancers Harald Kreutzberg and Yvonne Georgi before enrolling at the School of American Ballet in New York. Hawkins became a charter member of Lincoln Kirstein's Ballet Caravan in 1936, but in the summer of 1937 he met Graham at Bennington College, and his fate was sealed: A year later, he became the first man to join Graham's company.

For the next thirteen years, Hawkins danced numerous sensual duets with Graham in her works. His ideas about design and composition became increasingly important to her. Though he was fifteen years her junior, the couple married in 1948. Two years later, they divorced, and Hawkins left the company to pursue his own choreographic ideas.

Hawkins suffered many injuries while working with Graham. In his new dances he hoped to eliminate unnecessary bodily stress by achieving unity of body and mind, a principle he discovered through Zen Buddhism. Hawkins also hoped to establish a more significant presence for the man in modern dance, moving away from anything resembling the passive ballet partner. His movement quality struck some as androgynous.[6]

Erick Hawkins rehearses with Martha Graham, 1950. *Associated Press*

To encourage harmony between dance and music, Hawkins only choreographed to music composed for him—frequently by Lucia Dlugoszewski, who became his wife. *Here and Now with Watchers* (1957) embodied his new aesthetic: Ceremonial and cyclical, it felt Eastern in its slow, deliberate pace. Some viewers found it boring. But it marked a clear departure from Graham's theatrics. "The concept Graham began to articulate explicitly in the late 1940s—the dancer not only as suffering hero, but as divine acrobat—is, clearly, far from Hawkins's vision," critic Deborah Jowitt said:

> Striving, ardent, mortifying the flesh, achieving more than human feats of strength and daring: that's not how Hawkins sees the dancer. [His dancers] move with idyllic peacefulness, as if they've entered into a compact with the force of gravity—promising to tease it only in brief delighted forays into flight, disequilibrium, or accumulating momentum.[7]

Humphrey-Weidman Disciples

Eleanor King, Sybil Shearer, and José Limón

ELEANOR KING

Beautiful and perfectly proportioned—she had a side job as an artist's model—Eleanor King became an admired dancer with the Humphrey-Weidman Company in the 1930s. King was also very well-read, and when she began choreographing she often based her dances on works of literature. Her first major piece, *Icaro* (1937), a retelling of the Icarus story, mixed modern steps with variations on the "free dance" of ancient Greece. (Her Icarus was Jack Cole, who would become a pioneer of American jazz dance [see Chapter 9].)

In 1936 King went to Colorado for the summer to teach at the Perry-Mansfield Performing Arts School and Camp. She found herself drawn to the West's wide-open spaces, and to the rich cultures of the local American Indian tribes. She was also beginning to feel that modern dance needed to move

outside of New York, that its tight geographic focus was causing inbreeding.[8] In the summer of 1943 she traveled to the Cornish School of Art, Music and Drama in Seattle. She ended up staying in the city and opening her own studio.

King's works began to reflect her new environment. *Spirit Dance* (1945) was based on her observations of the Northwest Indians. Rather than try to reproduce their ceremonies, however, she created a psychological meditation, a movement study of a woman possessed by a supernatural being. In 1947 and 1948 King mounted "One World in Dance," a series of weekly performances that showed off the diverse dance heritage of the West Coast. Participants included American Indian, Peruvian, Colombian, Ecuadorian, Scottish, Swedish, and Mexican dancers who had settled in the region. "There are no barriers between types of dance," King said. "Any style, any period, any idea can be used. . . . The idea creates the form, the scope is absolutely unlimited."[9] Dance as idea, whether originating in the mythic forms of literature or the living forms of culture, became King's signature.

King ultimately settled in Santa Fe, New Mexico, where she worked and taught until her death in 1991.

OPPOSITE: Eleanor King in *Transformations*, 1955. *Howard Whitlach, courtesy Cross-Cultural Dance Resources Collection, Arizona State University*

BELOW: King in the studio, 1978. *Jane Grossenbacher, courtesy Cross-Cultural Dance Resources Collection, Arizona State University*

SYBIL SHEARER

After experiencing Holm, Humphrey, and Weidman's techniques at a 1934 Bennington College summer session, Toronto-born, New York-raised Sybil Shearer started studying with Doris Humphrey, and joined the Humphrey-Weidman Company in 1935. Shearer admired Humphrey because "her pupils were urged to dance, not just do exercises," she said. "The idea was the important thing."[10] That focus on ideas was central to Shearer's choreography, as it was to King's: Shearer saw modern dance as a way of looking at the world—a point of view—and not as a technique.[11] Her works frequently mixed the sacred and the secular, and her programs often alternated comedic and sober pieces. She earned a reputation as a gently rebellious artist, an independent individualist.

A year after a successful solo debut in 1941, Shearer unexpectedly moved to Chicago, where she taught at the present-day Roosevelt University and continued to perform. Like King, she was dissatisfied with the New York dance scene. In the Midwest, which she had visited on tour, she discovered a sense of freedom that she had found missing amid New York's busyness. Shearer found a small but loyal audience in the Midwest, where she developed an expressive style she called "liquid acting," in which the whole body is involved in the creation of a character.

JOSÉ LIMÓN

Born into an artistic Mexican family in 1908, José Limón arrived in New York in 1928 to study painting. A year later, after seeing a performance by German dancer Harald Kreutzberg, he had a lightning-bolt revelation: He was meant to be a dancer. Reading Isadora Duncan's *My Life* confirmed the feeling. In his own distinctive words, Limón described his revelation:

> Early in the year nineteen hundred and twenty-nine I was born at 9 East Fifty-Ninth Street, New York City. My parents were Isadora Duncan and Harald Kreutzberg.

OPPOSITE: Sybil Shearer in *Without Wings the Way is Steep* from *Fables and Proverbs*, 1961. The *Chicago Tribune* called the performance a "mesmerizing, spine-tingling experience." *Courtesy the Morrison-Shearer Foundation*

BELOW: José Limón dances during his all-soldier revue, Camp Lee, Virginia, 1943. *Getty Images*

They were not present at my birth. I doubt that they ever saw one another or were aware of their responsibility for my being. Presiding at my emergence into the world were my foster parents, Doris Humphrey and Charles Weidman. It was at their dance studio and in their classes that I was born. I had existed previously in human form for twenty years. But that existence was only a period of gestation, albeit a long one, longer than that of an elephant.[12]

He enrolled at the Humphrey-Weidman school. Though a late starter, Limón—tall and handsome, with a powerful build—was a welcome addition to the Humphrey-Weidman Company, which he joined after less than a year of study. Limón matured under the careful guidance of Humphrey, who respected his fervent idealism and encouraged him to choreograph. In 1937 he was one of the first Bennington College dance fellows.

Limón began developing a signature style, which was clearly related to Humphrey's but added the thrusting, off-center movements that came most naturally to his weighty body. His choreography frequently probed his Mexican heritage. *Danzas Mexicanas* (1939), a suite of solos, represented five different types of Mexicans: Indian, *conquistador*, peasant, *caballero*, and revolutionary. According to the program notes, the 1942 *Chaconne* was based on a dance that originated in Mexico before becoming more refined in Spanish courts. Essentially abstract, *Chaconne* was, more than anything else, an embodiment of its powerful Bach score, at once emotional and formally majestic.

Limón joined the army during World War II (and almost immediately made a new dance for a soldier revue, with a chorus of twelve infantrymen). Upon his return from armed services in 1945, he decided to form his own company. By that point Humphrey had moved on from Weidman; Limón asked her to serve as his co-director. She began

Limón rehearsing with Betty Jones and Ruth Currier, both members of his company, 1950. *Gjon Mili/Time and Life Pictures, Getty Images*

choreographing for Limón's group, and he brought several of her older works into its repertoire.

The José Limón Dance Company's first dancers—Lucas Hoving, Pauline Koner, Betty Jones, and Limón himself—had four entirely distinct onstage personalities, whose differences formed the basis of several of Limón's works. His most famous piece, *The Moor's Pavane* (1949), whittled the story of *Othello* down to its emotional core. Hoving's compact, pale Iago was the perfect foil for Limón's massive, dark Othello. The beautifully theatrical dance included no mime. Instead, each character had a distinctive way of moving that defined his or her personality, while repeated circular patterns evoked the tangled series of events that bound the dancers together. The Hoving-Limón partnership inspired several other works in which Limón rethought the role of the man in modern dance, giving him more dimension and masculine power.[13]

Limón died of cancer in 1972. His company was the first modern group to survive the death of its founder. It still performs the works of both Humphrey and Limón, a continuous lineage that exists nowhere else in modern dance.

Holm Disciples
Valerie Bettis, Glen Tetley, and Alwin Nikolais

VALERIE BETTIS

Houston-born Valerie Bettis began as a ballet student, but, unhappy, she traveled to New York to study with Hanya Holm. An exuberant dancer, Bettis learned discipline and precision in Holm's classes, and performed with Holm's company for three years in the 1930s. After a promising debut solo recital in 1941, she choreographed her breakthrough work, *The Desperate Heart*, in 1943. Sunny moments of remembered happiness pierced the otherwise gray, sorrowful piece, which featured sweeping, seemingly impulsive gestures. *The Desperate Heart* was set to a poem by John Malcolm Brinnin, who read at each of its early performances; moving to text would become one of Bettis's signatures.

Glamorous and naturally dramatic, Bettis danced on Broadway and in films as well as in modern works. She had a successful acting career, replacing, for example, the formidable Lotte Lenya in *The Threepenny Opera* in 1955. She also choreographed dances for Rita Hayworth in the films *Affair in Trinidad* and *Salome*. Bettis ultimately made use of all of her varied experiences, exploring the theatrical aspects of dance and the kinetic expressiveness of theater.

GLEN TETLEY

Glen Tetley first encountered dance while studying medicine at Franklin and Marshall College in Pennsylvania. He moved to New York to take classes with Holm and Graham. Eventually Tetley became Holm's teaching assistant, and danced in several of her Broadway productions, including *Kiss Me Kate* (1948) and *Juno* (1949). But he also developed an interest in ballet, which he studied with Antony Tudor and at the School of American Ballet. A charter member of the Joffrey Ballet, Tetley danced briefly with American Ballet Theatre and Jerome Robbins's Ballets: USA, as well.

Given his background, it might seem unsurprising that when Tetley formed his own company in 1962, he created works that blended modern dance

Valerie Bettis, 1948. *Nina Leen /Time and Life Pictures, Getty Images*

and ballet. The combination, however, shocked much of the dance world at the time. Modern dancers disliked the classical arabesques and pirouettes Tetley included in his first major work, *Pierrot Lunaire*, set to Arnold Schoenberg's song cycle; its Graham-like torquing of the torso puzzled the ballet world.

Around the time Tetley formed his troupe, Nederlands Dans Theater invited him to be a guest choreographer. He found that his hybrid style, which was intensely physical and often lushly sensual, met with less resistance in Europe, and he began to focus more of his energy overseas. In 1969, after disbanding his company, he moved to The Hague to become co-director of Nederlands. He assumed director-ship of the Stuttgart Ballet in 1974. Running a more traditional ballet company shifted his allegiances; increasingly his choreography became weighted toward the classical.

After leaving the Stuttgart in 1976, Tetley freelanced for compa-nies—primarily ballet companies—around the world. His dances for American Ballet Theatre include *Sphinx* (1977) for Martine van Hamel and *Contredances* (1979) for Natalia Makarova and Anthony Dowell. Tetley returned to North America to act as artistic associate for the National Ballet of Canada in the 1980s. He died in Florida in 2007.

ALWIN NIKOLAIS

Before the summer of 1936, Alwin Nikolais, who was born in a small town in Connecticut, had done a little of everything. He'd explored music, playing piano for ballet classes and silent films; he'd worked in local theater, where he learned how to light a stage; he'd experimented with puppetry; he'd dabbled in various forms of dance. During that criti-cal summer, at Bennington College, Nikolais was exposed to the theories of the Big Four. He immediately embraced them.

Nikolais studied with Humphrey, Graham, and Holm, but was most drawn to Holm. He found her class to be less about personal style and more about the development of a solid foundation—the "everydancer's" technique.[14] After a stint in the army during World War II, Nikolais studied intensively with Holm, and later became her teaching assistant.

Soon Nikolais began to form his own thoughts about teaching and choreography. Specifically, he explored the idea of a "decentral-ized" technique, in which the center of the body is not, as it is in clas-sical ballet, supportively rigid, but rather fluid and changeable. He also rejected the idea of dance as an exploration of the psyche. "I wanted man to identify with things other than himself," he wrote. Instead, he proposed a theory of dance as metaphor, looking beyond the personal to the universal.[15]

Nikolais's first important work, 1953's *Masks, Props and Mobiles*, used multiple types of media to create a world that made bodies barely recognizable; in one section, dancers wriggled inside large sacks of stretchy fabric, creating metamorphosing sculptures as they moved. The piece took full advantage of Nikolais' experiences with lighting and

Glen Tetley's *Voluntaries*, originally choreographed for the Stuttgart Ballet in 1973, performed by the Australian Ballet, 2003. *Nick Laham, Getty Images*

puppetry. It was the first of many of his works to involve this kind of transformative stagecraft, "dances of sorcery . . . in which the dancers may be engulfed by an entranced landscape of light, jitter on the edges of a fragmenting universe . . . [or] be imprinted with whirling patterns."[16] The works were "about" abstraction. But some critics charged Nikolais with dehumanizing dancers, a complaint that would plague him for much of his career.

Nikolais achieved mainstream fame thanks to *Allegory* (1959), another fantastical work that used tricks involving light, color, sound, and shape to create "a carnival of anthropomorphic illusions and visual delights."[17] Its particular wizardry seemed tailor-made for television, and it was presented on a late-night variety program, *The Steve Allen Show*, in 1959. The broadcast was a huge success. Nikolais' company ended up making eight appearances on the program, proving to mainstream audiences that modern dance could be accessible.

Nikolais essentially built his style on the body of his foremost dancer, Murray Louis, who had extraordinary muscular control. Louis also became a choreographer, and he and Nikolais's companies shared a building and a school for the latter half of Nikolais' life. Louis' best pieces showcased his witty sense of humor—particularly the 1964 *Junk Dances*, a satiric depiction of a household strewn with the ridiculous gadgets that modern-day advertising deems indispensable. After Nikolais' death in 1993, the Nikolais-Louis Foundation consolidated the two companies; in 1999 the foundation closed down its performing arm and began an association with the Ririe-Woodbury Dance Company in Salt Lake City, Utah. Ririe-Woodbury still performs several of Nikolais' and Louis' works, to great acclaim.

OPPOSITE: *Noumenon Mobilus,* choreographed by Alwin Nikolais in 1953 and performed by Juan Carlos Claudio and Brandin Scott Steffenssen of the Ririe-Woodbury Dance Company in 2004. *Laurent Paillier, photosdanse.com*

BELOW: Nikolais's *Crucible* (1985), performed by the Ririe-Woodbury Dance Company, 2004. *Laurent Faillier, photosdanse.com*

INNOVATIVE CHOREOGRAPHERS

The West Coast
Lester Horton

Los Angeles was a young city in 1928, the year Lester Horton arrived. A town obsessed with money and superficial appearances—it was the home of the burgeoning film industry, after all—L.A. was nevertheless where Horton found substance. There he was able to do what many New York dancers could not: develop a solid technique that shaped the body distinctively yet was malleable enough to serve the needs of many types of dancers.

Horton was born in Indianapolis in 1906. Part American Indian, he was fascinated by tribal dance; he attended local Indian ceremonies and absorbed as much as he could. He also studied ballet and Denishawn-style modern dance. After moving to Los Angeles, he began working with Japanese dancer and choreographer Michio Ito, further diversifying his already varied training.

Horton assembled a small group of dancers to explore the ideas he wanted to choreograph, most of which were inspired by "primitive" cultures. He developed a technique rooted not in steps but in ritual, and took a holistic approach to the body. Horton hoped "to create a system which would correct physical faults . . . having all the basic movements which govern the actions of the body, combined with a knowledge of the origin of movement and a sense of artistic design."[18] The resulting style involved deep bends at the knees, swinging through the body, and an emphasis on off-balance positions—particularly the "lateral T," in which a dancer stands on one leg, extending the torso at a ninety-degree angle while

OPPOSITE: Isadora Duncan, José Limón, Katherine Dunham, and Bob Fosse were commemorated by the US Postal Service's "Innovative Choreographers" stamps, 2012.

BELOW: Lester Horton Dance Company in *The Painted Desert*, 1934. The work celebrated Navajo, Hopi, Apache, and Zuni ceremonials.

counterbalancing that force by sending energy outward through the raised leg.

The Lester Horton Dancers first performed in 1932. Horton saw his company as a democracy, not a dictatorship; he wanted a group of individuals, not a cultish following with a particular "Horton look." He also cultivated a multiracial group, which was essentially unheard of at the time. The Horton company included black, white, American Indian, Javanese, and French dancers. His star was the fearless Bella Lewitzky, the daughter of Russian-Jewish immigrants.

Though a gifted teacher, Horton had no training in composition, and as a result his pieces were sometimes heavy on theater but light on content. His best-known work, *Salomé* (1934), was a boldly erotic imagining of Oscar Wilde's play. Other classics include *The Beloved* (1948), an eerie depiction of an abusive marriage, and *To José Clemente Orozco* (1952), a tribute to the fiery Mexican artist who also inspired Anna Sokolow.

The Horton Group's performances eventually became famous in the L.A. community, attracting movie stars and the film-world intelligentsia. Since money was tight, Horton made use of his Hollywood connections, ultimately working on nineteen films. He temporarily disbanded his company in the early 1940s to take on movie jobs, but by 1948 he had amassed enough funds to open the Horton Dance Theater in Hollywood—the first American stage devoted solely to dance.

After Horton died of a heart attack in 1953, his company floundered and eventually disbanded. His legacy lives on in the work of one of his most distinguished dancers, Alvin Ailey.

Race in American Modern Dance
Katherine Dunham, Pearl Primus, Donald McKayle, and Alvin Ailey

In the late 1930s and early 1940s, non-white dancers began to discover an outlet in modern dance. Led by Katherine Dunham and Pearl Primus, two anthropologist-performers, black dance in particular found a home in the modern community, making its way out of the vaudeville hall and onto the concert stage. Later, Donald McKayle and Alvin Ailey created dances that explored the black experience in America. Ailey's works were especially powerful: While rooted in black culture, they spoke directly to audiences of all colors.

KATHERINE DUNHAM

The strikingly beautiful Katherine Dunham—in the 1940s, her legs were rumored to be insured for a million dollars—broke new ground for black dance. She was, according to dance critic Wendy Perron, "the first American to present dance forms from the African diaspora on a concert stage, the first to sustain a black dance company, the first black person to choreograph for the Metropolitan Opera. . . . She could have had her own TV show called *Dance Roots*."[19]

Growing up in Illinois, Dunham had little formal dance training until her late teens. She studied anthropology at the University of Chicago, where she was inspired by the work of professors Robert Redfield and Melville Herskovits, who believed that knowledge of African culture was crucial to understanding African American culture.

After graduation, Dunham received a research fellowship that allowed her to spend a year and a half in the West Indies studying traditional dances. There she embraced the idea of dance as ritual, as a meaningful connection to a higher power. The concept transformed her. Upon her return to the United States, she created her first significant dance, *L'Ag'Ya* (1938), based on a Martinique folktale about a traditional rhythmic fighting dance. One of her best-known works, *Shango* (1945), portrayed a Haitian possession ritual in which she had participated. (Eventually Dunham would become a priestess in the Haitian *vodoun* religion.)

Dunham was also fascinated by black dance in America, especially the vibrant Harlem scene. Her revue *Tropics and "Le Jazz Hot": From Haiti to Harlem* opened at New York's Windsor Theater on February 18, 1940, supposedly for a one-night performance. Its blend of dances from the West Indies and Cuba with American social dances, such as the cakewalk and ballin' the jack, proved irresistible, and the show ended up staying at the Windsor for thirteen weeks. A year later Dunham co-choreographed the Broadway show *Cabin in the Sky*—an all-black, jazz-inflected retelling of the Faust legend—with George Balanchine. She was a sensation as the show's lead, siren Georgia Brown.

In 1943 Sol Hurok, the producer who had brought the Ballet Russe de Monte Carlo to the United States a decade prior, presented Dunham's company in *Tropical Revue* on Broadway, a production that "sent the critics thumbing through their thesauruses for synonyms of 'torrid.'"[20] While some of the material from *Tropical Revue* was recycled from *Tropics and Le Jazz Hot*, the show added the

shimmying Melanesian "Rara Tonga" and sensual rumbas from Mexico and Chile, as well as a section called "Rites of Passage," inspired by various puberty and fertility rituals. (The latter proved controversial enough to be banned from some performances when the show toured to Boston.) *Tropical Revue* was colorful, provocative entertainment, and its two-week New York run was extended to seven months.

Dunham ran the Dunham School of Dance and Theater in Times Square for a decade beginning in 1945. The school taught not only dance but also anthropology and languages. In addition to prominent dancers, it attracted its share of celebrities, including Eartha Kitt, Marlon Brando, James Dean, and Warren Beatty.

Though Dunham never thought of herself as a serious, formalist artist—she wanted her programs to be engaging and accessible—racial tensions in the United States spurred her to activism. In 1944, while her company was on a tour stop in Lexington, Kentucky, she discovered a "For Blacks Only" sign on a bus and pinned it to her dress during a performance.[21] In 1951 she choreographed *Southland*, which depicted the lynching of a black man falsely accused of raping a white woman. In the 1960s Dunham moved to East St. Louis, at the height of racial unrest in that city. Though she frequently faced threats and even bomb scares, she taught martial arts, drumming, and dance to a group of black teenagers, keeping them away from the turmoil of the streets. Even in her eighties, Dunham continued to make waves, going on a hunger strike in protest of the government's policy prohibiting Haitian refugees from staying in the United States. She died in 2006, at age ninety-six.

PEARL PRIMUS

Dunham and Pearl Primus had similar goals and academic interests, but remarkably different personalities. Primus came to the United States from Trinidad as a toddler. While studying biology and premedicine at Hunter College in New York, she made a name for herself as a track and field star. She accidentally stumbled upon dance at Hunter, and also developed an interest in African dances and cultures. Primus began studying with Graham, Weidman, and Humphrey, while simultaneously conducting anthropological research on dance in Africa and the African origins of Southern black religious ceremonies. Her first choreographic works, performed at the 92nd Street Y in 1943, showed remarkable range for a relatively inexperienced dancer. "If ever a young dancer was entitled to a company of her own and the freedom to do what she chooses with it," wrote *New York Times* critic John Martin, "she is it."[22]

In 1944 Primus traveled to the Deep South to research African American religious dances. During her trip she visited sixty-seven churches. Increasingly, she became committed to the idea of dance as communication rather than entertainment. Four years later, she received a research fellowship allowing her to spend nine months formally studying dance in Africa. She ended up staying for more than a year, living among the peoples of Angola, Congo, Cameroon, Ghana, Liberia, Nigeria, Senegal, Tanzania, Rwanda, Burundi, Sierra Leone, Côte d'Ivoire, and Benin. She persuaded elders to resurrect old dances, and documented her findings using film and dance notation. (She also introduced many Africans to the music of Mozart, Stravinsky, and Gershwin.)

Upon her return to New York, she founded the Pearl Primus School of Primal Dance, where she taught many of the dances and rituals she had observed during her travels. In 1951 she performed again at the 92nd Street Y, presenting several works based on her experiences in Africa—including *Fanga*, inspired by the Liberian dance of welcome, which would become one of her best-known pieces. By 1952 Primus had put together a full program of these dances, *Dark Rhythms*, which she presented at venues around New York.

In addition to her concert dances, Primus worked on Broadway, in opera, and in television. Beginning in the 1940s, she wrote a series of academic and popular articles discussing African and African American dance. She held firm to her belief that dance was a language of its own; in 1978 she established the Pearl Primus Dance Language Institute, and the same year she successfully argued that dance could be used to fulfill her doctoral language requirements at New York University. In 1986 she became a professor of ethnic studies at the Five Colleges (Amherst, Smith, Mount Holyoke, Hampshire, and the University of Massachusetts).

Throughout her career, Primus was able to show African traditions in a light that revealed their connections to American heritage, making them engaging and acceptable to both black and white audiences. "I dance not to entertain, but to help people to better understand each other," she said. "It is inappropriate to ask when I shall stop dancing. I expect to dance in the courts of the ancestors."[23]

DONALD MCKAYLE

First inspired to dance by a Pearl Primus concert, Donald McKayle went on to work with the likes

of Martha Graham, Anna Sokolow, and Merce Cunningham. He also had a successful Broadway career, performing in *House of Flowers* (1954) and *West Side Story* (1957).

McKayle was one of the first choreographers to dramatize the black American experience in dance. His breakthrough work, *Games* (1951), based on his childhood memories, depicted children at play in a crowded sea of tenements; their chanted songs and dialogue were interrupted by the arrival of violent policemen. *Rainbow Round My Shoulder* (1959) drew from the rhythms and stories of chain-gang workers in the South.

Though contextually specific, these dances spoke to a universal humanity. "All [his] best works deal, not with abstractions, but with people," said critic

P. W. Manchester; they are "living, laughing, suffering, bitter, protesting, superbly human beings."[24]

ALVIN AILEY

During junior high school, Alvin Ailey was dragged against his will to a Ballet Russe de Monte Carlo performance. Surprised to find himself absorbed in the dance, he began frequenting the theater scene in Los Angeles, to which he had moved with his mother at age eleven after an early childhood spent in poverty in rural Texas. Ailey was particularly enthralled by the polyrhythmic isolations of the Afro-Caribbean dances in Katherine Dunham's *Tropical Revue* and by her company's vivid theatricality.

Already an artist—he grew up drawing and playing the tuba—Ailey started training with Lester

Horton as a teenager. Horton became his mentor and shaped him into a strong dancer with a warm, oversized presence. Ailey joined Horton's group in 1950, though he dropped in and out several times while studying languages at the University of California, Los Angeles. In 1953 he rededicated himself to the company, only to find himself assuming the role of director when Horton died later that year.

Though Ailey tried to maintain the Horton group, the effort fizzled, and in 1954 he moved to New York City, along with fellow Horton star Carmen de Lavellade, to perform on Broadway in Truman Capote's *House of Flowers*. In New York he began studying with Graham, Holm, Weidman, and Sokolow, soaking up the city's diverse influences.

Ailey's goal was to create a color-blind group, like Horton's, but during his early years on the East Coast he found a foothold in a group of black dancers who supported one another.[25] In March 1958, Ailey and six of these dancers presented a concert at the 92nd Street Y that included Ailey's soulful, heartfelt *Blues Suite*, based on memories of his childhood in Depression-era Texas. The critical response was overwhelmingly positive. Later that year Ailey founded a permanent group of about a dozen dancers.

OPPOSITE: Alvin Ailey, Ella Thompson, and Myrna White in *Revelations*, 1961. *Jack Mitchell, courtesy Alvin Ailey Dance Foundation, Inc. © AADF*

RIGHT Judith Jamison, star dancer and future artistic director of Alvin Ailey American Dance Theatre, in *Revelations*, 1967. *Jack Mitchell, courtesy Alvin Ailey Dance Foundation, Inc. © AADF*

The Alvin Ailey American Dance Theater (as the company was eventually known) began amassing a diverse repertoire, ranging from older works by Ted Shawn to dances by Dunham and Primus, along with Ailey's own pieces. The company added Hispanic, Asian, and white dancers. Ailey established a vibrant school in New York, where students could learn many different dance styles.

Ailey's timing was good: The Civil Rights movement was picking up steam, and grants and other forms of funding were being set aside for artists of color. In 1962 the Ailey company was chosen to participate in John F. Kennedy's President's Special International Program for Cultural Presentations, which sent the troupe to the Far East and Australia. Later The Alvin Ailey American Dance Theater toured Brazil, Paris, London, Senegal, and West Africa, representing the State Department.

In 1960 the company premiered Ailey's masterwork, *Revelations*, which established Ailey as the preeminent dance voice of the African American experience. Set to choral versions of traditional black spirituals, *Revelations* embodied the powerful religious unity that buoyed generations of enslaved blacks. Its style, formally based in the techniques of Horton and Graham, also captured the idiomatic mannerisms of Southern black communities. But this wasn't an insular dance, for black audiences only. "Its roots are in American Negro culture, which is part of the whole country's heritage," Ailey said. "The dance speaks to everyone. . . . Otherwise it wouldn't work."[26]

The idea of "speaking to everyone" was in keeping with Ailey's hope to make modern dance popular again. At a time when many of his contemporaries were moving away from narrative and toward a kind of aggressive abstraction that frequently baffled audiences, Ailey wanted his company's performances to be both moving and entertaining. "I'm interested in putting something on stage that will have a very wide appeal without being condescending; that will reach an audience and make it part of the dance; that will get everybody in the theater," he said.[27] Some found his dances too commercial. But as critic Marcia Siegel said, Ailey "doesn't vulgarize and cheapen the modern idiom." Instead, he "avoids the strangeness and choreographic idiosyncrasy that made people think modern dance was 'difficult' and presents a very clear, unambiguous event."[28]

The demand for Ailey's dance-for-everyone approach crossed stylistic boundaries. He made *Feast of Ashes* for the Joffrey Ballet (1962), choreographed *Antony and Cleopatra* for the new Metropolitan Opera House (1966), and created

three works for the Harkness Ballet. As he became better known, he was able to collaborate with luminaries such as Duke Ellington, who composed the score for Ailey's *The River*, commissioned by American Ballet Theatre.

Ailey died of a rare blood disease at age fifty-eight in 1989. Judith Jamison, one of his dance company's star dancers, succeeded him as director. Under Jamison's direction, the group moved away from its original theatrical aesthetic. The caliber of the dancers, many of whom came up through the thriving Ailey School, increased exponentially. When choreographer Robert Battle took over the company in 2011, he set out to prove that the extraordinary movers of Alvin Ailey American Dance Theater could essentially do anything. The group's repertory now includes not only classics such as *Revelations* and *Blues Suite*, but also Jiří Kylián's balletic *Petit Mort* and Ohad Naharin's eccentric, improvisation-fueled *Minus 16*.

New Paths
Merce Cunningham and Paul Taylor

Whereas most choreographers of this period were still in conversation with the established dance orthodoxy, Merce Cunningham and Paul Taylor became active dissenters. Though intimately familiar with the Big Four's conception of modern dance—each performed in Martha Graham's company—they weren't sold on it. They sought new ways of thinking about dance, and specifically about dance's relationship to music.

MERCE CUNNINGHAM

Though his works would come to be known for their incisive austerity, Merce Cunningham started out in the flash-and-dazzle world of vaudeville. Growing up in Washington State, Cunningham studied tap and ballroom with Maude M. Barrett, who attended his family's church and ran the Barrett School of the Dance. He began performing with Barrett's daughter, Marjorie, and the trio went on the road for a short vaudeville tour when Cunningham was a teenager. Noticing his elegant bearing and articulate hands and feet, people frequently mistook him for a classically trained ballet dancer.

Cunningham enrolled at George Washington University, but left after a year to study at the Cornish School (now Cornish College of the Arts) in Seattle. Invigorated by the new environment, he performed in a work by Lester Horton and took classes with Bonnie Bird, a former member of Graham's company.

In 1938 a new accompanist arrived at Cornish School: the young composer John Cage. A year later, Cage published his essay "Goal: New Music, New Dance," which proposed that dance free itself from music—that music and dance, though performed together, might demonstrate no explicit relationship to each other. Working with Cage, who occasionally took over Bird's composition classes, "was a revelation," Cunningham remembered. "Suddenly there was something very precise and very strict to work with. He simply made us make things—you had to think about it, not just have some feeling about what you were going to do next, but *think* about it, and that was an extraordinary experience."[29]

Though Cage impressed Cunningham, it would be several years before the two would begin to collaborate in earnest. After Graham saw Cunningham perform during the 1939 Bennington summer session, she offered him a place in her company. He moved to

New York. For the next six years he earned acclaim in Graham's works, particularly as the fire-and-brimstone Preacher in *Appalachian Spring* and as March in the Emily Dickinson tribute *Letter to the World*, which showed off his preternatural jump. Noticing his singular talent, Graham encouraged him to take classes at the School of American Ballet, an uncommon step for a modern dancer of the time (and especially for a Graham dancer, since Graham was notoriously protective of the "purity" of her dancers' technique).

By 1942 Cunningham was finding neither Graham nor ballet fulfilling. He began giving himself classes, combining Graham's weightiness and solidity with ballet's speed and precision, developing the seeds of what would become Cunningham technique.

He also started working with John Cage, who had recently arrived in New York. The pair gave their first concert together at the Humphrey-Weidman Studio on 16th Street in 1944. "I date

Merce Cunningham Dance Company (with Cunningham, right), *Persepolis Event*, 1972. *Photographer unknown, courtesy the Merce Cunningham Trust* my beginning from this concert," Cunningham wrote.[30] He performed six solos, all with unconventional music by Cage. Though Cunningham's choreography still had, like the work of the early moderns, a psychological element, it was threaded only loosely to Cage's rhythmic pieces. "I have never seen a first recital that combined such taste, such technical finish, such originality of dance material," wrote critic Edwin Denby.[31] Cunningham, only twenty-five, had found his voice. He left the Graham company in October 1944. "He stayed," Graham said, "as long as he viably could."[32]

Cage's truly radical ideas about music and the relationship between music and dance spurred Cunningham onward. In the early 1950s, Cage began using chance procedures—frequently the flip of a coin—in his composing, and Cunningham considered their applications to choreography. His first work involving chance, *Sixteen Dances for Soloist and Company of Three* (1951), used a coin toss to determine which section would be performed first; the fourteenth dance "used charts of separate movements for material for each of the four dancers, and let chance operations decide the continuity."[33] *Dime a Dance* (1953) was a grab bag of solos, duets, and trios, totaling thirteen pieces in all. Seven were danced at each performance, with audience members picking cards from a deck to determine which made the cut.

Though some critics found them gimmicky, chance procedures made Cunningham performances invigoratingly unpredictable. More frustrating to audiences was the increasing dissociation between music, or even rhythm, and dance in Cunningham's work. "Cunningham tears down the signposts that allow the viewers of a dance to orient themselves in time," wrote critic Terry Teachout.[34] Cunningham, however, found the break liberating. "A formal structure based on *time*," he said, rather than music, "frees the music into space, making the connection between the dance and the music one of individual autonomy connected at structural points. The result is the dance is free to act as it chooses, as is the music. The music doesn't have to work itself to death to underline the dance, or the dance create havoc in trying to be as flashy as the music."[35]

For all their seeming arbitrariness, Cunningham's works were highly structured. A demanding choreographer, he often made nearly impossible requests of his skilled dancers. No matter how fiendish the steps, however, a sense of unrufflable cool prevailed during Cunningham group performances. Critic Deborah Jowitt called his style "superbly civilized and elegant."[36] Both he and Cage were deeply influenced by Zen Buddhism—by its

discipline and serenity, its idea that an awakened soul could see everything as art.[37]

In 1954 artist Robert Rauschenberg began collaborating with Cunningham. He became Cunningham's designer and production manager, roles he would hold for the next decade. From that point on, the Cunningham company worked regularly with prominent artists, who supplied imaginative and frequently elaborate decor, costumes, and lighting. Andy Warhol's giant silver Mylar pillows floated through *Rain Forest* (1968); for *Walkaround Time*, the same year, Jasper Johns created an oversized version of Marcel Duchamp's avant-garde multimedia sculpture *The Large Glass*.

Cunningham continually pushed forward. In the 1960s he began staging "Events," performances in unconventional spaces featuring excerpts from various dances, sometimes performed simultaneously in different areas. The performances created new perspectives on his choreography. He started experimenting with filmmaker Charles Atlas in the 1970s, and the two created not only video documents of Cunningham's works, but inventive re-imaginings of them for film, adopting increasingly sophisticated technology as it became available. In the 1990s, faced with the limitations of his own aging body, Cunningham began using a computer program, LifeForms, to generate movement. Toward the end of his life, he made his company classes available online, so that students everywhere could see and begin to understand his intricate, exacting technique.

In April 2009 Cunningham staged his final work, *Nearly Ninety*, a collaboration with alternative band Sonic Youth, former Led Zeppelin bassist John Paul Jones, and mixed-media sound composer Takehisa Kosugi. He died in July of that year. While the Cunningham Trust continues to oversee performances of his works by various companies, Cunningham's own group disbanded, per his request, a year and a half later. Critic Joan Acocella wrote of *Nearly Ninety*:

> For his anti-classicism and his anti-lyricism, together with his more ingratiating qualities, notably the cleanness and intensity of his dances, he will always be recognized as the foremost representative of high modernism—the Joyce-Pound-Beckett kind—in the history of modern dance, and as a creator of beauty and meaning on their level.[38]

Continued on page 159

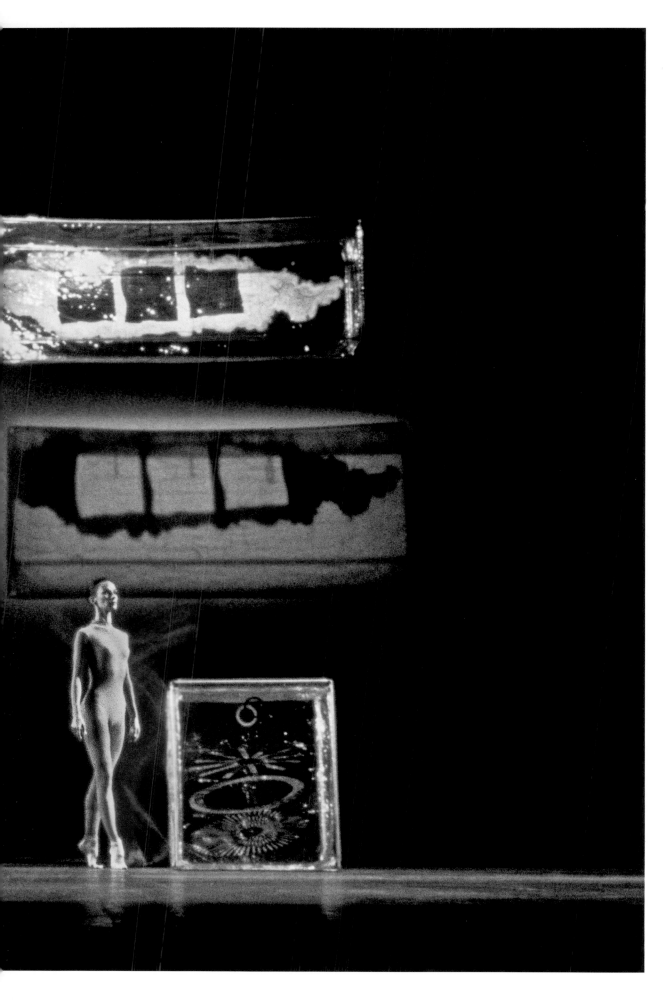

Carolyn Brown in Merce Cunningham's *Walkaround Time*, 1968. Décor by Jasper Johns after Marcel Duchamp's *The Large Glass. James Klosty*

ABOVE: Rambert Dance Company performs Taylor's *Roses*, 2001.
© Jane Hobson, Alamy

OPPOSITE: Paul Taylor Dance Company in *Profiles*, c. 1979. *Photofest*

Continued from page 155

PAUL TAYLOR

After a lonely, turbulent childhood in Wilkinsburg, Pennsylvania, Paul Taylor arrived at Syracuse University thanks to a swimming scholarship. He planned to study painting. Instead, he discovered dance books in the school library and began exploring a new creative pursuit. Tall and athletic, with canny instincts and a commanding sense of self, Taylor found he was a natural dancer.

He earned a scholarship to the American Dance Festival summer session at Connecticut College in 1952, where he encountered Graham, Humphrey, Limón, and Horst. Taylor then moved from Syracuse to New York City to study at Juilliard. Impatient after a year there, he left to work on Broadway and in television commercials, while training further with Graham and Antony Tudor. In 1953 he spent the summer working with Cunningham and Cage at Black Mountain College in North Carolina, and he continued to perform with the Cunningham

company through the following year. Taylor became, and remained, a great admirer of Cunningham's, but chance procedures didn't interest him. He started experimenting with his own choreography.

Taylor joined Graham's company in 1955 and stayed until 1962, creating roles—usually brawny, conquering hero types—in many works, including *Clytemnestra* (1958), *Acrobats of God* (1960), and *Phaedra* (1962). In the 1959 *Episodes*, a collaboration between Graham's company and the New York City Ballet, Taylor performed an extraordinary solo choreographed by Balanchine. During rehearsals Mr. B famously asked him to move "like fly in glass of milk."[39] Afterward, Balanchine asked if Taylor would like to join New York City Ballet, but Taylor, uncertain about the ballet world and eager to pursue his own ideas about dance, declined.

Taylor's first breakthrough as a choreographer came in 1956 with *Four Epitaphs*. Set to early recordings of New Orleans jazz pieces—specifically, funeral music—the piece revealed Taylor's bizarre, eerie sense of humor. Costumed in full-body black unitards and mirrored, scuba-like hoods designed by Rauschenberg, the dancers shuffled, slumped, and spasmed, unsuccessfully attempting to connect with each other in a way both grotesque and distinctly human. It was the beginning of a pattern that would develop further in Taylor's later works: the complex commingling of light and dark, comedic and tragic.

In 1957 Taylor presented *Seven New Dances* at the 92nd Street Y. The program established his reputation as a radical. He was curious about pedestrian movement. What was and what wasn't dance? Ultimately he found few boundaries between the two. In one solo, *Epic*, Taylor, dressed in a business suit, moved only very subtly over the course of 20 minutes, as a telephone operator announced repeatedly, "At the tone, the time will be . . ." The evening's most controversial piece, *Duet*, featured Taylor and Toby Armour holding perfectly still for the entirely of Cage's silent score *4'33"*.[40] After the performance, Graham shook her finger at Taylor and called him a "naughty boy." Louis Horst's review in *Dance Observer* was four inches of blank space, signed "L. H."

The program was a purposeful rejection of both Graham and ballet—a kind of slate-cleaning—and it earned Taylor a degree of fame (or infamy). Eventually, however, he tired of such extremism. "The more he danced and choreographed, the more a powerful and complexly fluid dance momentum engaged him," said critic Edwin Denby. "His gift defined itself as one not for anti-dance but for pro-dance."[41]

Aureole (1962), set to Handel, marked Taylor's turning point. It was his first time using baroque music. The resulting work, costumed in simple, pure white, was balanced, expansive, jubilant. This was a dance audiences felt they understood, and the response was overwhelming. "What Taylor offered in *Aureole* was . . . dance which lived in its music as a bird in the air," wrote critic Clement Crisp. "Here was dance which proposed an image of its dancers, of humanity, as courteous, loving, generous-spirited. Civilised. Oh, so civilised!"[42]

That "civilized" aspect troubled Taylor. Some critics went so far as to call *Aureole* a ballet, despite the fact that Taylor had purposely avoided balletic vocabulary. After *Aureole*, many ballet dancers, including Rudolf Nureyev, announced their eagerness to tackle Taylor. Even later, when he began to choreograph pieces expressly for ballet companies, Taylor remained ambivalent about ballet. After setting *Aureole* on the Royal Danish Ballet, he composed an imaginary letter:

Classic Ballet,

Keep away, keep building your creaky fairy castles, keep cloning clones and meaningless manners, hang on to your beanstalk ballerinas and their midget male shadows, run yourself out of business with your tons of froufrou and costly clattery toe shoes that ruin all chances for illusions of lightness, keep on crowding the minds of blind balletomanes who prefer dainty poses to the eloquent strength of momentum, who have forgotten or never known the meanings of gesture, who would nod their noses to barefoot embargos ("so grab me" spelt backwards). Continue to repolish your stiff technique and to ignore a public that hungers for something other than a bag of tricks and the empty-headedness of surface patterns.

Just keep it up, keep imitating yourself, and, *please*, go grow your own dance makers. Come on, don't keep trying to filter modern ones through your so-safe establishment. We're to be seen undiluted, undistorted, not absorbed by your hollow world like blood into a sponge.

Yours truly,
A Different Leaf on Our Family Tree[43]

For his own company, Taylor began building a staggeringly diverse repertoire. In addition to singing, sunny works like *Aureole*, there were inky-dark pieces like *Big Bertha*, in which an all-American family is torn to pieces by an evil carnival animatron who turns their wholesome family outing into a maelstrom of violence and incest. Changeable as his imagination could be, over time Taylor developed a kind of equilibrium in his dances, "an inscrutable balance of wit, solemnity, tenderness, and cruelty . . . wit in his blackest works as well as in his lightest, tenderness in his wickedest dances, dark currents in his blithest."[44]

Taylor retired from dancing in 1974. The change seemed to release something in him. The following year, he choreographed his masterwork, *Esplanade*, to a series of Bach violin pieces (two of which Balanchine had used in *Concerto Barocco*). It was in part a return to his earlier pedestrian experiments—much of the choreography involved simple walking and running—and yet there was a beautiful poignancy to its storytelling. The first unsettling adagio, in which the dancers appeared unable

Aileen Roehl, Michelle Fleet,
Robert Kleinendorst, Jamie Rae
Walker, and other dancers with
Paul Taylor Dance Company in
Taylor's *Esplanade. Paul B. Goode*

to touch each other, was offset by a series of tender, innocent pas de deux in the fourth section. The finale was an exuberant daredevil romp in which the dancers slid on the floor and took flying leaps into each others' arms.

Taylor, the author of more than one hundred dances, credits his eternal restlessness to the fact that he has "always had ten thousand ideas about everything . . . [and] always [been] very confused."[45] In a sense he is one of the last connections to the old moderns; in another sense, thanks to that restlessness, he is entirely his own being. He continues to choreograph for the Paul Taylor Dance Company

(renamed Paul Taylor's American Modern Dance in 2014) as well as other companies, and many consider him the greatest living choreographer.

Though the works of Cunningham and Taylor continue to speak to audiences today, by the 1960s, both had lost their "revolutionary" status. They looked, as the generation following them claimed, like the new establishment, celebrated by the mainstream. That next generation would take the ideas first investigated by Cunningham and Taylor to previously unimaginable extremes.

Chapter Seven
Postmodern Dance and Beyond

The Garden of Earthly Delights, choreographed by Martha Clarke, with Whitney Hunter on the floor and Sophie Bortolussi in the air. *Richard Finkelstein, courtesy Martha Clarke*

"NO to spectacle no to virtuosity no to transformations and magic and make-believe no to the glamour and transcendency of the star image no to the heroic no to the anti-heroic no to trash imagery no to involvement of performer or spectator no to style no to camp no to seduction of spectator by the wiles of the performer no to eccentricity no to moving or being moved." —*Yvonne Rainer*[1]

"All those nos would become my yeses." —*Twyla Tharp*[2]

The Concert of Dance #1, held on July 6, 1962, at the Judson Memorial Church in downtown New York, inaugurated a new era for modern dance. A collection of pieces asked, "What is dance, and when does it become *not* dance?" The three-hour performance was the culmination of two years of work in a composition course led by young musician Robert Dunn. Held at Merce Cunningham's studio, and attended mostly by Cunningham-sympathetic dancers—but also by the likes of Robert Rauschenberg and *Village Voice* writer Jill Johnston—Dunn's course, with assignments that rejected the rigid structure of traditional composition courses, unleashed rampant, violent creativity. Though the class had a structure of its own, Dunn's ultimate goal was "clearing . . . a space of nothing in which things could appear and grow in their own nature."[3] A sense of restless permissiveness, of why-don't-we and what-about-this, pervaded.

In the Concert of Dance #1, Dunn's students collaged more than twenty un-virtuosic, un-dancerly pieces, with the basic building blocks being walking, running, and everyday gestures. One solo was done in a hammock; another had a dancer listing a series of addresses aloud; yet another featured an untrained performer standing on his head while pulling out his hair.[4] It was a reflection of the social and political upheaval beginning to shake the world outside the studio walls, and a dismissal of the rules that had previously shaped the dance world.

The concert marked the beginning of postmodern dance. The members of what would become known as the Judson Dance Theater had different aesthetics, but they shared the same radical ideas about choreography. The only thing that made a dance a dance, they argued, was that it was framed as one.[5] Frequently their performances were frustrating, and sometimes they were boring, but they were always challenging, always forcing audiences to reconsider the value of tradition. Johnston, one of movement's greatest advocates—and, as alumna of Dunn's class, an insider—described a series of 1963 Judson concerts as "a big, pliable, inchoate matrix of independent, original activity which knows itself

Meat Joy, a Judson "Happening" by artist Carolee Schneeman, which incorporated raw fish, sausages, wet paint, and scrap paper, 1964.
Tony Ray-Jones, SSPL, Getty images

even while looking for itself. . . . a free-wheeling phalanx which is more than enough to fill that uncomfortable vacuum left by the decline, around 1945, of the first modern dance."[6]

Yet after several years, the Judson movement began to lose steam. Most Judson dances were born of curiosity, not in the interest of building a repertoire; they were doors that needed to be opened only once. Eventually younger choreographers felt all the rules that needed to be broken had been broken. Analytic post-modern dances, according to dance historian Sally Banes, "threatened to become an exercise in empty formalism."[7] "It's like bubble gum," said choreographer Twyla Tharp in 1971. "You can keep on chewing for ten hours but after about a minute and a half you've got all the good out of it."[8] (It didn't help that the movement was never terribly appealing to audience members. "Paradox: making art more like life doesn't necessarily make it more accessible or more popular," wrote critic Deborah Jowitt. "In fact, the reverse is likely to be true.")[9]

But the freedoms the Judsonites had earned for dance and dancers remained. Gone were the old pretenses, the emphasis on showmanship, the assumption that only one body type was fit for dancing. Though some choreographers eventually returned to technical polish and theatrical spectacle, many of them retained the laidback, slightly wrinkled, honest vulnerability of the Judson performers.

As the permissive 1960s and 1970s passed into the conservative, intractable 1980s and 1990s, dance artists looked for order, exploring narrative and character. Many reconnected with music. In an increasingly pluralistic world, modern dance also absorbed influences from popular culture and made greater use of multimedia. Style resumed its primacy over substance, with choreographers developing distinctive voices but not necessarily distinctive philosophical approaches to dance. After a period of purposeful plainness, beauty was in again.

Here is a closer look at some of the most influential artists in, around, and inspired by the Judson movement.

SIMONE FORTI

Though choreographer Simone Forti worked outside the official Judson tribe, her pieces explored similarly radical approaches. In 1956, after studying psychology and sociology at Reed College in Portland, Oregon, she moved to California, where she first discovered dance. Unencumbered by any previous technical training, Forti was able to fully embrace Ann (later Anna) Halprin's improvisation classes in San Francisco.

Halprin, who had moved away from the modern-dance mainstream a few years earlier, forswore traditional dance instruction—she disliked the unnatural stylistic habits it instilled in dancers. Instead, she led her students through tumbling and hiking exercises to build their strength and stamina. In her improvisation sessions, she helped dancers enter a near-trance state in which they could access unexplored areas of their brain, unlocking new dance impulses.

After four years, Forti felt she had absorbed all she could from Halprin and moved to New York City. She studied with Martha Graham and Merce Cunningham, but found their strict techniques didn't suit her. ("I *would not* hold my stomach in," she remembered.)[10] After spending some time teaching at a nursery school, where she was struck by the children's simple, natural movements, she began taking Dunn's composition course at the Cunningham studio.

Forti found Dunn's method similar, in many ways, to Halprin's, but the class also introduced her to conceptual dance and spurred her to choreograph. In December 1960 she premiered *See-Saw* and *Rollers*, both inspired by children's playground games—a subject that would continue to fascinate Forti for several years. The seminal *Huddle* (1961) represented another facet of her early work: the idea that a dance is an object, to be viewed the way a sculpture might be seen in a gallery.[11] In the piece, six or seven dancers formed a circle, placing their arms around each others' waists to create a sturdy

Simone Forti, 2010. *Chris Felver, Getty Images*

structure; one at a time, they crawled up and over the huddle before rejoining it, as spectators walked around them, observing the work from all sides.

Several of Forti's later dances, continuing in a different vein her preoccupation with unaffected movement, channeled the motions of various animals and plants. Throughout her career, she has valued the real and the everyday, the presentation of the familiar in an unfamiliar context.

YVONNE RAINER

Yvonne Rainer's prolific creativity and aggressive polemic made her one of the most influential Judson choreographers. Initially she wanted to be an actor, and she moved from San Francisco to New York to pursue that dream in 1956. Dissatisfied, she began taking dance classes, studying Graham technique and ballet, though she found herself limited by her lack of flexibility. In 1960 Rainer traveled back to San Francisco to attend Halprin's summer workshop, where she met several other soon-to-be

Judsonites. Upon her return to New York, she started taking classes at the Cunningham studio, including Dunn's composition class; ultimately Rainer helped organize Judson Dance Theater.

Her choreography frequently combined basic walking and running with idiosyncratic gestures, suggesting tiny snapshots of daily life reshuffled and reassembled. "These things can be as diverse as the mannerisms of a friend, the facial expression of a woman hallucinating on the subway, the pleasure of an aging ballerina as she demonstrates a classical movement, a pose from an Etruscan mural, a hunchbacked man with cancer," Rainer said.[12] Her goal of demystifying dance led to her famous "No Manifesto," quoted at the opening of this chapter— a repudiation of the theatrical traditions she found phony and limiting.

What remained, after all of Rainer's "nos," was *Trio A*, first performed in 1966 (as *The Mind Is a Muscle, Part I*). A landmark work, it was to become a Rainer emblem. Instead of musicality, development,

LEFT: Yvonne Rainer. *Courtesy Performing Artservices, Inc.*

OPPOSITE: Steve Paxton and Barbara Dilley, 1973. *Courtesy Performing Artservices, Inc.*

Judson mentality, and established a direction some postmodern dancers would follow for the next fifteen years. It ultimately appeared in seven other Rainer works, and many artists paid tribute to it in their own choreography.

In the early 1970s Rainer's interests shifted from dance to films, and in 1974 she stopped choreographing. But she returned to choreography in 2000, at the invitation of Mikhail Baryshnikov, and has been making dances ever since. Rainer has been remarkably generous with her repertoire, encouraging students to pass along works like *Trio A*.

STEVE PAXTON

Steve Paxton was a high-school gymnast when a friend's dance teacher, noticing Paxton's natural gifts, offered him a scholarship. In summer 1958 he attended the American Dance Festival at Connecticut College, where he encountered Graham, Doris Humphrey, José Limón, and Cunningham, and was immediately taken with the latter. Paxton came to New York to train with Cunningham; he simultaneously began working with other like-minded performers and studying composition in Dunn's class. He joined the Cunningham company in 1961 and stayed through 1964, even as he was working with the Judson Dance Theater.

Paxton's experiences in the Cunningham group shaped his perspective on choreography. Disliking the hierarchical structure of the company, which he saw as autocratic, he embraced a populist stance. Walking became the foundation of his work, because everyone could do it—just as everyone could eat, drink, smile, and get dressed and undressed, the material Paxton would mine for nearly two decades. In *Flat* (1964), he removed almost all of his clothing and hung it on hooks he'd taped to his body; in *Satisfyin' Lover* (1967), a large group of dancers and non-dancers walked one by one across the space, stopping in the center to stand or sit, according to a written score. The people, he argued, were the dance. It was a point he made especially effectively in *Word Words* (1963), a response to a comment that all the Judson dancers looked alike. Paxton and Rainer, both nude, performed identical phrases side by side, so that the emphasis was not on the choreography but on the differences in their physical forms.

In 1972 Paxton and several other dancers began experimenting with duets, playing with the give and take of shared body weight and relying on mutual trust. The result became known as contact improvisation, and seemed to propose not only an alternative technique but an alternative lifestyle, one governed

character, and virtuosity—all of the nos—in *Trio A* Rainer focused on simplicity, neutrality, and specific tasks.[13] The dance, a four-and-a-half minute phrase initially performed as a set of three solos danced simultaneously by Rainer, Steve Paxton, and David Gordon, looked elementary but was actually quite complex in its coordination. Its intricate series of movements was executed without any differentiation in dynamics between steps, an instruction that precluded dancerly interpretation. The dancers "stitch together the modules that make up the sequence without the . . . phrasing that would shape the material into peaks and transitions," said critic Deborah Jowitt, "substituting an uninsistent delivery that gives every moment equal importance and irons out even the dynamic inflections that inform everyday movement."[14]

An essay in steady motion freed of style and expression, *Trio A* embodied one strain of the

by the freedom of improvisation and the cooperation of support.[15] Paxton continued to explore improvisation for many years, although in recent decades he has returned to formal choreography.

DAVID GORDON

David Gordon was the Judson group's master of irony—and something of a renegade. Born and raised in New York City, he attended Brooklyn College and went on to study with Cunningham and several other outside-the-mainstream modern dancers. His inquisitive mind quickly found inconsistencies in the inflexible structure of Louis Horst's composition class at the Connecticut College summer session. (Looking for trouble, he named one of his works for Horst's course *The Spastic Cheerleader*.)

Discovering, however, that he was more interested in making dance than in refining his technique, Gordon enrolled in Dunn's class in New York. In keeping with his belief that the artist is, by nature, a rebel, he attended the course only sporadically, and took Dunn's assignments less seriously than his classmates did. But he was inspired by the other minds he encountered in the class.

Gordon had an ongoing fascination with show business. In *Random Breakfast* (1963), he included references that ranged from Judy Garland to Milton Berle's imitation of Carmen Miranda, partly in genuine tribute to the stars he admired, and partly to unpack the source of the world's fascination with celebrity. The casual, rough-around-the-edges Judson setting, and the mundane movements and gestures Gordon used to thin out his showbiz stew, threw the strangeness of the culture of glamour into high relief. *Random Breakfast* and several of his other dances, wrote Banes, "are not entertainments, but artworks that analyze and criticize entertainment."[16]

In the late 1970s Gordon formed his own group, Pick-Up Company, and began developing "a technique of understatement that concealed . . . careful design."[17] While making *Not Necessarily Recognizable Objectives* (1977), he incorporated occurrences from rehearsals—falls, mistakes, laughter—into the formal choreography; during performances, his skilled dancers made it difficult for the audience to determine what was planned and what was truly accidental. A mid-performance argument that sounded genuine, for example, turned out to be highly choreographed (as viewers discovered later, when it was repeated word for word). Yet again he proved to be "a supreme ironist, subverting impressions as fast as he project[ed] them"—the throughline of his work.[18]

LUCINDA CHILDS

Lucinda Childs, a choreographer of sharp, structural intelligence, first began studying dance seriously with Hanya Holm at age fifteen. At Sarah Lawrence College, she majored in dance and studied with Cunningham, a visiting teacher. She found that he "elucidated a kind of particularity and clarity in dance," and came to New York to take classes with him during school breaks.[19] After graduation she moved to Manhattan to continue her studies, and there, at the Cunningham studios, she met Rainer. Rainer invited Childs to join the Judson Dance Theater, for which Childs went on to make thirteen pieces, while continuing to train in ballet and Cunningham technique. "I never gave up the classical training, but I also committed myself totally to the Judson experience," she said. "In the morning you'd go to ballet class and in the afternoon you'd carry mattresses and that kind of thing."[20]

One of Childs's most extraordinary works related strictly to the "carrying mattresses" side of the equation. *Street Dance* came out of Dunn's 1964 composition class. After beginning in Dunn's studio, Childs and another dancer disappeared in a freight elevator, only to reappear outside the studio windows, pointing out various objects on the city street as the audience, still upstairs in the studio, listened to taped instructions. Rather than create an environment, Childs simply helped the audience discover an existing one.

In 1966 she abandoned the flagging Judson collective. Frustrated by the lack of resources, she left dance to become a schoolteacher. Five years later, however, equipped with government funding, she started her own company, Lucinda Childs Dance.

Childs was a lead performer in the 1976 Robert Wilson/Philip Glass opera *Einstein on the Beach*. Her Act I solo, in which she walked back and forth along a series of diagonals while executing an irregular series of drum-major-esque arm gestures, haunted audiences, in no small part because of Childs' mesmerizing onstage presence. Over time her own dances began to incorporate movement sequences that required great precision and composure, though they still maintained a sense of "haiku-like" spareness.[21] Childs' 1979 masterwork *DANCE* was—much like its Philip Glass score—propulsive, rhythmic, and hypnotically repetitive. Its seemingly never-ending series of low, fleet traveling jumps was echoed by a video projection of the same dancers performing the same steps, a shadowy mirror of the action onstage. (In later performances with different dancers, the same video would be used, allowing the ghosts of the original cast to live on.)

Lucinda Childs Dance Company performs *Concerto*, 1994. © *Julie Lemberger, 2014*

TRISHA BROWN

Of all the Judsonites, Trisha Brown's career has had the greatest longevity and range. After a childhood in Washington State spent climbing trees and taking informal dance lessons, she studied modern dance at Mills College and the Connecticut College summer sessions, working with Horst, Limón, and Cunningham at the latter. She was hired to organize a dance program at Reed College in 1958, but soon tired of traditional teaching methods and began developing her own style.

In summer 1960 she attended Halprin's summer workshop, alongside Rainer and Forti. She remained in touch with them in New York, where, in Dunn's class, she found permission to fully exercise her restless mind. Brown began creating works that overlaid improvisation with intriguing, frequently rule-based structures. In *Rulegame 5* (1964), for example, five dancers walked along seven parallel tapes, changing levels (from standing upright to crawling on their stomachs) at the end of each tape. The simple setup forced the performers to devise ways to work around each other as they crossed paths, generating complex, engrossing patterns.

Brown began experimenting with "equipment pieces"—involving everything from ropes to pulleys to oversized pegboards—in 1968. She used various apparatuses to reorient both dancers' and viewers' relationships to natural forces, especially gravity. Audiences who watched the 1971 *Walking on the Wall*, in which a series of harnesses allowed dancers to walk on the walls of the Whitney Museum, might have felt as if they were the ones standing on a building, watching pedestrians below them on the sidewalk. The equipment pieces were a "response to the limitation of sitting and looking into a box," Brown said.[22] "I always feel sorry for the parts of the stage that aren't being used. I have in the past felt sorry for the ceilings and walls. It's perfectly good space, why doesn't anyone use it?"[23]

Eventually she tired of the method (or at least of lugging around ropes and harnesses) and started making dances based on the sequential accumulation of gestures. *Primary Accumulation* (1972) featured a performer lying on the floor and executing a series of thirty basic movements: turning the head, lifting the knee, brushing the hair behind the ear.

Continued on page 173

Trisha Brown in *If you couldn't see me*, with costume by Robert Rauschenberg, 1994. © *Julie Lemberger, 2014*

THE MYSTICS

The 1970s saw the development of another strand in postmodern dance: the idea of dance as a mode of spiritual expression. Often works in this vein fostered a sense of community among their participants, a connection with a higher spiritual power through group dance.

Deborah Hay was one of the original Judsonites—she presented a piece during the Concert of Dance #1. But during the late 1960s and early 1970s her work moved away from the theatrical and toward the metaphysical, especially after Hay discovered tai chi, the ancient Chinese form of kinetic meditation. "I transcended my body and no longer felt responsible for my own movement," she said of practicing the discipline. "I began to let go of all I had learned, and to trust a new thing called flow, or myself, or the universe."[24]

Hay hoped to combine the reflectiveness of tai chi with familiar, everyday movements, allowing large groups of people to experience the kind of joy she found in the Buddhist practice.[25] She created a series of "Circle Dances"—all meant to be done by a group standing in a circle—as described in her book, *Moving Through the Universe in Bare Feet*. Made to be experienced rather than watched, Circle Dances led participants through a series of exercises that gradually resulted in heightened awareness. A dance might begin with visualization activities to be completed with the eyes closed, progress to include some form of contact between individuals, and end by looking outside the group, calling attention to its relation to the surrounding space. Though the Circle Dances felt mystical, they had no religious overtones; Hay often set them to popular songs. They were cousins not of sacred rituals but of old folk dances.

Laura Dean, another proponent of the idea that dance was meant to be communal and reflective, performed with the Paul Taylor Dance Company for a year before beginning to choreograph in 1966. By the early 1970s she was creating meditative dances of very simple movements repeated many times, as often indicated by their names: *Stamping Dance* (1971), *Square Dance*, *Circle Dance*, and *Jumping Dance* (all 1972). The rhythmic insistence of Steve Reich's music inspired several of her works, a fascination that continued throughout her career. Sometimes Dean pared her dances down even further, composing her own minimalist scores and relying on precise, sustained spinning to create a sense of communion among the dancers.

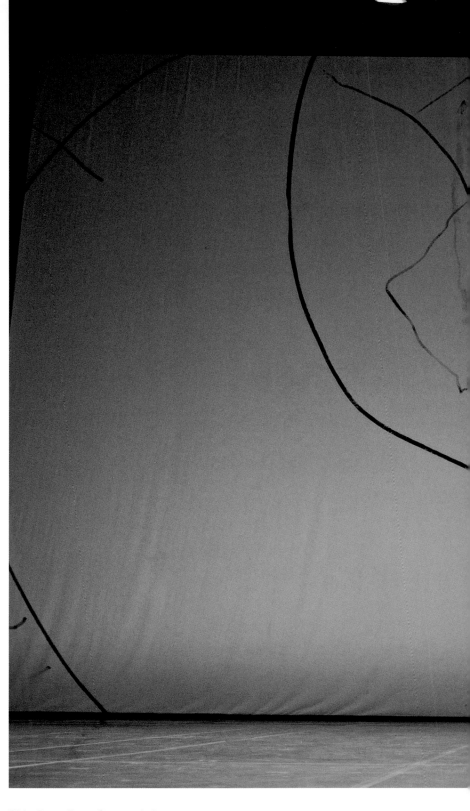

Trisha Brown Dance Company in *Le Yeux et L'âme*, 2011. © *Laurent Paillier, photosdedanse.com*

Continued from page 169

The actions were added one at a time—1, 1 2, 1 2 3, and so forth—to spellbinding effect. In the following year's *Group Primary Accumulation*, four dancers executed the sequence, never ceasing even as two "disruptive" performers carried them around, stacked them on top of each other, and propped them against walls.

In the late 1970s, reacting in part to the fact that critics often focused on her compositional process rather than her dances, Brown circled back to the loose, fluid style that had characterized her own earlier dancing. Her years working within formal, eminently logical structures added new polish and depth to its kinetic appeal. "She cultivates a soft, relaxed stance, offering a new look to rival the pristine verticality of Cunningham," wrote dance critic and former Brown dancer Wendy Perron.

> We see movements travel through the body like a wave. But we never see where in the body the movement is initiated. Trisha is a master at deflecting the eye. Before you realize it, you've missed it, and something

else grabs your attention. . . . The stream of motion can be exhilarating kinetically—and philosophically. It seems to speak of universal motion, of an inevitability that is not about fate but an embrace of the ongoingness of life.[26]

Beginning with the 1979 *Glacial Decoy*, Brown also returned to proscenium stages, costumes, and spectacle. She began a series of collaborations with major artists; for the 1983 *Set and Reset*, Laurie Anderson composed a driving score, and Robert Rauschenberg, whom Brown knew from her Judson days, created a set of transparent wing panels at the sides of the stage, which made it unclear when the dancers were and weren't "performing." In the 1990s, surprising many critics, she began choreographing to existing music, using pieces by Bach (*M.O.*, 1995) and Anton Webern (*Twelve Ton Rose*, 1996), and even Monteverdi's opera *Orfeo* (1998). But the thrust of her work remained compositional, architectural. After a series of small strokes, Brown presented her final two dances in 2013, and then

stepped down as director of her dance company. The group continues to perform works from all phases of Brown's career.

By 1964 many of the original members of the Judson group had fallen away. That autumn, a new group of students enrolled in Dunn's composition class, beginning a second wave of dance experiments that built upward and outward from the frame constructed by the movement's pioneers.

MEREDITH MONK

Meredith Monk's works transcend genre, combining dance, theater, and music to create dream-like universes. A droll 1969 program note encapsulated her romantic, stream-of-consciousness approach to art:

MEREDITH MONK was born in lima Peru/grew up in the West riding horses/ is Inca Jewish/lived in a red house A COMMERCIAL: SHE WILL PRESENT A NEW WORK: "TOUR: DEDICATED TO DINOSAURS" ON MARCH 4 IN THE ROTUNDA OF THE SMITHSONIAN

Meredith Monk in *The Games,* a futuristic musical theater piece in which individuals must compete in games in order to survive, 1984. *Photograph by Robert R. McElroy, Getty Images*

INSTITUTION IN WASHINGTON, D.C.
Started dancing lessons at the age of three
because she could not skip/did Hippy Love
Dance at Varney's Roaring 20's Topless
Club in California/has brown hair.[27]

Monk was indeed born in Peru, in 1942, though she grew up in Connecticut. A student of eurhythmics and ballet, she was also a musician from a very young age, and started composing at sixteen. Monk arrived in Manhattan after graduating from Sarah Lawrence College, just as the first stage of the Judson rebellion was coming to an end.

Rather than eschew spectacle, Monk chose to rethink it, exploring the expressive nature of theatricality. In one of her first major works, *16 Millimeter Earrings*, she wore a giant Japanese lantern over her head and projected a film of her face on top of it, creating an artificial distance between herself and the audience; later she showed footage of a burning doll, which was echoed at the conclusion of the work when flames were projected on Monk as she sang "Greensleeves." Her presentation of these tableaux might initially seem haphazard, but over the course of a dance a sort of poetic logic would emerge. "These pieces aren't fragments: each is polished, clear, complete in itself," wrote Deborah Jowitt. "The point is that each of these molecules acquires heightened significance or resonance when it's juxtaposed to other events in the work, set in particular contexts, repeated or varied."[28]

Frequently Monk tailored works to nontraditional sites. *Juice* (1969) was performed in three parts: the first inside the cavernous Guggenheim Museum, the second a few weeks later at Barnard College's Minor Latham Playhouse, and the third, later still, at Monk's downtown loft. The scale of the performance grew or shrank to fit its space. She also often composed her own music, creating chimerical, wordless melodies that made remarkable use of her expressive voice. *Education of the Girl Child* (1973), which she called an "opera," used both an unconventional space—the Cathedral of St. John the Divine in New York's Morningside Heights neighborhood—and Monk's music. In its second section, she moved along a spiral path that represented a lifetime, or, rather, a lifetime in reverse: Her body and voice transformed as she progressed from old age to childhood, "from remembering to knowing to wondering."[29]

KENNETH KING

Like Monk, Kenneth King made dances that returned to symbolism and expression but in a distinctly postmodern way. Trained as an actor, King presented his first dance works while still a philosophy major at Antioch College. He saw dance as a philosophical endeavor, a way to express the feeling that human experience is fragmented.[30] To that end he often appeared as one or more alter egos. His roster of personae included Sergei Alexandrovitch, a young Russian dancer; Zora A. Zash, an entrepreneur who discovered Sergei; Mater Harry a transvestite spy; Pontease Tyak, the custodian for the TransHimalayan Society for Interplanetary Research; flamboyant actress Tallulah Bankhead; and Patrick Duncan, Isadora Duncan's dead son. In *High Noon* (1974), a shattered portrait of Nietzsche, King became Nietzsche himself, then Nietzsche protagonist Zarathustra, then Dionysus; according to the program, the cast also included several of his alter egos. Sometimes the playacting felt like a teasing joke, but it was always in the service of a larger idea. King's works frequently involved wordplay and multimedia, especially video—he was a member of the underground film scene.

DOUGLAS DUNN

Douglas Dunn, a Cunningham dancer from 1969 to 1973, came to dance by an unusual route. While he was a student at Princeton, a friend took him to visit an ill professor of Chinese literature, thought to be on his deathbed. The professor, an arts enthusiast, immediately told Dunn he should study ballet. Dunn dismissed the suggestion and eventually forgot the conversation. The professor, however, later recovered and, undaunted, convinced Dunn to enroll at a local ballet studio.

Dunn was an elegant mover whose choreographic style was difficult to pin down. He made dances about dancing, and about choreographing— dances that analyzed themselves.[31] He presumed

Douglas Dunn and Dancers perform *Pulcinella*, 1984. Dancers, from left to right, are Jon C. Mensinger, Mitch Kirsch, William Douglas, Kate Nesbitt, and Susan Blankensop. © *Beatriz Schiller, 2014*

an intelligent spectator, creating works that didn't impose on audiences but rather opened a line of dialogue. In *101* (1974), he constructed a maze of rough-hewn wood boxes that filled his entire loft; then, over the course of two months, for several hours each day he opened the space to audiences, who might find him lying on top of the structure in a kind of trance. His vigil became a tribute to the hours of work that go into creating a piece—in this case, the maze itself.

Later in his career, Dunn's interests turned to artistic collaboration, and he created works with filmmakers Charles Atlas and Amy Greenfield, poets Anne Waldman and Reed Bye, and visual artists Mimi Gross and Carol Mullins.

GUS SOLOMONS JR

On the fringes of the Judson group was Gus Solomons jr. Solomons began studying dance seriously as a sophomore at the Massachusetts Institute of Technology, where he was an architecture major. After moving to New York in 1962, he shared a studio with Meredith Monk and Kenneth King; occasionally they created work together. Solomons performed with Graham, Pearl Lang, Donald McKayle, and Cunningham. The latter's work was an especially good showcase for Solomons's elegant physicality. He stayed with the Cunningham

company until a back injury forced him to leave in 1968.

That year he began choreographing in earnest. He experimented with chance- and rule-based systems, and many of his pieces seemed to reflect his background in architecture: Their clear demarcations of space and meticulous patterning evoked the sleekness of modern buildings.[32] Frequently he would invite the audience to participate, as in *Kinesia #5* (1968), a solo in which he asked viewers to shuffle their feet or clear their throats at specific points in the dance, rather than scattering those noises unselfconsciously throughout it. *Two Reeler* (1968) took the idea of audience participation to an even greater extreme. It was simply a series of taped instructions for movements, which those present could either do or not do. Eventually Solomons would also become a thoughtful, incisive dance critic, and in 1996 he founded Paradigm, a company for older dance artists.

TWYLA THARP

Twyla Tharp also began as a Judson fringer, but went on to have an exceptionally rich and diverse career. Born in Indiana and raised in California, where her parents owned a drive-in movie theater, Tharp had some dance training as a child, but became truly engrossed in dance and performing while studying

RIGHT: Twyla Tharp in *Fever*, 1993.
© *Julie Lemberger, 2014*

OPPOSITE: Gus Solomons jr in his work *Private Parts*, St. Mark's Church in New York, 1994. © *Julie Lemberger, 2014*

THE GRAND UNION

In 1969 Yvonne Rainer began work on *Continuous Project—Altered Daily*, a piece for six dancers composed of a collection of "chunks" and "insertables." These snippets of choreography could go anywhere, and their order was determined by the dancers. The dancers knew some of this material well; some they had just barely rehearsed; some they actually learned during the performance. The atmosphere was casual, with the dancers frequently stopping to discuss a certain passage of movement or to try a variation on a particular step. It was a perpetual work in progress, a manifestation of the choreographic process itself.

As Rainer and her group continued to perform *Continuous Project—Altered Daily*, Rainer began to feel ambivalent about her leadership role. Hoping to make the work more cooperative, she gave the dancers more and more agency. The experiment resulted in the Grand Union, a collective of choreographer-performers who gave brilliantly unpredictable improvisatory concerts from 1970 to 1976. Its rotating cast included Trisha Brown, Douglas Dunn, Becky Arnold, Steve Paxton, Barbara Dilley, Nancy Lewis, Yvonne Rainer, David Gordon, and Valda Setterfield. All took turns leading the group, trying to figure out its relationship to authority. By 1972, after two years of experimenting, they had "evolved a flexible, open, generous improvisatory format."[33]

Grand Union dancers Douglas Dunn, David Gordon, Steve Paxton, Trisha Brown, and Barbara Dilley. *Photographer unknown, courtesy Douglas Dunn and Dancers*

A Grand Union performance had no set goals. It was simply a period of physical and intellectual playtime for its gifted ensemble, though the results were often surprisingly coherent. Lines of choreographic logic would emerge, develop, and suddenly be discarded, only to pop up again later. Characters played out miniature, inscrutable dramas. Often the dancers poked fun at themselves and the stereotypes associated with their kind of work. Frequently they returned to familiar bits of old choreography. (Gordon has said that, when stumped for what to do next, he would start going through Rainer's *Trio A*.)[34]

While some criticized the dancers for falling too easily into predictable parts—Brown the deadpan comedian, at Barnard College in New York. After graduating she danced with the Taylor Company for two years, leaving in 1965 to pursue her own choreography.

Tharp was an iconoclast from the beginning. She and her admirers had little reverence for the older Judsonites. "We were younger than they and had issued no manifestos," she said, taking a jab at Rainer's "No Manifesto." "Most importantly, we had the gall to *dance*. That was definitely not chic.... At heart [the Judson dancers] were very puritanical because they refused to enjoy the challenge, the juice of moving."[37]

Instead, Tharp developed a style that fused technical accomplishment with postmodern freethinking. Her early pieces were often quite difficult—spare, opaque, stubborn workings-through of problems, which she later admitted were "aggressive and unpleasant [in a way that was] defensive."[38] As her work matured, however, it became both more bountiful and more accessible. The turning point was *Eight Jelly Rolls* (1971), set to the jazzy ragtime of Jelly Roll Morton. Breezy and whimsical, the dance maintained throughout a solid foundation in classical technique, which kept Tharp organized even as she riffed on dozens of other dance styles, especially popular crazes. Working with well-known music seemed to unlock something in her, to give her permission to play. Over time she choreographed to pieces by Scott Joplin, Fats Waller, Chuck Berry, Paul Simon, Randy Newman,

Grand Union members Barbara Dilley, Steve Paxton, Nancy Green, David Gordon, and Trisha Brown, 1973. *Courtesy Performing Artservices, Inc.*

Gordon the rabble-rouser, Paxton a "gentle Jesus"—Grand Union presentations were routinely rich and satisfying.[35] The dancers "are such colorful and memorable characters that we are drawn to their performances again and again, as though to a new installment of a soap opera," Wendy Perron wrote. "We follow their triumphs, disappointments, dares, and frustrations almost too keenly to be bearable. We feel the challenge of spontaneity, the chaotic assortment of possibilities as we do in our own lives. We know that there is no plan."[36]

and the Beach Boys, as well as Bach, Mozart, Haydn, and Brahms.

Within a few years, Tharp had honed her new style blade-sharp. While she never lost the intellectual rigor that characterized the best of her early choreography, Tharp's works were now also theatrical, appealing, virtuosic. As described by scholar Elinor Rogosin:

> [Tharp] first creates the calm center which is the core of the classical ballet idiom, and then, like a naughty child asking, "Is this really all dance can do?" knocks everything off center. . . . She brilliantly uses the shifts of weight that support a

dancer's movement and flow through the body in a walk, run, balance, leap, jump, and on to an infinity of possibilities. . . . [She has] a twentieth-century, American feeling of time, for things that are fast, shifting, and essentially rootless.[39]

Tharp was creating dances designed to charm and to impress. The style appealed to ballet companies; she eventually developed a productive, innovative relationship with the ballet world (see Chapter 8), as well as a presence on Broadway (see Chapter 9).

As the arc of Tharp's career demonstrates, virtuosity eventually returned to the dance world after

EIKO AND KOMA

The Japanese husband and wife duo Eiko and Koma brought an Eastern sensibility to American modern dance. Growing up amidst the devastation of postwar Japan, they watched their ancient culture struggle to adapt to the Western materialism forced upon it.[43] Both joined choreographer Tatsumi Hijikata's Butoh company, a radical group that rejected all Western influences and created dances that frequently involved grotesque imagery. The pair also studied with a Mary Wigman disciple in Germany before coming to the United States in 1976.

Eiko and Koma works, as they developed in America over the next decades, became meditations on the elemental. Frequently nude or dressed in rags, the duo performed in almost incomprehensible slow motion; from the near-stillness emerged shapes evoking primitive creatures, inanimate beings, anthropomorphic abstractions. The stark, pitiless nature of their physicality was sometimes ugly or depressing, but it also invited empathy. Their rich, theatrical stage pictures continue to be deeply engrossing.

OPPOSITE: *Men's Stories,* choreographed by Lar Lubovitch in 2000 and performed by the Lar Lubovitch Dance Company. *Steven Schreiber, courtesy Lar Lubovitch Dance Company*

its Judson-era purge. The cloak of casualness, the most persistent remnant of the 1960s revolution, only made it seem more spectacular. "Compared to the glossy athletes of modern ballet, [this group of modern dancers] may appear refreshingly homespun, but there's no mistaking the value many of them place on strength, speed, endurance, expertise," said Deborah Jowitt. There was also a renewed interest in narrative and emotion as contexts to anchor dance. "The old narrative structures won't do," Jowitt wrote, "but neither, perhaps, will the coolness and casualness dancers once so carefully cultivated."[40]

The new attitude in modern dance was that anything was possible. A full spectrum of dance doctrines had been tested throughout the 1960s and 1970s. Now the choreographer's stylistic, rather than philosophical, voice returned to the fore.

LAR LUBOVITCH

A graduate of Juilliard, Lar Lubovitch worked with ballet, modern, and jazz companies before forming his own group in 1968. Frequently using the music of Bach and Handel, he created dances with rounded edges—soft, supple, and, like his own performing manner, generously extroverted. In 1975 he began using music by Philip Glass and Steve Reich, and his style contracted to reflect their simple repetitions. By the 1980s, however, he had returned to his roots in symphonic music, and to the smooth plasticity it inspired. His *Concerto Six Twenty-Two* (1986) was one of the first modern works to include a pas de deux for two men. The gently romantic

duet, created at the height of the AIDS epidemic, hit a nerve with audiences.

In addition to leading his own company of talented dancers, Lubovitch has choreographed for several ballet companies, and he did the staging for Stephen Sondheim's musical *Into the Woods* on Broadway in 1987. "Lubovitch has created dances so warm and sensuous and pretty," wrote critic Jennifer Dunning, "he seems to have created a new category—dance to bask in."[41]

PILOBOLUS, MOMIX, AND MARTHA CLARKE

In 1971 three Dartmouth College students with little dance experience made an unusual work, *Pilobolus,* for their dance composition class. Jonathan Wolken, Robb (later Moses) Pendleton, and Steve Johnson were intelligent, athletic, witty guys, and their creation—named for a barnyard fungus—was a tribute to the power of the group. Almost constantly linked, they counterbalanced and cantilevered each other into fantastical gymnastic feats. Alwin Nikolais disciple Murray Louis discovered the trio at a college dance festival. As Deborah Jowitt noted, the Dartmouth group's "lyrical, slow-motion Rorschachs and . . . play of opposing forces . . . have a lot in common with some of Nikolais's own illusion-games with limbs and heads and torsos."[42] Louis sponsored the New York debut of Pilobolus Dance Theatre in December 1971.

The group lost Johnson to medical school just before its New York performance, and Lee Harris and Robby Barnett, students from the same Dartmouth composition class, joined. Their playful, intensely physical works quickly attracted a following. Critic Anna Kisselgoff wrote:

> It isn't footwork or what its members call "dancey dance" that makes Pilobolus what it is. Rather, it is the kinetic and visual impact of the shapes into which the dancers mold themselves. It is, for instance, the sight of one dancer carrying two above him, of one human form cantilevered out from another, of bodies hurtling through space and caught casually, of centipede-like conglomerates of arms and legs, of sculptural chains of bodies and of everchanging forms flowing out from each other with energy and humor.[43]

In 1973 Martha Clarke and Alison Chase entered the Pilobolus circle. The dynamic of the company shifted away from the overt athleticism and occasionally juvenile humor of its early days, and toward works of strange, poignant narrative symbolism. The surreal *Untitled* (1975) featured two demure ladies (Chase and Clarke) in period gowns who suddenly sprouted long, hairy legs—the legs of the men hidden beneath their skirts. Later the women grew visibly pregnant and gave "birth" to these men, their sons or, possibly, their fantasy lovers.

That spirit of innovation—sometimes purely mischievous, sometimes getting at a deeper truth—continues to characterize Pilobolus, which has become, unusually for a dance company, a popular success. The Pilobolus aesthetic, like Nikolais', is television-friendly, and the company has appeared on numerous broadcasts and in several commercials. Their ingenious shadow play at the Oscars in 2007 earned them mainstream celebrity.

In 1980 Pendleton and Chase pulled away from Pilobolus to form their own group, MOMIX, which has a similar aesthetic. Martha Clarke also broke away from Pilobolus. An admirer of Anna Sokolow and Antony Tudor—she had worked with both—Clarke hoped to synthesize the physical, visual world with the emotional unseen. Her

Pilobolus in a 2013 performance of *Ocellus,* initially created in 1972. *Grant Halverson*

ABOVE: Pilobolus in *Untitled*.

RIGHT: MOMIX Associate Director
Cynthia Quinn in *White Widow*,
1994. *John Kane, Silver Sun Studio,
Courtesy MOMIX*

breakout work was *The Garden of Earthly Delights* (1984), based on Hieronymus Bosch's triptych painting. With ten dancers, a few simple props, inventive lighting, period instruments, and flying rigging, Clarke "conjured a vision of the medieval realm of the blessed and the damned in events that were by turns droll, sensual, coarse, and nightmarish."[44] In a sense her works were cousins of those of Meredith Monk, fractured collages at once enigmatic and deeply moving.

BILL T. JONES AND ARNIE ZANE

African American Bill T. Jones and Italian Jewish Arnie Zane first met in 1971 at the State University of New York, Binghamton. Enrolled in the same contact improvisation class, they immediately formed a partnership, creating dances with wild kinetic outbursts, and over time courageously choreographing works that celebrated their lives as gay men. Jones, with his regal onstage presence, was the better dancer of the two; Zane, slight and self-conscious, was less

Bill T. Jones with the Bill T. Jones/Arnie Zane Dance Company, 1994. *Ted Thai, Time and Life Pictures, Getty Images*

fond of performing, though he could be quick and funny onstage. But both fervently believed in the power of dance as an instrument for social change. For the next seventeen years they created works that explicitly addressed issues of race, sexuality, culture, and class.

In 1982 they founded the pointedly diverse Bill T. Jones/Arnie Zane Dance Company—which included dancers and actors of varying sizes, ages, and races—and began creating ambitious, evening-length works. Zane died from complications of AIDS in 1988, but Jones continued choreographing, keeping the company's name. His work turned increasingly personal—and increasingly aggressive. He believed the world had become a "garbage heap." His dances about censorship, homophobia, and alienation sometimes browbeat audiences by incorporating family photos and confessional performance art.

HIV-positive since 1985, Jones in the early 1990s began hosting "Survival Workshops" for people with terminal illnesses. The result was 1994's *Still/Here*, which used excerpts from workshop participants' confessions. Their emotional voice-overs haunted the work's ten dancers. The piece met with great success—it was chosen to open the Bill Moyers PBS series *Healing and the Arts*—but it also generated heated controversy. *New Yorker* dance critic Arlene Croce refused to see *Still/Here*, calling it "victim art." "By working dying people into his act, Jones is putting himself beyond the reach of criticism," she said. "I think of him as literally undiscussable—the most extreme case among the distressingly many now representing themselves to the public not as artists but as victims and martyrs."[45]

Though deeply hurt by the criticism, Jones pushed onward, never backing away from his thought-provoking, push-button aesthetic. He has worked with Trisha Brown, Laurie Anderson, and writer Toni Morrison. In 2007 he won a Tony Award for his choreography for *Spring Awakening*, a musical about the turmoil of adolescent sexuality; three years later, he earned another choreography Tony for *Fela!*, based on the life of Nigerian musician and composer Fela Kuti. That same year, the Bill T. Jones/Arnie Zane Dance Company merged with the downtown Dance Theater Workshop, forming a combined producing-and-presenting organization now known as New York Live Arts.

GARTH FAGAN AND JAWOLE WILLA JO ZOLLAR

Black identity is just one of the diverse issues Jones's work addresses, but both Garth Fagan and Jawole Willa Jo Zollar have spent their careers exploring that single, ever-complicated problem. Born in Jamaica, Fagan studied with Graham, Limón, and Alvin Ailey, and developed a hybrid style that incorporated elements of modern dance, Afro-Caribbean movement, street dance, and ballet. While he avoided the folkloric subject matter of earlier black dance, his works "epitomized the combination of strength, élan, dignity, and communal spirit of the best black dancing."[46] Many of his greatest works were done to jazz, like *Griot: New York* (1991), a montage of images of urban life set to a commissioned score by Wynton Marsalis. He has choreographed for numerous companies participating in the ongoing conversation about black identity in dance, including Alvin Ailey American Dance Theater and Dance Theatre of Harlem.

Zollar, who studied with a disciple of Katherine Dunham, founded Urban Bush Women in 1984. Zollar brought an avant-garde sensibility to black dance, creating mixed-media works that used spoken text, percussion, singing, and visual art to explore folk traditions and the black woman's experience. Unafraid to tackle issues like abortion and homelessness, Zollar found moments of hope and dignity in even the most desperate subjects. *Praise House* (1990), one of her best-received works, used a gospel choir and imagistic texts to create an abstract portrait of African American painter Minnie Evans. On the other end of the spectrum, *Batty Moves* (1995) celebrated the black woman's well-rounded buttocks.

MOLISSA FENLEY AND ELIZABETH STREB

The 1980s also saw the emergence of aggressively physical choreographers, who believed physicality *was* style. After graduating from the Mills College dance program, Molissa Fenley began creating works of sustained frenetic speed that required incredible stamina, as epitomized by her 1980 piece *Energizer*. In addition to taking regular dance classes, her dancers ran and did calisthenics to ensure they could survive her pieces. Fenley frequently earned criticism for the fact that her choreography, while aerobically impressive, was relatively simple; some saw its explosive energy as a distraction from its thinness.

Elizabeth Streb, an alumna of Fenley's company, would face similar critiques throughout her career. Taking Fenley's physicality to an even more daring extreme, she sought to replicate the thrilling velocity of skiing or motorcycling in her dances. Every one of her works involved elements of risk: Dancers jumped from high platforms, swung from trapezes, bounced on trampolines. She also enjoyed exploring nontraditional venues, staging performances in

malls, at gyms, even on the Coney Island boardwalk. Over time she pulled far enough away from the dance mainstream that she asked to be called not a choreographer but an "action specialist." (Her 2010 autobiography is titled *How to Become an Extreme Action Hero*.)

MARK MORRIS

Perhaps the most traditional of the post-Judson choreographers was Mark Morris, whose works demonstrate a respect for the past even as he puts his own distinctive spin on older forms.

Morris first began choreographing as a teenager in Seattle, when his dance teacher, Verla Flowers, assigned him portions of the studio's recital to develop. Around the same time, Morris became a member of a Balkan dance group, the Koleda Folk Ensemble, an experience that would have a profound effect on his style. Even in his earliest works, the folk-dance sense of community was ever-present. "I want it to look as though these are people who are dancing, as in folk dance or ethnic dance, where people are answering the call, 'Come on, let's dance!'" he said later. "That's probably the first thing that human beings did when they stopped throwing rocks at each other, and the history of

dance begins with them, the first people who joined hands together."[47]

Morris arrived in New York City in 1976. He danced briefly with Eliot Feld Ballet, Lar Lubovitch, Hannah Kahn, Laura Dean, and Twyla Tharp—just long enough to absorb each choreographer's approach. But he was unimpressed by most of the postmodernists. "Mark didn't want to be part of some phony avant-garde art scene," said Robert Bordo, a designer who worked with Morris.[48] Morris summed up his experiences of postmodern dance in his characteristically hyperbolic way: "A guy sits alone onstage in a spotlit chair, tells you his life story, then flicks his hands a couple of times to let you know it's a dance."[49]

By 1980 Morris was presenting his own choreography, creating work extremely rapidly; he averaged nearly six pieces a year for many years. With *Gloria* (1980), set to Vivaldi, and *New Love Song Waltzes* (1982), set to Brahms, he announced his intention to reclaim the classics and classic themes, and to rework them "for modern bodies and souls."[50] Those bodies, the bodies of his dancers, though eloquent, were not especially virtuosic. They were the real bodies of real people.

STREB Extreme Action dancers perform in London, 2012. *Jan Kruger/ Getty Images for BMW*

Similarly "real" was his approach to music. Though Morris showed a strong fidelity to melody and rhythm—so much so that critics accused him of "Mickey Mousing," referring to the ponderously literal movements of animated cartoons— he never let great classical compositions overawe him. "Morris has always been in the habit of using fine old classical music, which tends to put audiences in a worshipful mood," wrote critic and Morris biographer Joan Acocella, "and then setting it to steps that have a blunt, vernacular look, which disturbs that worshipful mood and leaves spectators wondering, 'Is he making a joke?' "[51] Sometimes he was. More frequently he was just expressing his honest reaction, as a modern artist, to a timeless work.

After years of living on the financial edge, in 1988 Morris became resident choreographer of the well-funded Théâtre de la Monnaie in Brussels, where

Mark Morris and Teri Weksler perform *One Charming Night*, 1988. © Beatriz Schiller, 2014

L'Allegro, Il Penseroso ed Il Moderato, performed by Mark Morris Dance Company, 2010. © Geraint Lewis, Alamy

until recently Maurice Béjart's Ballet du XXe Siècle had presided. The transition was not an easy one. Béjart was a Belgian hero, but during press interviews Morris spoke candidly about his dislike for Béjart's flamboyant choreography, which did not endear him to the Belgian public. "Mark Morris, Go Home!" read a Brussels newspaper headline (in English) after one of Morris' premieres. Thanks to the resources available to him at Théâtre de la Monnaie, however, Morris was able to create his most ambitious works to date. L'Allegro, Il Penseroso ed Il Moderato (1988), a masterpiece set to Handel, was presented on a grand scale, with dozens of scrims and drops, a huge cast clad in flowing, brightly colored chiffon costumes, and a full orchestra with opera singers. The Hard Nut, his brilliant deconstruction of The Nutcracker, featured lavish comic-book sets by cartoonist Charles Burns; Mikhail Baryshnikov was scheduled to dance in its premiere, though an injury prevented him from doing so. (Baryshnikov did later appear with Morris's company and still does occasionally. He and Morris also collaborated on the experimental White Oak Dance Project after Morris's Brussels contract ended in 1990.)

Morris's choreography became more precise and balletic in Brussels. Though he had conflicted feelings about ballet dancers—he has called them "dead virgins" and accused them of being uneducated and immature—his company began to use ballet vocabulary "as a sort of Latin," a structure on which to build.[52] When he returned to the United States, he started creating works for ballet companies as well as his own group. Many of them analyzed and subverted ballet conventions, or "show[ed] a marked self-consciousness about *being a ballet*."[53] In *Drink to Me Only With Thine Eyes*, created for American Ballet Theatre in 1988, Morris made an extended joke about the ballet hierarchy. Hidden in the twelve-dancer piece, which ostensibly had no stars, was Baryshnikov, the biggest ballet star in the world.

Morris is as savvy a businessman as he is a choreographer. By 2000 he had gathered enough funds to begin constructing the Mark Morris Dance Center—not only a home for his company, but also a vibrant school, which has become a New York dance hub. One of the most popular choreographers in modern dance, he has reached institutional status.

What's next for modern dance? The answer is unclear. Like Morris, many choreographers are still squeezing juice from relatively traditional formats. David Parsons, a longtime Taylor dancer, has created more than sixty handsome, well-constructed pieces for his company, including his signature solo, *Caught* (1982), which made ingenious use of a strobe light so that the dancer appeared to be floating above the stage. Stephen Petronio, a Trisha Brown alumnus, constructs limb-lashing, densely packed works that play with the concepts of transition and flow. Larry Keigwin has found popular and critical success combining rigorous modern dance structures with an arch, campy cabaret sensibility.

Others are navigating the sticky territories between dance and theater, or between dance and visual art. Artists like John Jasperse and Miguel Gutierrez, both talented movers, make works that might not be called dance but rather choreographic art—multimedia presentations that revolve around composition, pattern, and rhythm, and frequently incorporate improvisation. These are cerebral works, meant to be thought about as much as seen. In a way they return to the unbounded explorations of the Judson era, while still acknowledging all that has come between.

Fort Blossom revisited (2000/2012), choreographed and designed by John Jasperse. With, from left to right, Lindsay Clark, Erika Hand, Burr Johnson, and Ben Asriel. *Lindsay Browning, lbrowningphotography.com, courtesy John Jasperse*

Chapter Eight
Ballet after the Boom

William Forsythe's *The Second Detail.* © 2009 Laurent Paillier, photosdedanse.com. All rights reserved

"I speak the language [of ballet]. I don't recite the language."
—*William Forsythe*[1]

Following the deaths of George Balanchine, Jerome Robbins, and Antony Tudor, the ballet world suffered a loss of momentum. Rather than take new risks, some choreographers seemed haunted by those great men's ghosts, and merely mined and re-mined the styles they had developed. America's ballet companies, once fly-by-night organizations, were also newly institutionalized, with boards and marketing committees to answer to. Choreographic experimentation had become a higher-stakes game.

As ballet's popularity increased and American children flocked to studio classes, the caliber of ballet technique improved dramatically. By the 1980s professional companies could choose from a wealth of aspiring dancers and could afford to hire only the most "perfect" bodies. The corps de ballets of major groups achieved a uniformity that was both breathtaking and stultifying. While the standards for the average *Swan Lake* swan maiden or *Giselle* Wili had never been higher, gone were many of the distinctive personalities that animated early American ballet. Audiences worshipped the seemingly unlimited capabilities of the Superdancer. "Like the sleek-formed, well-muscled new beauties who glow in the ads and fashion magazines, like the increasing numbers of driven people who spend their lives training for triathlons, they reflect our current infatuation with expertise, with endurance, with prowess," wrote critic Deborah Jowitt. "We have upped our prescribed (and needed) dose of virtuosity."[2]

The new ballet dancer could do anything—and that versatility became an asset to directors and choreographers, because "anything" included non-balletic dance. Beginning with Twyla Tharp's

Boston Ballet performs *Swan Lake*, 2004. *Evan Richman/Boston Globe, Getty Images*

Deuce Coupe in 1973, postmodern dancemakers began to enter the ballet arena. They provided an intriguing new perspective on what classical dance might encompass. Ballet companies also started to add modern repertoire to their programs, works by pioneers Merce Cunningham, Paul Taylor, and Mark Morris. Though some of these experiments were more successful than others, the dissolution of stylistic boundaries helped lift ballet out of its post-boom doldrums.

As the turn of the century approached, some choreographers, with fewer and fewer limitations to

Pacific Northwest Ballet in *Diamonds*,
choreography by George Balanchine.
© *The George Balanchine Trust.*
© *Angela Sterling*

contend with, chose to embrace anything and everything that inspired them. For them, ballet became a foundation on which to build works that defied categorization. Others found in traditional neoclassical forms the structure they needed in a world of overwhelming options. Decades after Balanchine's death, they were not haunted by his specter. Rather, they were inspired anew by his choreographic principles.

From fairly early in the history of modern dance, some wondered whether a union of ballet and modern might be just what each style needed. Elements of modern dance could reinvigorate ballet, relaxing its sometimes prissy formality; ballet could lend a bit of glamour and sparkle to no-frills modern.[3] Still, the ballet-postmodern marriage was an unlikely one. Postmodern choreographers' emphasis on creating for the moment, rather than for perpetuity, clashed with ballet's focus on curating and maintaining a repertory. The artist who was first able to bridge the gap between the two worlds was, fittingly, a choreographer who was herself somewhere in the middle: Twyla Tharp.

By 1971, the year she created *Eight Jelly Rolls* (see Chapter 7), Tharp had moved away from the spareness of her thorny early works and toward a rich, theatrical style that incorporated dance of all types, from ballet to boogaloo. Robert Joffrey, the first ballet director to recognize the cross-genre appeal of Tharp's work, asked her to make a piece for the Joffrey Ballet. The result, 1973's *Deuce Coupe*, became a sensational hit. Tharp chose to use soothingly familiar songs by the Beach Boys, a decision that immediately put hesitant ballet fans at ease. Her six dancers joined fourteen of the Joffrey's, prompting witty physical jokes about the differences—and similarities—between their styles.

There were more similarities than differences, in fact. Tharp developed a mix-and-match hybrid vocabulary that, rooted in the common ground of social dances, revealed new qualities in every dancer onstage. "Along with the proprieties of ballet," she wrote, "I [blended] a vernacular style composed of running, skipping, sliding, and tumbling, plus all those magical steps . . . —the mashed potato, the slop, the go-go—the whole of this funneled through a little bit of Broadway show biz."[4]

Three years after this success, Tharp created *Push Comes to Shove*, the work that definitively crowned her a ballet-world darling, for American Ballet Theatre. Her secret weapon in the piece was recent Soviet arrival Mikhail Baryshnikov, a dancer eager to explore new ways of moving. Discovering that Baryshnikov was a master mimic, Tharp assigned him some of her personal movement mannerisms: herky-jerky stops and starts, breakneck sprints, slouchy shufflings. Baryshnikov-as-Tharp proved wittily irresistible. In typically insouciant fashion, Tharp also alternated ragtime pieces with a Haydn symphony and created a choreographic echo of the madcap musical mixture by veering from vaudeville-style tricks to quotations from ballet classics.

Over time Tharp's breezily colloquial style became a little too recognizable—and too frequently imitated. *Nine Sinatra Songs* (1982), created for her own dancers but later adopted by several ballet companies, saw Tharp heading in a different direction. Set to a selection of popular Frank Sinatra ballads, it evoked a dreamy, nostalgic world with no place for satire or irony; the women dancers wore gowns by Oscar de la Renta. Formal and entirely classical, *Bach Partita* (1983), made for American Ballet Theatre, was, in a way, a tribute to Balanchine, showing yet another facet of Tharp's range.

Baryshnikov and Judith Fugate rehearse *Push Comes to Shove* at the Hollywood Bowl, 1979. *Joan Adlen, Getty Images*

"One for My Baby (And One for the Road)," from *Nine Sinatra Songs*, performed by the Washington Ballet, 2012. *Katherine Frey /The Washington Post, Getty Images*

In the 1980s, as she became increasingly engaged with classicism, Tharp began recruiting ballet dancers for her own company. *In the Upper Room* (1986), created for Twyla Tharp Dance, illustrated the tensions between modern Tharp and ballet Tharp in a strikingly literal way. The piece, with a driving score by Philip Glass, featured sneaker-clad "stompers" facing off against a balletic "bomb squad." Both groups expended massive quantities of energy in their efforts to outdo each other and match the relentless, propulsive throb of the music.

In addition to Tharp, other postmodernists—David Gordon, Lucinda Childs, and Laura Dean among them—made forays into the ballet world. But postmodern dance wasn't the only influence reshaping the look of American ballet. Ballet companies had begun to import works by European choreographers, who had developed their own synthesis of ballet and modern dance, creating a better-blended mixture than America's frequently lumpy soup. Rather than view modern as a mode for personal expression, European choreographers used its techniques as organizational vocabularies, which allowed the style to get more naturally and completely with ballet.[5] As the earthy, calligraphic works of Europeans like Jiří Kylián, Mats Ek, John Neumeier, and Nacho Duato made their way into American ballet company repertories, they in turn inspired American choreographers.

Though he had a European sensibility, William Forsythe was actually an American choreographic export. Born in New York City, he trained at the Joffrey Ballet School; as an apprentice with the Joffrey company he was influenced by the works of Balanchine. He decamped in 1973 for Germany's Stuttgart Ballet, where he first encountered ballets by Kylián, Neumeier, and John Cranko. Encouraged by Stuttgart director Marcia Haydée, Forsythe began experimenting with choreography.

From the beginning, Forsythe operated under the assumption that classical ballet was as lost as the hierarchical model of society upon which it was founded; it had been abandoned along with the rational, linear perspectives that artists of all kinds discarded during the twentieth century.[6] But he never forsook it entirely. Instead, Forsythe twisted and warped the geometries of ballet, searching for the point at which the form became unrecognizable. "If dance only does what we assume it can do, it will expire," he said. "I keep trying to test the limits of what the word choreography means."[7] Forsythe went beyond Balanchine's (relatively speaking) genteel probing of ballet's possibilities. Like a mad scientist, he dissected classical

technique and then reassembled it, making his own ballet Frankensteins. Frequently he used aggressive electronic scores and disorienting side lighting. He also played with the conventions of balletic stagecraft, lowering the curtain in the middle of a work or having his dancers talk.

Though Forsythe choreographed for American companies—several of his works would eventually become staples of the American ballet repertoire—European audiences embraced his extremes more readily. In 1984 he assumed directorship of Ballett Frankfurt, which he led until 2002. While he made Germany his home, he found an especially receptive public in Paris. In 1987 he created *In the middle, somewhat elevated* for the Paris Opéra Ballet. *In the middle*'s provocative evocation of the intensity of the ballet studio provided a showcase for rising virtuoso Sylvie Guillem and helped revitalize the notoriously stuffy company's image. Ballett Frankfurt also had a series of brilliantly successful seasons in Paris beginning in 1989, which made Forsythe a household name in Europe.

Over time Forsythe became increasingly interested in experimental theater, incorporating film, song, sculpture, and text into his works. Frankfurt's municipal authorities, who wanted a more classical company, became irritated, and in 2002 they asked him to leave Ballett Frankfurt. Though the decision provoked widespread dissent, Forsythe departed—unwilling, he said, to present ballet as a "fine dining experience."[8] In 2004 he founded the Forsythe Company in Frankfurt. He continues to make new pieces for the smaller, streamlined group, removed from opera house politics.

Forsythe Company performances seem entirely unballetic. While creating *I don't believe in outer space* (2008), for example, Forsythe asked the dancers to blindfold themselves and memorize their apartments' layouts; that became the movement material he mined for the work. Yet the ballet foundation remains, however abstractly. "An idea from one domain can exist in another, and thrive just as well, but in a different form," Forsythe said. "Something as fundamental to ballet and classical music as counterpoint survives in my work in translated form, even if I choose not to use other associated elements."[9]

The swirl of post-Balanchine, post-literal, post-ballet boom influences also produced several choreographers who remained in America. Among the most successful were Gerald Arpino (see Chapter 5), Eliot Feld (see Chapter 5), Karole Armitage, and Alonzo King.

Karole Armitage earned the moniker "punk ballerina" early in her career, and while it's no longer

a fitting description of her work, at the time it was especially apt. A student of classical ballet, she performed with the Ballet du Grand Théâtre de Genève in Switzerland—a company then devoted exclusively to Balanchine works—before returning to the United States to study with Merce Cunningham. She danced with the Cunningham company from 1976 to 1981, becoming one of its most distinguished dancers.

In 1979 Armitage achieved sudden notoriety after presenting a concert in a New York City high school gymnasium. Pairing overwhelmingly loud electronic noise with dramatic lighting, neon costumes, and movements of extreme dynamic force, she seemed to embody urban chic. Her choreography made it clear that she had a deep understanding of classical technique, yet her sensibility, filtered through her years with Cunningham, was modern.

Audiences and, initially, critics responded with hot enthusiasm. Arlene Croce, reviewing the 1981 piece *Drastic Classicism*, described the Armitage experience as "an hour or more of frenzied classical dancing to a deafening rock score . . . [in which] classical values that were flayed alive stayed alive."[10]

Like Forsythe, Armitage achieved even greater acclaim in Europe, to which she relocated for several years after her early successes. When she returned to the United States in 1986, she renounced her first dances as immature and founded the small, subdued Armitage Ballet (renamed Armitage Gone! Dance in 2004). The slick classicism of her newer works showed little of her former rebelliousness.

Though choreographer Alonzo King came out of and continues to work within the ballet tradition, his dances also include multicultural and spiritual influences. King danced with several ballet

companies, but in 1982, eager to explore chore-ography, he founded the San Francisco Bay Area–based Alonzo King LINES Ballet—named not only for the lines created by dancers' bodies but also for "the interconnectedness of everything."[11] For his group of admirably versatile dancers, he began making works with diverse references: Eastern chants, Indian ragas, Bach and Handel, jazz, folk music. His movement vocabulary metamorphosed to reflect each cultural channel, but always maintained its connection to classicism.

In the early 1980s New York's three major ballet companies were all struggling to define—or rather, redefine—themselves. The situation seemed most urgent at the Joffrey Ballet.

After canceling its 1977 season because of financial constraints, and a year later disbanding for six

months, the Joffrey took up residency at the Music Center of Los Angeles, becoming the first bicoastal ballet company. It was a bold experiment, and for some years, it seemed, a successful one. With no other competition in the area, the Joffrey had L.A. ballet patrons' pockets at their disposal.

With a new lease on life, the Joffrey continued its much-lauded work reviving lost classics (see Chapter 5). In 1987, after years of research and preparation, the company presented a meticulous reconstruction of Vaslav Nijinsky's *Le sacre du printemps* (1913)—a work so sensational that it caused a riot at its Paris premiere, and that for years was thought to be irretrievably lost. Dance scholar Millicent Hodson pieced it together step by step, using a smattering of sources that included backstage photos and a score marked by Nijinsky's assistant. While the result

Three Theories, choreographed by Karole Armitage in 2010 and performed by Armitage Gone! Dance company members Emily Wagner and William Isaac. *Julieta Cervantes, courtesy Karole Armitage*

was an interpretive rather than an absolute recon-struction of the original—there were just too many holes to fill—it was, nevertheless, an astounding achievement. (On the night of the premiere at the Music Center, a strong earthquake hit Los Angeles, which some thought to be an appropriate seismic response.[12]) The Joffrey also acquired a number of works by British choreographer Frederick Ashton, many of which had been long since dropped by their home company, London's Royal Ballet. The troupe filled out its repertoire with pieces by Kylián, Forsythe, and Cranko, and with Gerald Arpino's continuing stream of youth-centric works. By 1985, according to critic Jennifer Dunning, the company had "succeeded in building the most provocative and interesting collection of ballets on the interna-tional ballet scene."[13]

Alonzo King with Alonzo King LINES dancer Laurel Keen. *R. J. Muna, courtesy Alonzo King LINES Ballet*

The Joffrey of the 1980s was a "democratic" company—full of strong, versatile, game-for-any-thing dancers, but essentially starless. Because its technical standard was lower than that of other companies its size, the Joffrey tended to bleed its top talents, including Maximiliano Zomosa, Francesca Corkle, and Tina LeBlanc. The group was also some-times criticized for trying to do too many things at once. "In a single evening," wrote Arlene Croce, "the Joffrey can attract three publics—the balletomanes, the avant-garde, and the media-aware, just-curious-about-ballet crowd. The problem is that these pub-lics swiftly tire of one another."[14]

In the early 1980s Robert Joffrey discovered he had AIDS. Fearful that the news would scare away potential patrons and harm the company's image, he kept quiet about his illness, a decision that angered many in both the dance and gay communi-ties. On March 25, 1988, he died. After a tense few months of back-and-forth negotiations, Arpino was named his successor. But soon the company faced instability yet again: It was asked to leave the L.A. Music Center in 1991, and its relationship with New York City Center became strained by rising rent. Hoping the Midwest would prove to be friendlier territory, the Joffrey moved to Chicago in 1996. It was the beginning of yet another new era for the embattled company.

Though the Joffrey Ballet of Chicago, as it was now called, struggled financially during the first few years after the move, eventually it settled into its new home. Arpino retired in 2007. (He died the follow-ing year.) Ashley Wheater, a British dancer who had spent four years performing with the Joffrey in the 1980s, became artistic director. Under Wheater the company has attracted increasingly refined dancers, among them the elegant Victoria Jaiani. The Joffrey is now on more solid monetary footing, and in 2008 it moved into a state-of-the-art new facility, the Joffrey Tower.

American Ballet Theatre went through a simi-larly dramatic period of transition beginning in 1980, when longtime directors Lucia Chase and Oliver Smith were dismissed. Mikhail Baryshnikov, fresh off his year of working with Balanchine at New York City Ballet, replaced them. Though the superstar had little managerial experience, he had a distinct vision of the type of company he wanted to run, and his prestige helped him implement his ideas quickly. He also took no salary from ABT after 1983, which gave him more independence.

Baryshnikov's vision was not, as some had feared, to turn American Ballet Theatre into another haven for Balanchine's neoclassical style. Instead of a single artistic perspective, he wanted a single coherent style: the precise, pure Russian style he believed to be best.[15] He also disliked the star system that had been key to the company's success in the past (and that was, ironically, the reason he'd come to American Ballet in the first place); he believed it gave a select few dancers far too much power over the artistic staff. It wasn't that he didn't like stars, he said, but rather "star self-indulgence."[16]

Under Baryshnikov, the overall level of technique at American Ballet Theatre improved dramatically. "Baryshnikov is presiding over a new Ballet Theatre—one in which every corps member performs impeccably," said Arlene Croce. "A clean style is always pleasant to see. But scrubbing away impurities isn't enough to make dancing interesting."[17] To add that interest, Baryshnikov commissioned works from postmodern artists or crossovers. His classical dancers sometimes had trouble adjusting to these choreographers' sensibilities, but when choreographer and dancers were able to meet in the middle—as in Mark Morris's *Drink to Me Only with Thine Eyes* (see Chapter 7)—the results were electric. Baryshnikov also added works by Cunningham, Paul Taylor, and Kylián to the repertoire.

For a time, people complained that Baryshnikov had "deglamorized" American Ballet Theatre. The level of technique may have been higher, but the level of personality was far lower, and audiences felt the loss. Though he groomed several ballerina protégées, limpid Susan Jaffe became the only breakout star, and only after several years. In the later 1980s,

The Joffrey Ballet in the reconstructed *Le sacre du printemps*.
Roger Mastroianni,
courtesy Joffrey Ballet

Talented dancers like Amanda McKerrow, here with John Gardner in Antony Tudor's *The Leaves Are Fading*, enlivened American Ballet Theatre in the 1980s. *AP Photo/Misha Japaridze*

however, Baryshnikov seemed to ease up on the reins. He acquired Kenneth MacMillan's *Romeo and Juliet* and *Sleeping Beauty*, great star vehicles that delighted balletomanes. Amanda McKerrow, winner of the 1981 gold medal at the International Ballet Competition in Moscow, enlivened the company's principal ranks. Alessandra Ferri, an Italian ballerina of incomparable dramatic ability, joined soon afterward; she formed a thrilling partnership with young Argentinian guest star Julio Bocca. The Mariinsky Ballet's Altynai Asylmuratova also began making guest appearances. Glamour, it seemed, was back.

In 1990 Baryshnikov left the company, possibly to allow more time for the acting opportunities he'd begun to pursue (see Chapter 9).[18] American

Ballet cast about aimlessly, coming perilously close to financial disaster, until former dancer Kevin McKenzie was appointed director in 1992.

Under McKenzie, the old star model returned in force. He had no qualms about presenting full versions of warhorse classics, which became the foundation of American Ballet's repertoire. Attracted by opportunities to tackle prime roles like Giselle and *Sleeping Beauty*'s Aurora, world-class dancers arrived to fill out the group's principal roster. From Russia came Nina Ananiashvili and Vladimir Malakhov; from Latin America, José Manuel Carreno and Paloma Herrera; from Spain, Ángel Corella. Homegrown dancers Julie Kent and Ethan Stiefel reached celebrity status, which only intensified

LEFT: Ángel Corella and Paloma Herrera in *Swan Lake*, 2005. *Gene Schiavone, Associated Press*

OPPOSITE: Julie Kent as Medora in *Le Corsaire*. *Beatriz Schiller/ Time and Life Pictures, Getty Images*

after both starred in the 2000 film *Center Stage* (see Chapter 9). American Ballet Theatre became a company ruled not by a choreography-centric vision but by a dancer-centric one. The approach helped return the group to financial health.

McKenzie also worked to maintain the other wings of the theater's repertoire, such as the hybrid contemporary works brought in by Baryshnikov and the dances by Antony Tudor and Agnes de Mille that had defined the company's early history. But these pieces often got short shrift, performed in smaller programs during the company's brief fall season at New York City Center. To fill the cavernous Metropolitan Opera House's seats each spring and summer, McKenzie needed star power and spectacle.

The theater became best-known as America's home for ballet in the grand, old-world style.

After the turn of the century, McKenzie further burnished the company's roster by adding a stable of high-wattage guest stars, who would descend upon the Met for a few performances each season. Buzz around these shows—which offered rare opportunities for Americans to get a glimpse of Russian sensations Natalia Osipova and Ivan Vasiliev, or exquisite Royal Ballet ballerina Alina Cojocaru—frequently reached a feverish pitch. It was a savvy, pragmatic move, though some of the company's permanent members resented the fact that guest stars were performing the roles they themselves were eager to dance. Established principals, on the other hand,

Misty Copeland performs with Prince at Madison Square Garden during the "Welcome 2 America" tour, 2011.
Kevin Mazur, WireImage

seemed to rise to the challenge represented by the visiting celebrities. Gillian Murphy blossomed from a singularly competent technician into a singularly incisive artist; Brazilian Marcelo Gomes became ballet's most gallant, attentive partner; and the diminutive Herman Cornejo proved that his brilliant virtuosity was coupled with expressive power.

With the return of the star dancer came the idea of the dancer as brand. Several artists in American Ballet Theatre's upper echelons began amassing engagements on the strength of their own names around the United States and abroad. Sometimes it seemed as though half of the theater's principal roster was absent at any given time. In 2011 principal David Hallberg, a dancer of extraordinary purity and exemplary line, signed a contract with the Bolshoi Ballet—a sort of reverse defection. He continues to split his year between Moscow and

New York, an international superstar with no single allegiance. Misty Copeland, an African American soloist, has achieved mainstream fame thanks to her eloquent articulation of the struggles black dancers face in ballet—and thanks to her concert performances with Prince.

Surprisingly, one of the company's most important recent triumphs has been acquiring not a star dancer but a star choreographer. Russian-born Alexei Ratmansky, for several years a director of the Bolshoi Ballet, had a prolonged flirtation with New York City Ballet in the early 2000s, but signed an artist-in-residence contract with American in 2009. Ratmansky is known for creating ballets at once human and mysterious, works that look at ballet's oldest traditions through modern eyes. Frequently audiences recognize his characters— they are people we know, and yet, as depicted in

Ratmansky's choreography, they transcend type. His 2010 *Nutcracker* gave the company a version of the classic to rival Balanchine's. While Balanchine's heroine, Marie, remains a child throughout the ballet, Ratmansky transformed his Clara into a grown-up princess who shows us that she still remembers what it's like to be young.

In 2004 American Ballet Theatre also revived in earnest its on-again, off-again school. The Jacqueline Kennedy Onassis School began attracting young dancers eager to learn not a specific style, as they would at the Balanchine-centric School of American Ballet, but rather an unmannered, flexible technique that promised to make them attractive to a variety of companies. The theater also created a teacher-training curriculum, to spread its uniform standard to schools across the country.

After Balanchine's death, New York City Ballet seemed rudderless for several years. Peter Martins, the distinguished dancer appointed Balanchine's successor, faced a daunting task:

properly maintaining the Balanchine legacy while also determining a new, fruitful direction for the company. Jerome Robbins initially served as co-director, but retired from the position in 1990. The subsequent deterioration of his health meant that there were few new Robbins ballets to bolster the New York City Ballet repertoire. (Robbins died in 1998, shortly after re-staging his 1965 *Les Noces* for the company, a heroic effort.)

Martins began commissioning new ballets at a breakneck pace. He brought in strings of fluent neoclassical choreographers to create works for various festivals, including the Diamond Project, which ran every few years from 1992 to 2006. Most of these ballets, however, were poor imitations of Balanchine camouflaged by the slickness of the European style.[19] They burst and disappeared like so many fireworks—not only artistic but financial disappointments. Martins, a highly competent choreographer, also added his own ballets to the pile. The structural integrity of his works

American Ballet Theatre in Alexei Ratmansky's *Nutcracker,* one of the first major works Ratmansky created for the company as its artist in residence. *Linda Davidson/The Washington Post, Getty Images*

Boston Ballet in Wheeldon's *Polyphonia*, 2013. *Nigel Norrington/Associated Press*

was impressive, as was the fact that his pas de deux often demonstrated a remarkable equality of the sexes. But too often Martins ballets seemed sketchy and strangely soulless.

Though not the mentor Balanchine had been to his dancers, Martins was a generous giver of opportunities. He entrusted even the greenest company dancers with major parts—and with all the new ballets he commissioned, there were plenty of parts to go around. Under Martins' direction, Darci Kistler, the last of Balanchine's prodigies (and eventually Martins' wife) continued to develop the sparkling sweetness that first captured Mr. B's attention. Kyra Nichols became a dancer of serene stylistic purity.

Damian Woetzel proved a charming, easy cavalier, and Nikolaj Hübbe, from Denmark, combined an immaculate technique with dramatic power.

Perhaps the company's greatest 1990s discovery was Christopher Wheeldon. Born and trained in Britain, Wheeldon joined New York City Ballet in 1993 and soaked up the company's Balanchine repertoire. He began choreographing for the ballet in 1997. From the beginning he showed an aptitude for stage geometry, for crafting kaleidoscopic patterns that shifted and clicked into place. In 2001 Wheeldon had a breakthrough moment with *Polyphonia*, set to the rhythmic thickets and tangles of several Gyorgy Ligeti piano pieces. At once chaotic

and ordered, *Polyphonia*, performed in simple leotards and tights, seemed like Wheeldon's answer to Balanchine's *Agon* (see Chapter 5). Martins made Wheeldon the ballet's first resident choreographer that same year. Though he later left—first to direct a small company of his own, Morphoses, and eventually to become artistic associate at the Royal Ballet in his native Britain—Wheeldon continues to choreograph frequently for American companies.

In 2011, following Kistler's retirement, the New York City Ballet reached a pivotal point: None of its dancers had been hired by Balanchine. But there was no generational crisis. Every year a fresh crop of School of American Ballet graduates, trained in the

Balanchine style, entered the company, bringing an infusion of talent and enthusiasm. Balanchine had wanted a school before a company, and the School of American Ballet continued to be the motor that drove the troupe forward. Instead of an American Ballet Theatre-style showcase, the New York City Ballet was a breeding ground.[20]

First among the outstanding dancers to emerge post-Balanchine was Wendy Whelan. With her sinewy, angular frame, Whelan did not have the archetypical ballerina "look," yet her distinctive form became the preferred canvas for many choreographers, including Wheeldon. Her cool, intelligent surface belied a warm soul, which radiated to the

surface in works by Robbins and Ratmansky. Maria Kowroski, who shared much of Whelan's repertoire, had The Body: endless, tapering arms and legs and luxuriant flexibility. Her voluptuous arabesques, in particular, seared the memory.

A flood of new talent has recently come of age at New York City Ballet—dancers who, though united by their Balanchine style, could not be more different. The explosive Ashley Bouder is complemented by the lithe, languorous Teresa Reichlen; the crisp, musical Tiler Peck; and the rapturously dramatic Sara Mearns. Brothers Jared and Tyler Angle have emerged as the company's resident princes, Daniel Ulbricht as its jaunty virtuoso, and Robert Fairchild as its contemporary go-to. The ballet has a promising choreographer, too, in soloist Justin Peck (no relation to Tiler). Still an active dancer, he carries the works of Balanchine, Robbins, Wheeldon, and Ratmansky in his body, but they seem to be an asset, rather than an intimidating hindrance, to his choreographic work.

Both American Ballet Theatre and New York City Ballet continue to struggle with the issue of diversity. American Ballet's Copeland has been an important spokesperson for the plight of black people in ballet, and NYCB has several male dancers of color—among them Craig Hall and the ebullient Amar Ramasar—in its ranks. But the problem is nearly as pervasive now as it was in 1969, when Arthur Mitchell founded the Dance Theatre of Harlem as a home for black ballet dancers.

Despite its successful stagings of *Swan Lake* Act II and *Giselle* (see Chapter 5), the Dance Theatre of Harlem struggled artistically in the late 1980s and early 1990s. The company faced a uniquely difficult situation: Given the charged history of race relations in America, there was no way to separate its artistic agenda from its sociopolitical one. Reviewers approached the theater with gloved hands; condescension was an ever-present possibility.[21]

Unable to find a consistent vision, and facing insurmountable financial difficulties, the Dance

Theatre of Harlem shut down in 2004. It would lie dormant for the next nine years (though its school remained open). The void it left was keenly felt. Several of its most talented members—including Alicia Graf Mack, a dancer of extraordinary facility—were unable to find jobs with other classical companies, though they were more than qualified for them.

The year 2009, however, brought hope. Former principal dancer Virginia Johnson became artistic director of the Dance Theatre of Harlem organization, taking over for Mitchell. Johnson proved a unifying leader. She assembled a new, smaller group of dancers, most of whom had trained at the theater's school. The revived Dance Theatre of Harlem gave its first performances in 2012, to enthusiastic audiences.

Ballet has depended on government funding for the past half-century, but in recent decades those resources have declined steadily. Nearly every ballet company was also hard hit by the recession that began in 2008. Many laid off dancers and shortened seasons to make ends meet. With the economic climate still uncertain, it seems that a rethinking of the American ballet company model is inevitable.

Several existing companies—small, flexible groups that tour widely—propose alternatives that might be the way forward. Aspen Santa Fe Ballet's two-home strategy (the company has annual seasons in both Aspen and Santa Fe) brings ballet to regions that couldn't support companies independently. The recently disbanded Trey McIntyre Project smartly chose to make low-cost Boise, Idaho, its home base, which helped its bottom line. New York City's sleek Cedar Lake Contemporary Ballet and Complexions Contemporary Ballet are hip, trendy alternatives to American Ballet Theatre and New York City Ballet, rather than competitors.

All of these groups present small-scale contemporary ballets. Though their dancers have strong classical training, the companies lack the resources to mount most major works of the American ballet repertoire. The standards of American ballet have never been higher, but it's hard to predict what its future might look like.

Dance Theatre of Harlem performs at the Fire Island Dance Festival, 2011.
Leandro Justen, PatrickMcMullan.com, Sipa Press, Associated Press

REGIONAL BALLET COMPANIES

During the 1960s and 1970s, as arts funding increased exponentially thanks to the Ford Foundation and the National Endowment for the Arts, ballet companies sprouted in cities across the United States. After a few decades, with technical standards on the rise, many of these began to rival even the top New York City troupes. By the mid-1980s it was possible to see an evening of world-class ballet in San Francisco, Boston, Houston, or Seattle—an extraordinary achievement for a country that had no ballet tradition fifty years earlier.

Foremost among the regional companies is the **San Francisco Ballet**. Founded in 1933, it is also the oldest continually operating ballet company in the United States. Led for thirty-two years by Lew Christensen, a former Balanchine dancer, the company achieved widespread visibility because of its frequent tours. Christensen had broad access to Balanchine's ballets, which formed a key part of the company's repertoire. He also made more than one hundred ballets himself, including two full-length *Nutcracker*s, and encouraged his dancers to choreograph. Following Christensen's death, former New York City Ballet principal Helgi Tómasson assumed directorship of the company in 1985. A strong, pure classical technician himself, Tómasson set about raising San Francisco Ballet's dance standards. He acquired several traditional full-length productions, commissioned works by numerous neoclassical choreographers, and created his own polished, if not distinguished, ballets. Tómasson also nurtured a number of extraordinary dancers, notably Evelyn Cisneros, Yuan Yuan Tan, Maria Kochetkova, and Sarah Van Patten.

Christensen's brother William, who was involved in the early direction of San Francisco Ballet, left California to create the country's first university ballet department at the University of Utah. A Ford Foundation grant allowed him to turn the department's small affiliated performing group, Utah Civic Ballet, into a professional company in 1963. Five years later the company was renamed **Ballet West**. A succession of directors assembled a repertory that included story ballets, works of dramatic theater, and pieces by Balanchine and Frederick Ashton. Recently the company achieved a degree of mainstream fame from the reality television show *Breaking Pointe*, though the series' melodramatic depiction of life in a ballet company generated some controversy.

Balanchine protégée Barbara Weisberger founded Philadelphia's **Pennsylvania Ballet** in 1964, with the support of Balanchine and a Ford Foundation grant. The first child student at the School of American Ballet, Weisberger was a gifted teacher, and her company quickly attracted talented dancers from nearby New York. In 1972 Benjamin Harkavy, former director of Nederlands Dans Theater, joined her as co-director, bringing a distinct European influence to the troupe. After a series of financial problems crippled the company, Weisberger and Harkavy both resigned in

1982. The company then had a somewhat lower profile, though its new director, Robert Weiss, restored much of its original Balanchine repertory. After a brief tenure by Christopher d'Amboise (son of beloved New York City Ballet principal Jacques d'Amboise), former company dancer Roy Kaiser took over the directorship in 1990. In 2012 Kaiser helped re-establish the company's on-again, off-again school.

As in Philadelphia, it took a talented teacher to establish a company in Boston. E. Virginia Williams, who opened her first dance school in the mid-1930s, started a small group in the Hub in 1958. In 1963, with help from the Ford Foundation, **Boston Ballet** turned professional. Williams hoped to create a "gallery of the dance" that included older classics, Balanchine ballets, and contemporary works. In 1980 Boston Ballet became the first American dance company to tour to China. Bruce Marks, who assumed direction of the company in 1985, continued Williams's multi-faceted approach. The company's 1990 "glasnost" *Swan Lake* marked the first collaboration between Soviet and American dancers on such a scale; after the fall of the Soviet Union, when Russian dancers began flooding the United States, many of them came to Boston. Finnish-born Mikko Nissinen, Boston Ballet's director since 2001, added more European works to the company's repertoire and appointed fellow Fin Jorma Elo as resident choreographer.

It took a few false starts before ballet truly took root in Houston, but in 1976 **Houston Ballet** finally found the right director in Britain's Ben Stevenson. Stevenson shaped a repertoire grounded in full-length fairy tales by Ashton, Cranko, and MacMillan, and created his own successful (though not critically acclaimed) version of *Cinderella*. He also established a strong school that served as a feeder for the company. Australian Stanton Welch, who became director in 2003, has added many contemporary ballets to Houston Ballet's repertoire, a reflection of his own choreographic sensibility.

Founded in 1972, Seattle-based **Pacific Northwest Ballet** picked up steam in 1977, when former Balanchine dancers Francia Russell and Kent Stowell took over its helm. Russell had previously traveled the world staging Balanchine works, and accordingly the company performed many Balanchine ballets. Stowell mounted his own versions of *Swan Lake* and *The Nutcracker*, the latter with ingenious sets and costumes by Maurice Sendak. In the late 1980s and early 1990s, fearless, gazelle-like dancer Patricia Barker made a particular impression in the company's Balanchine repertoire. Former New York City Ballet principal Peter Boal assumed directorship of Pacific Northwest Ballet in 2005. He brought New York City Ballet soloist Carla Körbes with him, and under his care she developed into an assured, authoritative principal. In 2013 Boal turned heads with his appointment of Twyla Tharp as the company's first artist-in-residence.

Pacific Northwest Ballet in Balanchine's *Agon*. © *The George Balanchine Trust. Photograph* © *Angela Sterling*

The youngest of the major regional companies, **Miami City Ballet** was founded in 1986. For some years the city had demonstrated an interest in forming a civic ballet troupe, and longtime New York City Ballet star Edward Villella was invited to create one from the ground up. He assembled a group of dancers who shared many of his own performance qualities—strength, spirit, courage. Villella's goal was to piece together a repertoire of masterworks, ballets whose value had already been proven. Balanchine formed the backbone. Quickly the company achieved a high profile, earning praise for the robustness and vitality of its performances of Balanchine standards. Despite his successes, Villella was forced out after a dispute with the company's board in 2011. Miami City Ballet's new director, former New York City Ballet dancer Lourdes Lopez, has expanded the company's repertoire to include newer ballets and premieres and hopes to forge a connection with Miami's large Latino community.

Chapter Nine

American Musical Theater

George Chakiris (center) in the film version of *West Side Story*, choreographed by Jerome Robbins, 1961. *Popperfoto, Getty Images*

"I wanted to find out at that time how far we . . . could go in bringing our crafts and talents to a musical. Why did we have to do it separately and elsewhere? Why did Lenny [Bernstein] have to write an opera, Arthur [Laurents] a play, me a ballet? Why couldn't we, in aspiration, try to bring our deepest talents together to the commercial theater in this work?" —*Jerome Robbins on* West Side Story[1]

Nobody entered the American ballet or modern dance scene expecting to turn a profit. Choreographers in the concert world developed philosophies based on what they believed was good for their art forms. Their works explored the ideas they hoped would move dance forward, regardless of the financial viability of the result.

Broadway was a different story. For its first few decades, showbiz dance developed haphazardly, driven not by high-minded choreographers but by hard box-office numbers. Rather than tell audiences what to think, Broadway choreographers tried their darndest to give 'em what they wanted. Dance artists were second-class citizens on the Great White Way for many years. Not until nearly halfway through the twentieth century did the term "choreographer" become widely used on Broadway. Before then, "dance directors," in the eyes of most producers, simply arranged people prettily onstage, perhaps adding a soft-shoe or two to keep audiences in their seats when the singers needed a rest.

Still, nearly every major choreographer worked in musical theater at some point, and many of them took their commercial jobs very seriously. "In the concert field, one creates out of a deep necessity to say something. . . . The ideas initiate with you," said Helen Tamiris, both a modern pioneer (see Chapter 4) and a frequent Broadway choreographer. "In the Broadway theater, that center is removed, so you contribute on another level. . . . It is a place where you use your taste, your knowledge of craft, your basic set of values based on material emerging from the author's script."[2]

Eventually, some Broadway directors and choreographers risked meddling with the traditional formula. Instead of simply creating a pleasant mixture of dance, music, and story, they began integrating all three, so that each component became essential to the greater whole. In works like *Oklahoma!*, *West Side Story*, and *Chicago*, the form achieved a kind of transcendence. These musicals weren't just a good time; they were conduits for powerful emotional truths. Rather than force audiences to choose between art and entertainment, they presented art *as* entertainment.

The Broadway musical's earliest ancestors were the minstrel and vaudeville shows that attained widespread popularity during the nineteenth century (see Chapter 3). Generally these variety evenings had no storyline; they were just mishmashes of the best dance, comedy, and musical acts a producer could put together at a given time in a given city. One of the first pieces of true "musical theater" presented in the United States was *The Black Crook*, which opened at New York City's Niblo's Garden in 1866 (and which brought dozens of European ballet dancers to the New York stage; see Chapter 5). *The Black Crook*'s plot may have been preposterous—it had to do with a wizard helping to reunite two medieval lovers—but it did have a plot. It also included many dancing chorines, precision-trained groups of beautiful women who offered well-drilled marches. *The Black Crook* marked the moment when a parade of chorus girls became an indispensable part of an American evening at the theater.

Dancers in *The Black Crook*, 1893.
Library of Congress

Several English comic operas also arrived in the United States before the turn of the century. The US premiere of W. S. Gilbert and Arthur Sullivan's ebullient *H.M.S. Pinafore* at the Boston Museum in 1878 caused a sensation. Over the following year, ninety companies across the country performed the light opera—or some version of it. Religious organizations and children's groups mounted their own productions; there was a Yiddish revision, and numerous parodies emerged.[3] *Pinafore*'s popularity ensured that other Gilbert and Sullivan comic operas, including *The Pirates of Penzance* and *The Mikado*, made their way across the pond as well.

On the more romantic end of the theatrical spectrum were Viennese operettas. (Americans Reginald de Koven, John Philip Sousa, and Victor Herbert also made contributions to the operetta genre.) American audiences swooned for their stories of passion. As in opera, dance in these productions was a diversion, not a part of the story; frequently a large chorus of comely women backed a soloist during dance interludes. The New York staging of *The Merry Widow* in 1907, however, demonstrated the power of dance as a plot mechanism. At one point, the show's two stars began moving dreamily toward each other, humming softly. Eventually their movements accelerated as the orchestra picked up their melody, and the scene blossomed into a heady, sweeping waltz—a moving metaphor for their surging feelings.

In 1905 the massive Hippodrome—a 5,000-seat juggernaut with fantastic stage capabilities—opened

LEFT: The Hippodrome, c. 1905.
Library of Congress

OPPOSITE: Chorus girls, c. 1899.
Library of Congress

London production of *The Merry Widow*, 1907.

in Midtown Manhattan. Directors of theatrical productions suddenly had the means to portray hurricanes, fires, floods, and elaborate military campaigns. Dancing had to be grand to stand out in the midst of such spectacles, and in many Hippodrome shows, as many as 280 chorus girls filled the stage. Numbers, rather than talent, created the best effect on such a scale; most of the dancers had little training beyond rudimentary ballet.

Seemingly never-ending lines of dancing girls also became the centerpieces of American revues, variety shows that were essentially, as dance historian David Ewen wrote, "vaudeville in fancy dress."[4] Revues differed from old-time vaudeville in that they frequently had custom scores and numbers conceived with some kind of unifying theme. Yet spectators still came primarily for the women, who paraded in glamorous ensembles that left little to

the imagination. One review of the 1915 *A World of Pleasure*, performed at New York's revue-centric Winter Garden, sniffed:

> Unless a girdle of beads be considered a costume, there are scenes in which the chorus may truthfully be described as wearing no clothes at all. Stockings are as obsolete at the Winter Garden as the steel armor of a mediaeval soldier. A dress not cut to the waist line at the back is a curiosity—an impudent attempt at unwelcome modesty.[5]

Nobody understood the power of beautiful women better than Florenz Ziegfeld. Ziegfeld modeled his shows after Paris' legendary Folies-Bergère, mounting a hugely popular series of revues, the *Ziegfeld Follies*, from 1907 to 1931. His pageants,

The Rockettes perform at Radio City Music Hall, 1930s. *Museum of the City of New York, Wurts Brothers, Getty Images*

with their rows and rows of dancing chorines, glorified the American girl—and surrounded her with the best singers, comedians, and solo dancers available. Ziegfeld's talented non-chorus dancers included Ann Pennington, whose "hoochy" derrière-shaking dances, straight from Harlem, brought down the house. Perhaps the most famous was Marilyn Miller, who grew up learning soft shoe dances from her building's black janitor.[6] Ziegfeld, noticing her aptitude and charisma, groomed Miller for the spotlight, and over time she became proficient in ballet. She developed a "happy dancing" style, in which classical steps frequently gave way to her own cheerful idiosyncrasies. Her charming act earned her some of the highest fees of any performer of the time.

Entrepreneurial producer Russell Makert saw the *Ziegfeld Follies of 1922*, and was inspired to start his own group of leggy chorus girls. Founded in 1925 in St. Louis, Makert's "Missouri Rockets" became the "Roxyettes" shortly afterward, when Samuel Roxy Rothafel brought the group to New York to perform at his Roxy Theater. In 1932 Rothafel moved the company to the newly opened Radio City Music Hall, where eventually it took on its third and final moniker: the "Rockettes."

"Over There" sheet music, 1917. With typical Cohan patriotism, the song encouraged young men to serve their country.

Rockette girls were not just pretty faces. They were well-trained dancers, as famous for their signature eye-high leg kicks as for the shapely legs doing the kicking.

Early twentieth-century America teemed with dancing girls, but not even the popular performances of stars like Vernon Castle (see Chapter 2) and Fred Astaire (see Chapter 3) could relax the nation's suspicious attitude toward men dancing. The boys who succeeded were, generally speaking, not virtuosos but rather song-and-dance everymen, nice guys who knew a few steps and a couple of tunes.

King of these performers was George M. Cohan, frequently called the "father of musical comedy." After starting out in vaudeville with his family's "The Four Cohans" act, George eventually began writing his own lyrics, music, and librettos. He frequently starred in the resulting shows. Not prodigiously talented in any one field—"I can write better plays than any living dancer, and dance better than any living playwright," he quipped—Cohan nevertheless created a new genre of entertainment, translating European-style operettas and comic operas into an American vernacular.[7] Cohan's characters included jockeys, ex-boxers, US senators, and manufacturers. His dancing oozed vaudevillian charm; his brassy dialogue had a jaunty Yankee edge to it. His songs frequently waxed patriotic: "You're a Grand Old Flag," "The Yankee Doodle Boy," and "Give My Regards to Broadway" are all Cohan classics. Onstage, Cohan became the aw-shucks-dontcha-love-me model for the likes of Donald O'Connor, Bob Hope, and Tommy Tune.

All-American though they were, Cohan's productions still used songs and dances as punctuation marks rather than part of the show's dialogue. For four years in the second decade of the twentieth century, on the other hand, New York's pint-sized Princess Theater hosted some of the first attempts to truly integrate all aspects of musical theater. Since the venue seated just three hundred people, it had to present small-scale shows. There, without spectacle to rely on, composer Jerome Kern and librettist Guy Bolton created several intimate musicals that made up for their lack of sparkle with sophisticated plots, meaningful songs, and plenty of Castle-style ballroom dances—all tied together by the thread of dramatic logic.

But it was *Show Boat* (1927) that truly crystallized the new American musical theater. *Show Boat*, with music by Kern and a book and lyrics by Oscar Hammerstein II, was based on Edna Ferber's novel about life on the Mississippi, a complicated story

Continued on page 223

Ziegfeld Follies chorus girls.
Alfred Cheney Johnston

Continued from page 219

that spanned fifty years. Dance director Sammy Lee, a vaudeville veteran, put together a review of dance development from the late 1800s through the 1920s, with nods to all the various social crazes: the cakewalk, the Charleston, the Black Bottom. The show also had a group of black performers, who appeared in a minstrel-like concoction on the showboat. Audiences responded enthusiastically, proving they could enjoy popular dances on the concert stage.

By this point, Hollywood films were creating competition for live shows. As the flashy movie business picked up steam, many Broadway producers

OPPOSITE: Helen Dowdy, Pearl Primus, and La Verne French in *Show Boat*, 1946. *Photofest*

BELOW: Fred Astaire reprised his Broadway role opposite Cyd Charisse in the 1953 film adaptation of *The Band Wagon*. © *Moviestore Collection Ltd., Alamy*

decided they needed more thoughtful, substantive, *Show Boat*-like musicals if they were going to continue to draw audiences. They could no longer rely on the second-rate musicians and librettists who, until then, had dominated musical theater. Instead, a new wave of talented artists became increasingly visible on Broadway: composer and lyricist Irving Berlin, composer and lyricist Cole Porter, and composer-lyricist teams Richard Rodgers and Lorenz Hart and George and Ira Gershwin. Books, too, achieved increasing coherence, ensuring that all of a show's elements worked together.

Albertina Rasch emerged as one of the most prominent musical theater choreographers during this fruitful Broadway era. A Viennese ballerina who had performed at the Hippodrome and studied with German modern dancer Mary Wigman, Rasch pulled from all aspects of her diverse background to craft a unique style. While everyone else was offering yet another kickline, she was creating witty ballets on pointe to ragtime music. Rasch's work for *The Band Wagon* (1931), starring Fred and Adele Astaire and ballet dancer Tilly Losch, earned high praise from *New York Times* dance critic John Martin, who gave Rasch much of the credit for "an appreciable increase in artistry and taste in the dancing of the musical comedies and revues."[8] In *Band Wagon*'s "The Beggar's Waltz," she created the sort of "dream ballet" that would later become a musical theater staple, with Astaire as a beggar fantasizing about performing with a glamorous ballerina, played by Losch. "Dancing in the Dark" featured Losch in a shimmering gold gown, which created a dazzling effect as she glided down a mirrored ramp on pointe.

George Balanchine first encountered musical theater while drifting around Europe after the death of Ballets Russes impresario Sergei Diaghilev in 1928. He choreographed several revues in London before decamping to America (see Chapter 5). His first real musical success, however, was the Rodgers and Hart production *On Your Toes* (1936). The show's plot followed backstage life at a ballet company—a subject of real interest to audiences thanks to the Ballets Russes' US tours. Balanchine's show-within-the-show, "Slaughter on Tenth Avenue," featured a Striptease Girl (ballerina Tamara Geva) and a Hoofer (vaudeville hero Ray Bolger) in an absurd comedy of intrigue. With the help of choreographer Herbie Harper, Balanchine mixed a potent cocktail of jazz, tap, ballet, and Bolger's rubbery "eccentric" dancing (which would become universally familiar three years later, when Bolger played the Scarecrow in the film *The Wizard of Oz*). "Slaughter on Tenth Avenue" so impressed audiences that Balanchine

later revived it as a standalone work for New York City Ballet. Several ballet companies still perform it today, a testament to its enduring appeal.

Balanchine made dances for several other Broadway shows, including *I Married An Angel* (1938)—starring his second wife, ballerina Vera Zorina—and the black musical *Cabin in the Sky* (1940), co-choreographed with Katherine Dunham (see Chapter 6). Some believed him to be wholly responsible for the success of the 1944 *Song of Norway*. The work's plot was so spare that Balanchine tacked a masterfully crafted ballet, also titled "Song of Norway," to its end, starring Ballet Russe de Monte Carlo luminaries Alexandra Danilova and Frederic Franklin, plus a troupe of other Ballet Russe dancers. "Balanchine's Broadway choreography does not falsify ballet as most musicals do on the grounds that adulteration is the first principle of showmanship," wrote critic Edwin Denby, apropos of *Song of Norway*. "Balanchine's numbers are simplified ballet,

but of the purest water."[9] After New York City Ballet solidified, however, Balanchine's attentions turned back to concert dance.

Setting the stage for Broadway's artistic explosion of the late 1940s and 1950s was *Pal Joey* (1940). The show owed its integrity not only to the infectious score of Rodgers and Hart, but also to its book, by John O'Hara. An enlargement of a series of stories O'Hara had contributed to the *New Yorker*, *Pal Joey* featured unrelentingly witty dialogue and exceptionally lifelike characters, whose likeability was even more remarkable given that they were all disreputable figures from the seedy world of Chicago show business. Choreographer Richard Alton, riffing on the show's shabby Chicago nightclub environment, created numbers that shrewdly satirized everything threadbare and passé in showbiz, especially gaudy showgirls.

In *Pal Joey*, everything rested on the shoulders of the title character, and luckily those shoulders

belonged to Broadway newcomer Gene Kelly. Displaying the buoyant charm that would later beguile movie audiences, Kelly sang, acted, and—especially—danced with an ease and bravado that made his should-be-despicable Joey a hero. While the production was a tad too cynical for its early audiences, later revivals would earn it the acclaim it deserved.

Most producers assumed *Oklahoma!*—a sweet, earnest adaptation of Lynn Riggs' down-home farmhouse play *Green Grow the Lilacs*—would be a flop. Even with a Rodgers and Hammerstein score behind it, the show seemed an unlikely success. One

fan described its problems as "No Girls, No Gags, No Chance."[10]

Yet audiences adored *Oklahoma!* (1943), which became the gold standard for musicals. The show's appeal hinged on its choreography by Agnes de Mille, who just a year earlier had demonstrated her mastery of the art of American dance storytelling in *Rodeo*. Like Rodgers' music and Hammerstein's lyrics, de Mille's choreography showed a constant commitment to the story, with every gesture a reflection of character. The extraordinary "dream ballet" that closed the second act, "Laurey Makes Up Her Mind," allowed dancing counterparts for the central

BELOW "The Farmer and the Cowman," *Oklahoma!*, 1943. *Photofest*

characters—Laurey, Curly, and the evil Jud—to express the roiling feelings beneath the relatively placid surface of their everyday lives. "The story is roughly about a girl's choice of partner for a picnic supper, not, one would think, an extraordinary crisis on which to base an entire evening," de Mille wrote. "The ballet, however, showed what was going on in [Laurey's] mind and heart, her terrors, her fears, her hopes; so in fact the happiness of her life, her life itself, depended on the choice."[11] (So effective was this mechanism that dream ballets, as dance critic Margaret Lloyd wrote, "afterwards became a public nuisance in the hands of copycats, 'til managers ran a mile from them.")[12]

In 1945 the same trio—Rodgers, Hammerstein, and de Mille—produced *Carousel*, a retelling of Ferenc Molnar's play *Liliom*. *Carousel* moved the story of a cocky carnival barker and his innocent love from Hungary to New England. The show's most significant dancing occurred in the second act, when Billy, its antihero, now dead, is given the chance to spend a day back on earth with his troubled, tomboyish daughter. In an extended dance sequence, he sees her being ostracized by her schoolmates, then watches as she becomes fascinated with a shabby visiting carnival troupe. Moving in a wavelike circular pattern, the carnival stagehands evoke carousel horses as the young woman begins dancing with one

of the group's young men. Their duet terminates in aggression and near rape; the girl is left weeping and alone. In that single well-edited sequence, de Mille told audiences all they needed to know—and feel—about the daughter's situation.

De Mille also choreographed *Brigadoon* (1947), the tale of a mysterious Scottish village that appears for just one day every one hundred years, with a book and lyrics by Alan Jay Lerner and music by Frederick Loewe. She melded Highland dance with ballet and expressive modern techniques, helping to create, as *New York Times* critic Brooks Atkinson wrote, "a plastic work of art that carries dialogue into dancing and dancing into music with none of the practical compromises of the Broadway stage.... [A] kind of idyllic rhythm flows through the whole pattern of the production."[13] Particularly impressive was the "Sword Dance" performed in celebration of a village wedding, a dynamic restyling of traditional Highland steps.

With this series of musicals, de Mille raised the standards of dancing on Broadway. Well-structured, fully integrated dances executed by concert-level performers became the norm. This was great news for most of New York's dancers, who could now count on steady, well-paid employment in musical theater. But the era of the Broadway hoofer, of the vaudeville baby, was over. Tappers disappeared from

ABOVE *Picture Post* magazine depicts the *Oklahoma!* dream sequence, 1947. *Raymond Kleboe/Getty Images*

Brigadoon, 1947. *Photofest*

musical theater stages until the 1970s, when, thanks to a resurgence of interest in the form, they returned in full force (see Chapter 3).

The late 1950s and 1960s, often called the Golden Age of the Broadway musical, gave rise to Jack Cole, a major choreographic force. A product of Denishawn, Cole also studied Indian *bharata nātyam* with master instructor Uday Shankar (musician Ravi's uncle). He went on to perform in a series of revues. For a while he had a fabulously unorthodox—and fabulously popular—nightclub act that fused modern dance with the exoticisms of East Indian and South American traditions, all set to swing music. Over time his style also brought together dances from Harlem, the Caribbean, and Latin America, a mixture so unlike anything else that it was immediately recognizable. Critic John Martin expressed his admiration in a review of the early Cole musical *Magdalena* (1948):

Cole fits into no easy category. He is not of the ballet, yet the technique he has established is probably the strictest and most spectacular anywhere to be found. . . . His art is strictly high-tension; it is nervous, gaunt, flagellant, yet with an opulent sensuous beauty that sets up a violent cross-current of conflict at its very source. The dancer . . . is a depersonalized being, an intense kinetic entity, rather than an individual. In this state of technical preparedness, which amounts almost to possession, he performs incredible movement.[14]

This was the beginning of modern jazz dance, which was entirely unrelated to the black jazz tradition (see Chapter 3). Sexy, aggressive, and tightly wound, Cole's jazz soon proved irresistible to audiences.

MODERN DANCE CHOREOGRAPHERS ON BROADWAY

The Ascot Gavotte scene in the film adaptation of *My Fair Lady*, 1964.
© *Warner Bros. Pictures, Photofest*

Beginning in the 1930s, several modern dance pioneers tried their hands at Broadway choreography. Doris Humphrey and Charles Weidman both choreographed theatrical shows to subsidize their concert dance work. Helen Tamiris created dances for eighteen shows between 1945 and 1957, most notably *Annie Get Your Gun* (1946), in which she grafted the Wild West's swaggering movement vernacular onto modern dance.

Hanya Holm took to the form especially well, gathering bits and pieces from diverse styles and unifying them through her own pure, energetic modern technique. For *Kiss Me, Kate* (1948), she incorporated soft shoe, folk dancing, jitterbugging, and ballet into delightfully spirited dances that added to the show's breezy, sardonic mood. Holm frequently used her ensemble dancers as actors, too, giving them dramatic personae that contributed to the overall development of the plot. In the racetrack "Ascot Gavotte" scene from *My Fair Lady* (1956), for example, the dancers' mincing movements artfully conveyed the mannered snobbishness of the British upper classes.

Kismet (1953) became Cole's first major Broadway success. Though set in a fictional Baghdad at the time of *The Arabian Nights*, its show-stopping "Not Since Nineveh" number featured the geometrical, filigreed look of Indian classical dance, set to brassy big-band music. The "Hindu swing" style wowed audiences and critics alike. Despite being less interesting choreographically, *A Funny Thing Happened on the Way to the Forum* (1962) and *Man of La Mancha* (1965) were also big hits for Cole.

While Cole admired the precision of ballet and frequently hired people with extensive ballet training, a Cole dancer had none of ballet's nose-in-the-air prissiness. His favorites—among them Carol Haney and, especially, Gwen Verdon, who was his assistant for a time—instead approached Cole's innovative choreography with ballet's strict attention to detail. Despite the enthralling crispness of the result, Cole never achieved unqualified success on Broadway. His dances, extraordinary as stand-alone showcases, lacked expressive potential.[15]

It was Jerome Robbins who would master the dramatic possibilities of the new jazz idiom. After the wild success of his *Fancy Free* (1944) for Ballet Theatre, Robbins and composer Leonard Bernstein decided to expand the ballet—which followed three sailors on leave—into a full musical. The result, *On the Town* (1944), was the product of close collaboration between composer and choreographer; its music and dance were essentially born together. Robbins' ballet experience informed his dances for the show, although for Broadway he expanded *Fancy Free*'s jazzier elements, creating fresh, funny, ebullient choreography.

More Robbins Broadway hits followed in quick succession: *Billion Dollar Baby* (1945), *High Button Shoes* (1947), and *Look, Ma, I'm Dancin'* (1948). Robbins earned special praise for *The King and I* (1951), set in Siam (present-day Thailand), in which he retold the story of Harriet Beecher Stowe's *Uncle Tom's Cabin*, using Siamese dance vocabulary. Over time, as his reputation grew, he earned authority over more and more aspects of his projects. By 1957 Robbins had the freedom to shape his most ambitious project yet—*West Side Story*—from start to finish, according to his singular vision.

West Side Story took nearly ten years to come to fruition. Around 1949, actor Montgomery Clift asked Robbins, his friend, for advice on how to

A Funny Thing Happened on the Way to the Forum, with Zero Mostel, far right, 1962. *John Dominis/Time and Life Pictures, Getty Images*

ABOVE: *West Side Story*, 1957.
Fred Fehl/Museum of the City of New York, Getty Images

RIGHT: The Dance at the Gym scene from *West Side Story*.
Hank Walker/Time and Life Pictures, Getty Images

play a modern Romeo in *Romeo and Juliet*. Struck by the idea of Shakespeare's star-crossed lovers in a contemporary setting, Robbins began formulating a musical. Initially he envisioned his Montagues and Capulets as the rival Italian and Irish gangs on Manhattan's Lower East Side—*East Side Story*. During the creative process, however, tensions began to heat up on the city's West Side, home to increasing numbers of Puerto Rican immigrants. Bernstein, the musical's composer, and book writer Arthur Laurents convinced Robbins to reimagine his plot.

Determined to create something authentic, Robbins traveled to street festivals and dance halls in Spanish Harlem and Brooklyn, where he observed the outsized personalities of young gang members. His choreography captured their predatory restlessness in a sharp, splayed-out jazz style, with every motion carefully calibrated to drive home the tragedy of the story. Bernstein wrote an uncomplicated score for the ensemble, leaving Robbins free to cast thirty-nine highly trained dancers who could bring his vision to vibrant life. During rehearsals, he used the principles of method acting, discouraging the actors who made up the rival Shark and Jet gangs from socializing with each other. (Eventually, the actress playing misfit tomboy Anybodys found herself walking home alone.)[16]

The resulting show simmered and spat, reaching a full rolling boil during Act One's dance at the gym, when the Sharks and Jets squared off in a blazing mambo. Gone were the dream ballets of the past. In Robbins' new onstage world, jazz dancing was the best way—the only way—to get at a dark, angry reality.

Though the first reviews of *West Side Story* admired the dancing, they weren't raves. *West Side* wouldn't take firm hold of the popular consciousness until the release of the film version in 1961.

Two years later Robbins had another hit with *Gypsy* (1959, with music by Jule Styne and lyrics by Stephen Sondheim). For the story of a 1920s stage mother's pathologically determined efforts to turn her daughters into stars, Robbins created dances inspired by the worlds of vaudeville and burlesque.

Fiddler on the Roof (1964), based on Sholem Aleichem's stories about a Russian Jewish village where traditional values are slowly eroding, was especially dear to Robbins—his parents were Russian Jewish immigrants. He incorporated traditional Jewish dancing into the choreography, visiting a Hasidic community in New York as part of his research. "[What] I contributed to [*Fiddler*]," Robbins said, "was to bring it into a place where I

felt . . . the deepest rituals of a people were enlarged to a ritual stage . . . that noble thing of a race holding itself together in the face of adversity and holding on to its roots."[17]

Following the success of *Fiddler*, Robbins left Broadway for twenty-five years and devoted himself instead to New York City Ballet (see Chapter 5). In the mid-1980s he began to feel anxious about his Broadway legacy, worrying that some of his works might be lost. What began as a preservation project ultimately turned into *Jerome Robbins' Broadway* (1989), a revue of his most remarkable dance numbers. In typical Robbins fashion, the show was expertly produced and tightly edited, offering a pristine look at his career's highest highs. "While 'Jerome Robbins' Broadway' may celebrate a vanished musical theater," wrote critic Frank Rich in the *New York Times*, "it does so with such youthful exuberance that nostalgia finally gives way to a giddy, perhaps not even foolish, dream that a new generation of Broadway babies may yet be born."[18]

Like Robbins, Michael Kidd also started out at American Ballet Theatre—where he performed in *Fancy Free*—and later found a home on Broadway. Kidd's hybrid of jazz dancing and athletic gymnastics introduced a new kind of male dancer to musical theater, one modeled in Kidd's own image, who could throw off a complex dance phrase and finish with a back handspring. A talented mimic, Kidd had an especially good eye for local idiosyncrasies. In *Guys and Dolls* (1951), he captured the cocksure swagger of Damon Runyon's wise guys in flashy jazz routines portraying crapshoots and horse races. Kidd's straightforward approach to choreography made his work broadly appealing. "Dancing should be completely understandable," he said. "Every move, every turn should mean something, should be crystal-clear to the audience."[19]

Bob Fosse, unlike most Golden Age Broadway choreographers, didn't come out of either ballet or modern dance. He was straight vaudeville. Fosse began performing in Chicago-area burlesque shows as a scrawny thirteen-year-old, an early entrance into a seedy world where he was frequently harassed by the older women dancers. That world never really left him; it seemed to seep into his bones. For the rest of his career, wrote dance historian Cecil Smith, "the spirit and marrow of Fosse's theatrics were the bump and grind."[20] Never an ideal dancer, Fosse nevertheless became a magnetic performer, adapting choreography to fit his own unusual body—turned-in, slouchy, bent-kneed. The hat he used to cover his growing bald patch eventually became

ABOVE: Michael Kidd and dancers rehearse *Guys and Dolls*, 1950. *Gjon Mili/Time and Life Pictures, Getty Images*

RIGHT: Bob Fosse, 1980. *Jack Vartoogian, Getty Images*

an inseparable part of him, like the cigarette that dripped perpetually from his lips.

During World War II Fosse served in naval entertainment units in the Pacific, before earning a contract with MGM and suffering through a disappointingly brief career in Hollywood. His first Broadway break came when co-director Jerome Robbins hired him to choreograph *The Pajama Game* (1954), an unlikely musical about labor troubles at a pajama factory. Fosse pulled out all the stops for "Steam Heat," a dance number theoretically meant to be a morale booster for the union strikers. Because "Steam Heat" was a nonintegrated routine, essentially irrelevant to the plot, Fosse didn't have to develop characters or move the narrative along; he was free to use all his old vaudeville-style hat tricks and pelvic thrusts. He turned his trio of dancers—led by the witty Carol Haney—into three Fosses, imbuing them with his unique style. "Accenting

steps with a slouch or a soft wrist," wrote Fosse biographer Sam Wasson, "[they] showed a tantalizing synchronicity of hot and cool, like slow-curling steam."[21] Though "Steam Heat" got a standing ovation at nearly every preview performance, it was almost cut—co-director George Abbott thought it extraneous to the show. Robbins, however, fought for the routine, and his effort moved Fosse.

In 1955 Fosse had his next success with *Damn Yankees*, a retelling of the Faust story. The musical paired him for the first time with Jack Cole dancer Gwen Verdon. In Verdon, Fosse found the perfect vessel for his crystallizing style; it fit naturally on her jazz-baby body. As siren Lola, Verdon added snap to Fosse's serpentine choreography. She would later become his wife and longtime muse, the keeper of his repertory.

Fosse soon began directing as well as choreographing musicals, allowing him to stamp entire

Jim Hutchison, Carol Haney, and Peter Gennaro perform "Steam Heat" in *The Pajama Game* on Broadway. *Photofest*

productions with his distinctive aesthetic. He found inspiration in cynical, unsentimental stories. Both *Sweet Charity* (1966) and *Chicago* (1974) centered on lightweight, sketched-out characters, but their damaged souls spoke most clearly through Fosse's fractured jazz movement. His line of beat-down prostitutes hanging languorously off a bar, in *Sweet Charity*'s chilling "Big Spender" routine, became an iconic theatrical image. (To get a grasp on each hooker's personality, Fosse hung out at the dime-a-dance halls in Times Square and talked to the girls.) "When you're dancing in one of Bob's shows, you're always dancing a paradox," said longtime Fosse dancer Ann Reinking. "In 'Big Spender,' you really want to get that guy to come to you, so from the waist up you're glamorous, you're wonderful. But from the waist down, you're tired and your legs are busted and your feet are hurt. 'Please God let me go home and get to sleep' and 'But I have to get the money' at once."[22]

During an era of sexual liberation, Fosse's sensual, exhibitionist style seemed to embody everything current. It spoke to an even larger number of people through his groundbreaking work as a film director, particularly in *Cabaret* and the autobiographical *All That Jazz*. Fosse's style also presaged

the choreographic trends that would shape the music video industry in the 1980s and 1990s (see Chapter 10). Michael Jackson, a huge Fosse fan—his signature white-socks-black-shoes combination was a Fosse signature first—actually asked Fosse to choreograph his "Thriller" video, though Fosse ultimately declined the offer. Fosse died in 1987. More than twenty years later, *Fosse*, a revue featuring his most memorable dance numbers, played to sold-out Broadway houses for 1,093 performances.

Gower Champion, another innovative choreographer-director of the 1960s and 1970s, was essentially the anti-Fosse. A former Broadway and film dancer (who frequently performed with his wife, Marge), Champion had a sunnier outlook on the entertainment world. The spit-polished production number—featuring large numbers of dancers in ever-unfolding, deftly organized patterns—became his trademark. Perhaps the best-known of these kaleidoscopic pageants was "The Waiters' Gallop," from *Hello, Dolly!* (1964). A multitude of tuxedoed waiters, thrilled by the news that their beloved former patron Dolly Levi was returning, executed a precision-timed culinary extravaganza. While running from the kitchen to the dining room and back again, they managed to balance

"The Waiters' Gallop," *Hello! Dolly*, 1964. *Photofest*

huge trays of food and set and clear tables instantly, all at a breakneck pace.

Champion's acclaimed final musical, *42nd Street*, opened the day he died, August 25, 1980. Based on the 1933 backstage movie of the same name, which followed an unknown's rise to stardom, *42nd Street* spiffed up 1930s tap routines with extraordinarily expert 1980s tap dancers. Its most memorable moment was its first. A rehearsal piano began playing the title song; soon it was accompanied by the percussive tattoo of tapping feet. Those feet were revealed slowly by a rising curtain, which paused on them before ascending further—eventually exposing forty dancers in ardent competition at a 1930s Broadway musical audition.

The most affecting backstage musical of the period, however, was *A Chorus Line* (1975), directed and choreographed by Michael Bennett. Bennett, who started out as a chorus dancer—he performed in the European company of *West Side Story*—choreographed skillfully, if not imaginatively. Rather than create a specific vocabulary, Bennett took a step back, focusing instead on the lighting, music, and personalities that would bring his dances to life. *A Chorus Line* explored the lives of seventeen dancers auditioning for a Broadway chorus, and it benefited from a deeply personal script. In a series of workshops, Bennett asked his dancers to tell him their stories, recording their responses and shaping the musical around the resulting transcripts. He wanted the dancers to play themselves, essentially. The bitingly honest but still warm-hearted outcome radiated authenticity. Bennett's concept "is bright—indeed, it glows like a beacon heavenward," wrote critic Clive Barnes.

> Like most great ideas it is simple. It is nothing but the anatomy of a chorus line. And the gypsies themselves—those dear, tough, soft-bitten Broadway show dancers, who are the salt and the earth of the small white way—are all neatly dissected. . . . Honesty is the policy of Mr. Bennett's show, and from opening to the stupendous closing chorus, it is, stamped indelibly, as Mr. Bennett's show. His choreography and direction burn up superlatives as if they were inflammable. In no way could it have been better done.[23]

A Chorus Line ran for an unprecedented 6,137 performances. Bennett had recreated the Broadway gypsy as a star. Thanks to an innovative arrangement that fundamentally made his dancers business partners in his ventures, he also made many of his own gypsies very wealthy indeed.

ABOVE: *A Chorus Line*, 2013 London Palladium production. © *Geraint Lewis, Alamy*
LEFT: "We're in the Money," *42nd Street*, 1980. *Photofest*

Bennett didn't live to see *A Chorus Line*'s closing date in 1990. He passed away from complications of AIDS in 1987. The end of *A Chorus Line*'s run signaled a shift in Broadway theater. The concept musical, with its integrated collage of book, music, lyrics, and dance, was on its way out. Ticket prices had been climbing steadily—from $15 in 1975, when *Chorus Line* opened, to $60 for *Jerome Robbins' Broadway* in 1989—and producers felt increasing pressure to justify that kind of expenditure with lavish shows. Grand spectacles, emphasizing the visual over the thoughtful, were on the rise.

A series of musicals originating in London's West End fit that bill exactly, and the 1980s and 1990s saw a veritable British invasion. Some of the new shows, particularly *Cats*, were choreographed from beginning to end. Others, including *The Phantom of the Opera* and *Evita*, barely had any dance at all. All relied on luxe stagecraft to make an impression, counting on grand sets to atone for amateurish book- and lyric-writing. Despite the critical scorn that vehicles like *Phantom* earned, however, in a way they revived Broadway. They were popular; they got people in seats.

Some of the later British works were also genuinely affecting. Based on the 2000 movie of the same name, *Billy Elliot*, which came to Broadway in 2008 after premiering on the West End, featured inspired choreography by Peter Darling. Dancing ingeniously knit the show's scenes together. *Billy Elliot* also presented a remarkable opportunity for three young dancers—initially, Trent Kowalik, Kiril Kulish, and David Alvarez—to share the choreographically demanding title role. (The boys won a special joint Tony Award for their performances.)

Americans, and American choreographers, reclaimed Broadway in the 2000s. Director/choreographer Susan Stroman's *Contact* (2000) proved that audiences would buy tickets for a pure-dance musical. Officially a "dance play," *Contact* had no dialogue and no plot through line. Instead, it presented three vignettes, which collaged pre-recorded music ranging from Tchaikovsky to the swing band Squirrel Nut Zippers. The first section, "Swinging," was an improvisatory musing on Jean-Honoré Fragonard's circa 1767 painting *The Swing*; much of the action occurred on a large swing. The second, "Did You Move?," followed a New York Italian gangster's wife as she fantasized about escaping her empty marriage. The work closed with "Contact," in which a lonely advertising executive became enchanted with a beautiful woman in a yellow dress—a spectacular dance role for performer Deborah Yates.

In 2002 the tidal wave that is Twyla Tharp hit Broadway. Already a mainstream success in the ballet and modern dance worlds, Tharp staked her claim to the Great White Way with *Movin' Out*, a rock musical set to songs by Billy Joel. In weaving Joel's Top 40 hits into a story that followed five friends through high school, the Vietnam War, and the war's aftermath, *Movin' Out*, like *Contact*, eliminated dialogue. Dance did the storytelling. And

Kiril Kulish in *Billy Elliot*, 2008.
David Scheinmann/Associated Press

Movin' Out, 2006 London
production. © *Lebrecht Music and
Arts Photo Library, Alamy*

Tharp's extraordinary dancers, nearly all poached from professional ballet companies, were more than up to the task. None allowed Joel's all-too-familiar oeuvre to drive the work into a series of clichés. As critic Ben Brantley wrote, "Each principal performer seems to have his or her own special dialogue with the songs; the dances become shaded personality sketches, expressing individual reactions to mass-marketed music."[24]

Tharp stumbled with the poorly received Bob Dylan tribute *The Times They Are A-Changin'* (2006), but returned to form with *Come Fly Away* (2010), another jukebox musical, this time highlighting the work of Frank Sinatra. She had been choreographing to Sinatra since the 1970s, and, though slightly overwrought, *Come Fly Away* evinced her deep connection to his work. It also revisited a few of her earlier duets from the ballet *Nine Sinatra Songs* (1982).

Recent talented musical theater choreographers have integrated much of Broadway's history into their well-polished works, nodding to the greats even as they develop their own voices. High-wattage energy drives their dances; weak spots are often camouflaged by sheer enthusiasm. Andy Blankenbuehler's choreography for *In the Heights* (2008), a musical set in New York's gritty Washington Heights neighborhood, incorporated the sizzle of salsa and the daredevil spirit of urban dance, all performed at top volume. Sergio Trujillo's dances for *Memphis* (2009) adroitly channeled the wop-bop-a-lu-bop buoyancy of the early days of rock and roll. And in *Newsies* (2012), based on the cult-favorite Disney movie, choreographer Christopher Gatelli made near-corny earnestness a virtue, creating vigorous, unironic dance numbers for the show's chorus of paper-peddling man-boys. Their acrobatic excesses proved irresistible.

Dance on Film

The history of dance on film is tied directly to the history of musical theater. For many years, film musicals were surefire box office hits, and the film and theater worlds shared directors, choreographers, and stars. But translating dance from stage to screen posed unique challenges. On film, "there is a loss of three-dimensional perception so closely linked to presence," wrote Agnes de Mille. "The camera can focus on a detail or a grand pattern, but not on both simultaneously."[25]

And so the art of choreographing for the camera began to emerge. The first director to confront these problems head-on was Busby Berkeley, who, though he had no formal dance training, became the most famous dance director in Hollywood during the 1930s. Rather than use multiple cameras to record the action from different angles, then cut the various shots together later, Berkeley used only one camera, which he moved along his lines of dancers to catch intriguing, unusual perspectives. The "dancing camera," in effect, became the star. Some of Berkeley's most successful efforts featured not a solo performer but rather large groups of anonymous dancers. The camera effects took center stage—as in the 1933 film *42nd Street*, with its prismatic groups of chorus girls.

Fred Astaire's dance films—particularly those in which he squired the glamorous Ginger Rogers—delighted audiences in the 1930s and 1940s (see Chapter 3). Astaire disagreed with Berkeley's dancing camera philosophy; he believed that either he should dance or the camera should.[26] Astaire was given a good deal of control over the way his performances were filmed. He chose to frame his dances tightly and photographed them without interruption, allowing audiences to see every detail of the choreography. These unadulterated depictions of Astaire's astonishing virtuosity made him one of the film world's biggest stars. Over the course of thirty-five years, Astaire performed in thirty-one movie musicals, in addition to dancing in television specials and taking the occasional role on Broadway.

In 1941 MGM signed Gene Kelly, fresh off his success in Broadway's *Pal Joey*. Kelly eventually became the studio's star choreographer and director, as well as its go-to dancer. He enjoyed creating dances tailored to the camera, works preoccupied not with the limitations of film but with its possibilities. Kelly frequently incorporated effects that were only possible onscreen. In *Cover Girl* (1944), for example, he used a double exposure to make it seem as though he were dancing a duet with himself. After the wild popularity of the British film *The Red Shoes* (1948) proved that audiences enjoyed seeing ballet on film, Kelly crafted a groundbreaking ballet number for the conclusion of *An American in Paris* (1951), with the young French ballerina Leslie Caron as his co-star. The spectacular seventeen-minute dream ballet—actually a robust mixture of ballet, jitterbugging, hoofing, and tap—took six months to rehearse and another month to film, and cost half a million dollars, a staggering sum in 1951. This kind of showstopping production number was to become a Kelly trademark. He created some of his best for *Singin' in the Rain* (1952): the title song, with Kelly splashing gleefully in puddles and wielding his umbrella like a cane; Donald O'Connor's brilliant vaudevillian antics in "Make 'Em Laugh"; and the fanciful "Broadway Melody Ballet," with the elegant, beautifully trained Cyd Charisse as a sultry siren whose legs deserved their own credits.

Choreographer Jack Cole also came to Hollywood, where he signed with Columbia Pictures in the 1940s. His more than thirty films included *Gilda* (1946), the adaptation of Broadway's *Kismet* (1955), and *Gentlemen Prefer Blondes*. The studio especially appreciated Cole's ability to bring the best out of stars like Rita Hayworth and Marilyn Monroe, and to craft numbers that showcased their varying performance abilities. "Diamonds Are a Girl's Best Friend" from *Gentlemen Prefer Blondes*, for instance, made the most of Monroe's lush

OPPOSITE: *Footlight Parade*, directed by Busby Berkeley, 1933. *Getty Images*

BELOW: Marilyn Monroe in *Gentlemen Prefer Blondes*, 1953. © 20th Century Fox, AF Archive, Alamy

sensuality. While at Columbia, Cole also set up a special training program for his dancers, who took classes in East Indian and Spanish dance as well as ballet, tap, and jazz.

The 1950s and early 1960s saw a flush of movie adaptations of stage musicals that frequently involved the original Broadway choreographers—with mixed success. For the film version of *Oklahoma!* (1955), Agnes de Mille brought her dream ballet to the screen essentially unchanged, but its misty magic didn't translate. The same could be said of Michael Kidd's adaptation of his *Guys and Dolls* dances for the 1955 movie starring Sinatra and Marlon Brando. The choreography Kidd designed expressly for the screen, in *The Band Wagon* (1953) and, in particular, *Seven Brides for Seven Brothers* (1954), fared much better.

As co-director of the movie version of *West Side Story* (1961), Jerome Robbins had more control than any other film choreographer, and he was able to effectively tailor his rough-and-tumble choreography to the medium. After the film exceeded its budget, however, Robbins was let go from the creative team. Though he claimed to be pleased with the finished product, he did not supervise the movie's final stages.

By the late 1950s, the movie musical was in decline. The decade marked "the great and crippling confrontation between the cinema and television," wrote dance historian John Kobal:

> The gogglebox could be said to have won. It weaned audiences from their movie-going habit. . . . Genres that failed to draw in proportion to their costs were abandoned, and the expensive musical was hit harder than most. TV, with its endless variety shows, though incapable of the breadth and size of the movie musical, began to drain the interest in [it].[27]

The exceptions to this rule were the movies of Bob Fosse. Fosse understood that in order to reinvigorate the movie musical, he had to completely reimagine it. His film adaptation of *Sweet Charity* (1969), which he directed as well as choreographed, hummed thanks to its artful, aggressive cutting. The story followed broken characters, and the camerawork echoed their brokenness by collaging hundreds of quick cuts, creating an overwhelming series of sensations that were powerful even as they approached incoherence. "I think that for my whole life I've been a frustrated painter," Fosse said. "The camera gives me a chance to finally do some 'painting.'"[28] Fosse continued to explore this kind of keenly claustrophobic filmmaking in *Cabaret* (1972), starring Liza Minnelli. Though he had not choreographed the original Broadway production, Fosse found that his insinuative jazz style fit the story perfectly, creating ironic commentary on the decadent Weimar Germany setting. Seven years later, in the autobiographical movie *All That Jazz*, Fosse used his filming philosophies to lay bare his own tortured, guilt-ridden soul.

Saturday Night Fever (1977) marked the closest Hollywood came, in the wake of the demise of the movie musical, to finding its own dance idiom.[29] John Travolta's disco gyrations, at once extroverted

Singin' in the Rain, 1952. © Metro-Goldwyn-Mayer, AF Archive, Alamy

and intimate, seemed designed for film; each dance felt like an extended flirtation with the camera. Like Fosse's bump-and-grind, *Saturday Night Fever*'s choreography augured the style that would reach new heights in music videos (see Chapter 10).

In 1977 *The Turning Point*, a pseudo-realistic depiction of life in the ballet world, was released. Written by playwright Arthur Laurents and directed by Herbert Ross with the help of his wife, former American Ballet Theatre dancer Nora Kaye, the film arrived right at the crest of the ballet wave, when the furor over Mikhail Baryshnikov was at its peak. While the movie's plot occasionally veered toward melodrama, its use of real dancers—including Baryshnikov, young talent Leslie Browne, and former Ballets Russes star Alexandra

Danilova—added depth and authenticity. Even better, it included large sections of compelling dance footage. In one remarkable scene, the dance studio reality (Browne rehearsing *Romeo and Juliet* with another dancer) blended seamlessly with both a fantasy world (Browne rehearsing with Baryshnikov) and the offstage reality (Browne and Baryshnikov, in bed together).

Several 1980s movies used dance as a primary mode of communication. In some ways *Flashdance* (1983), the story of a blue-collar welder who hopes to become a professional dancer, was a contemporary translation of *The Red Shoes*. "Why do you want to live?" said *Red Shoes* heroine Victoria Page, when asked why she danced; "When you give up your dream, you die," echoed *Flashdance*'s Nick Hurley.

ABOVE: The "Rich Man's Frug" in Bob Fosse's *Sweet Charity*. *Universal, Photofest*

OPPOSITE: Mikhail Baryshnikov in *The Turning Point*, 1977. © *20th Century Fox, Photos 12, Alamy*

Flashdance caused something of a scandal when it was revealed that several of its dance sequences were performed not by star Jennifer Beals but by two uncredited body doubles—one of them a man, Richie "Crazy Legs" Colón of the Rock Steady Crew (see Chapter 10).

Dirty Dancing (1987) required no body doubles. As Johnny Castle, a working-class ballroom instructor hired to teach affluent vacationers at a Catskills resort, Patrick Swayze made full use of his considerable ballet training. (Swayze actually had a short professional dance career with Eliot Feld's Feld Ballet.) He seemed to jump off the screen, especially in scenes with talented dancer Cynthia Rhodes, who played his dancing partner Penny. Jennifer Grey—daughter of original *Cabaret* emcee Joel Grey—also studied dance and was able to hold her own as Swayze's upper-crust love interest.

In 2000 the ballet world got a cult hit to rival *The Turning Point. Center Stage* followed a young dancer's trials and tribulations as a student at the fictional American Ballet Academy. Though not of *Turning Point*'s artistic caliber, *Center Stage*, like its predecessor, filled its primary cast with real dancers. Most were from American Ballet Theatre, with extras recruited from both ABT and New York City Ballet. Young dance student Amanda Schull (who would go on to perform with San Francisco Ballet) won the lead role; up-and-coming ABT dancer Sascha Radetsky played her love interest; ABT stars Ethan Stiefel and Julie Kent appeared as senior dancers, who performed excerpts from Kenneth MacMillan's *Romeo and Juliet* and Balanchine's *Stars and Stripes*. The climactic student showcase performance included choreography by Christopher Wheeldon and a fantastical ballet-meets-Broadway extravaganza created by Susan Stroman.

Robert Altman, known for his naturalistic films, approached the ballet world from a different angle in the 2003 film *The Company*. Composed of stories told by the dancers and choreographers of Joffrey Ballet—many of whom played themselves—the film also starred Hollywood's Neve Campbell, herself a former ballet dancer. For dance fans, the most compelling parts of the movie were its numerous excerpts from the Joffrey repertory, including pieces from Alwin Nikolais's *Tensile Involvement*, Gerald Arpino's *Trinity*, Moses Pendleton's *White Widow*, and Lar Lubovitch's *My Funny Valentine*.

Few movies have been as effective at imprinting ballet on the popular consciousness as *Black Swan* (2010), a warped psychodrama that followed a troubled ballet dancer's quest to find her darker side. Its fractured universe delighted film critics but angered many ballet fans, who disliked the film's exaggeration of the suffering-ballerina stereotype. Natalie Portman (who later married Benjamin Millepied, the film's choreographer) gave an impressive performance as the lead, earning an Academy Award. But more drama swirled when it was revealed that Portman had an uncredited body double, ABT soloist Sarah Lane.

Patrick Swayze and Jennifer Grey in *Dirty Dancing*, 1987. *© Great American Films Limited Partnerships, Vestron Pictures, Moviestore Collection Ltd., Alamy*

Ethan Stiefel, Amanda Schull, and Sascha Radetsky in *Center Stage*, 2000. © *Columbia Pictures, AF Archive, Alamy*

Beginning in 2006, the *Step Up* series gave the hip hop and commercial dance worlds the *Center Stage* treatment. Though all five of *Step Up*'s installments suffered from dubious premises and stilted scripts, they were nevertheless powerful vehicles for some of the Los Angeles dance scene's most exciting talents. The original *Step Up* introduced Channing Tatum, now a mainstream darling, and highlighted his considerable dance ability, honed during his years as a stripper. (Fans would see more of that talent in 2012's *Magic Mike*.) The series' third installment, *Step Up 3D*, was directed by innovative dance filmographer Jon M. Chu and featured a particularly dynamic combination of world-class hip hop dancers and stunning three-dimensional visuals.

Chapter Ten

Urban and Commercial Dance

B-boys in Brooklyn, 1984. *Michael Ochs Archives, Getty Images*

"Hip hop is a colorful culture. It's vibrant. It's a culture that just has to be larger than life. When you look at the graffiti characters and you see the way they're exaggerated, you know, *we* have to be exaggerated as b-boys. . . . We have to be blasting out off the page. Off the circle. Off the crowd. Off the blacktop. Off the wall. That's what it's about." —*B-boy Ken Swift*[1]

One day in the early 1980s, a group of teenagers from 175th Street in the Bronx was arrested for fighting in the subway. Only, they claimed, they weren't fighting. They were dancing. Hauled to the precinct office anyway, the dancers, members of the High Times crew, started demonstrating their moves for the cops: head spins, chin freezes, "the Helicopter," "the Baby." Unconvinced, an officer called them forward one at a time and quizzed them, asking for a chin freeze or a head spin on command. "As each kid complied, performing on cue as unhesitatingly as a ballet dancer might toss off an enchainement," the *Village Voice*'s Sally Banes wrote in one of the first stories about street dance, "the cops scratched their heads in bewildered defeat."[2]

Parts of that story, Banes noted, are probably apocryphal. Much of the early history of urban dance, like the history of hip hop music, "is a riddle wrapped inside an enigma stuffed inside a mystery hidden in a sock," wrote hip hop scholar Johan Kugelberg. "The more you read, the more people you talk to, the more likely you are to run into contradictions."[3] However hazy its origins, there's no denying its effects: Street dance has had an enormous impact on American culture.

As they gradually earned greater visibility, urban styles like breaking and funk boogaloo made their way from city street corners to television commercials and films. Some of the form's pioneers expressed unhappiness with street dance's journey into the mainstream. Many of its original qualities, they felt, were watered down or distorted to increase its appeal to suburban audiences. But in other ways, hip hop dance's relationship to the commercial world felt natural. It was, after all, invented by a generation raised on television, movies, and video games. Some of its steps were stylized pop culture references, and, like popular dance and music, hip hop dance was frequently presented in short, bite-sized chunks. "The very success of the form and of some of the dancers," Banes wrote, "seems an American dream-come-true that could only have been concocted in Hollywood."[4] Eventually commercial culture, absorbing hip hop and melding it with other forms, generated a rich dance genre of its own. Its widespread appeal created a larger, more diverse audience for American dance.

In the mid-1960s, as popular dances like the twist were sweeping the country (see Chapter 2), one craze in particular caught the attention of young dancers in California. The boogaloo, which heated up with the release of the instrumental song "James Brown's Boogaloo" in 1966, started out as a simple dance—a side-to-side step that involved rolling the hips, knees, and head, emphasizing the smooth, sensual rhythm of Brown's soul music.

A few years later came the advent of funk, with its faster, more insistent pulse. Brown, again, was at the lead: James Brown and the Famous Flames' song "Cold Sweat" (1967) crystallized the genre. A group of black teens in the San Francisco Bay Area, inspired by the distinctive groove of "Cold Sweat" and the sound of the other new funk songs, began reimagining the old soul boogaloo dance.

The result, funk boogaloo, looked and felt harder than its predecessor—all edges and stomping. (Its evolution also marked a reversal of the usual trend: Rather than a street dance working its way up to mainstream status, a mainstream craze inspired a street phenomenon.) Dancers found the style to be good clay, moldable and adaptable, and they began incorporating new steps that further transformed it. To accent particular beats, they developed the freeze, a sudden suspension of movement; "locking it down" meant freezing so hard that you jiggled.

In the late 1960s, Pete Terrace (aka Pedro Gutierrez) recorded his album *King of the Boogaloo* in New York. From the album cover: "In the late winter of 1966 a new dance explosion hit Spanish Harlem, New York— *the Boogaloo.*"

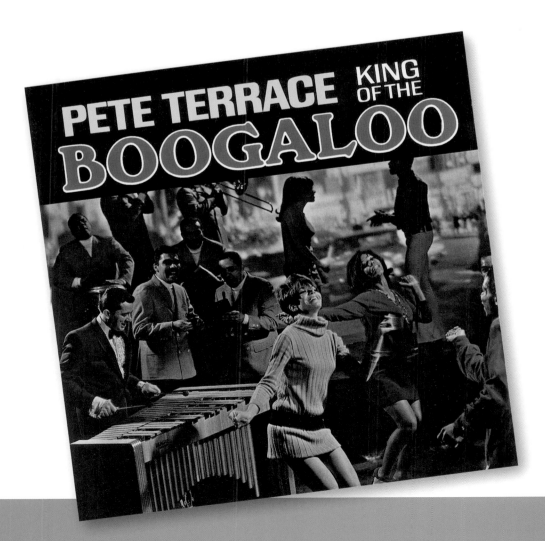

Old sci-fi movies were experiencing a revival in California's street culture at the time, and these inspired moves of their own—most notably the slide, which came directly from the Boris Karloff *Frankenstein* movies, and involved sliding smoothly forward and backward while maintaining a pseudo-robotic Frankenstein pose. Funk boogaloo dancers also looked to musical artists for ideas. The Temptations, choreographed by legendary tapper Charles "Cholly" Atkins (see Chapter 3), popularized a "stepping" style of clean, posed stops, spins, and slides. After seeing them on television, Bay Area funk boogaloo dancers added that, too, to their mix.[5]

Funk boogaloo simmered underground for several years. In 1977, the dance group Black Messengers—restyled for television as the Mechanical Device—introduced it to a larger audience when they appeared on *The Gong Show*, a send-up of amateur talent competitions. Their performance, in a style they called "Posing Hard Robotic Funk Boogaloo," was judged by the likes of J. P. Morgan and Phyllis Diller. It earned the top score of the episode.

Around the same time, in South Central Los Angeles, Don Campbell discovered dance while a commercial arts student at Los Angeles Trade Technical College. During dances in the school cafeteria, he attempted to mimic the popular styles his friends were doing—the funky chicken, the breakdown—and in the process he developed a style of his own. "I wanted to dance like [my friends], but I wasn't very good," Campbell remembered. "I used to freeze up or stop in the middle of [a] move. . . . They would laugh at me, but I would keep trying anyhow."[6] The stutter-start look, which Campbell refined and polished over time, became known as the "Campbellock," or just "locking." Locking on the beat produced a kind of visual percussion—with the body accentuating as well as illustrating a song's rhythm—that both audiences and dancers felt viscerally.

As he became more involved in L.A.'s dance scene, Campbell met Charles Washington, a.k.a. "Robot Charles." Washington had developed a style of bodily isolation that made him look mechanical, with abrupt "dimestops" giving the impression of motors starting and stopping—the robot. (He'd learned the rudiments of the technique from a young street mime, Robert Shields, who in turn had created a personal interpretation of an old 1930s "mannequin" pantomime.) Eventually Don Cornelius invited both Campbell and Washington to perform on his television show *Soul Train* (see Chapter 2), where they introduced locking and the robot to a national audience. Later Campbell formed his own group, initially called the Campbellock Dancers and later just The Lockers, which featured both lockers and robot-style dancers. The Lockers appeared regularly on *Soul Train*, and they also performed on mainstream white shows like *Saturday Night Live* and *The Tonight Show*, inspiring kids all over the country to take up their distinctive style.

The Electronic Boogaloo Lockers, eventually known simply as Electric Boogaloo, came out of Fresno, California, in the later 1970s. A second-generation group, they learned most of their locking- and funk boogaloo-based moves by watching groups like The Lockers on television. But they also invented several techniques of their own, including popping, which involved quickly contracting and releasing the muscles in one area of the body to create a sharp, percussive jerk, known as a "pop" or a "hit." Some of the group's members could do gymnastic flips, which they layered on top of their dances for greater effect. Electric Boogaloo appeared twice on *Soul Train* in 1979 before breaking up later that year.

From the 1970s gay club scene in Los Angeles emerged a style of urban dance with a different feel. Posing—later known as voguing—developed at the Paradise Ballroom, one of the city's first gay discos. Posing involved elements of locking, but added filigreed gestures of the arms and hands as they moved decoratively around the head. The dance was accented by freezes in vampy poses—often visual quotations from *Vogue* magazine or photos of old-Hollywood movie stars like Greta Garbo and Marilyn Monroe. Posing's deliberate camp lent street dance a theatrical flair.

A voguer in 1989. *Mario Ruiz/Time and Life Pictures, Getty Images*

ABOVE: House of Ninja dancers perform, 2008. *Astrid Stawiarz/Getty Images*

Punking evolved from posing and incorporated large, sweeping arm movements between freezes. Elements of Latin dances, like the cha-cha and mambo, gave posing a more expansive feel. Eventually straight black dancers began punking, and the dance took on a more masculine edge. Some added martial arts elements and even the knock-'em-dead tricks of old "flash" tap groups like the Nicholas Brothers (see Chapter 3). The result became known as "whacking" or "waacking."

About a decade later, the posing/punking style experienced a renaissance in Harlem's gay community. New York voguing, as it developed in the 1980s, incorporated the basic arm movements and freezes of the older forms, but placed a new emphasis on symmetry, precision, and graceful fluidity. New Way Vogue, which developed after 1990, took things a step further. It involved intricate illusions created with the hands and wrists, and frequently presented contortionist displays of shoulder flexibility—uncanny hyperextensions in which dancers pretended to move an imaginary geometric shape, like a box, 360 degrees around their heads. New York voguing was immortalized in the 1990 film *Paris Is Burning*, and in Madonna's "Vogue" music video the same year. The vogue community remains strong in New York, led by several competing "houses"; foremost among them is the House of Ninja. Founded by pioneering Vogue dancer Willi Ninja (born William Leake), the House of Ninja was continued after Willi's death from AIDS-related heart failure by his equally extraordinary protégés, including Benny Ninja (Benjamin Thomas) and Javier Ninja (Javier Madrid).

Meanwhile, in the Bronx, hip hop culture was beginning to germinate. By the late 1970s, New

York's South Bronx neighborhood had fallen into decline. Thanks in part to the construction of the intrusive Cross Bronx Expressway, the area felt the city's larger fiscal downturn especially keenly. A quick access route from the suburbs to the city, the Expressway meant that those with enough money could escape the city's noise and crowding and commute to work daily, while the rest remained stuck in an increasingly poor, run-down community. Homes were destroyed to make way for the raised portions of the road, adding to the deterioration of the area. Middle-class businesses moved out; the projects moved in.[7] The resulting neighborhood, while impoverished and crime-riddled, also represented an extraordinarily rich mixture of cultures—African American, Puerto Rican, Afro-Caribbean.

From the musical and artistic experiments of the "Boogie Down" Bronx kids, who met on the neighborhood's streets and at vibrant block parties, hip hop began to emerge. Building on the existing traditions of jazz, blues, disco, and funk, hip hop was the product of an array of cultural influences.

Though outsiders frequently assumed that hip hop was an expression of violence, another outlet for the gangs menacing New York's streets, early on the movement emphasized self-expression, originality, and respect. It became a way for the city's disenfranchised youth to articulate their creativity and individuality, establishing a positive community of their own creation.[8] Hip hop parties were relatively safe. In fact, sometimes they were held in community centers, like St. Martin's Church on 182nd Street and Cortona Avenue. Soon dance battles became their centerpieces—competitive events that featured all the excitement and theatricality of gang warfare without the brutality (though especially heated battles did sometimes devolve into fistfights). Young dancers began to form dance crews, held together by some of the same familial allegiances as gangs. "In the summer of '78," remembered Tee, a member of the High Times crew, "when you got mad at someone, instead of saying, 'Hey, man, you want to fight?' you'd say, 'Hey, man, you want to rock?'"[9]

DJ Afrika Bambaataa (originally Kevin Donovan) served as the face of the reactionary, anti-violence side of hip hop. Once a member of the Black Spades gang, he left that world and became a promoter of hip hop parties, eventually founding the music- and culture-oriented hip hop awareness group Universal Zulu Nation. Bambaataa encouraged his fans to use hip hop as a means to address their dire sociopolitical plight. He also urged them to practice tolerance. Frequently he would mix bits of songs by white groups like The Monkees into his DJ sets, later revealing to revelers that they'd danced to music they claimed to hate.[10]

Breaking—the currency of dance battles—was hip hop's physical embodiment. There are several possible sources for the term "breaking." Some said it referred to a dancer having a "break" while dancing, and losing his mind on the floor. The more common take was that it related to the bridge, or break, in a jazz song, when the musicians would improvise. DJs similarly created "breaks" for dancers in their sets, moments when all instruments except the rhythm section fell silent. A break was a signal to the b-boys to pull out their most impressive moves, saturating the silence with motion.[11]

"Breakdancing," on the other hand, was a word created by outsiders, a misleading umbrella term for a mishmash of urban dance forms. Members of the scene preferred to be called b-boys or b-girls rather than breakdancers, and they often referred to their craft as b-boying. "B-boying is, of course, its true name," according to dancer B-boy Ru. "It stands for 'bad-boy,' 'break-boy,' you know, 'best-boy.' You know, it stands for many things. That's the reason why it's just *b* and 'boy.' Because the *b* is actually a universal."[12]

Part of breaking/b-boying's appeal was that it could be credibly done by virtually any teenager with some free time to hone his skills, and maybe a more experienced friend to mentor him; no classes, no equipment, and no significant expenses were required. The best b-boys mastered a staggeringly diverse and vastly imaginative vocabulary. Much of early breaking came out of 1960s and 1970s dance trends from the worlds of funk and disco, and from West Coast styles—locking, popping, boogaloo—as seen on shows like *Soul Train*. Some of its more athletic movements had roots in *capoeira*, a Brazilian martial art, and in the martial arts films of Bruce Lee. There were shades of competitive gymnastics, as in the "flare," which involved supporting the body's weight on the hands while swinging the legs in continuous circles, just as a gymnast would on a pommel horse. More than anything else, though, breaking was about attitude. "Breaking is a way of using your body to inscribe your identity on streets and trains, in parks and high school gyms," wrote Sally Banes.

> It is a physical version of two favorite
> modes of street rhetoric, the taunt and the
> boast. . . . It is a subjunctive expression
> of bodily states, testing things that might
> be or are not. . . . But most of all, breaking

is a competitive display of physical and imaginative virtuosity, a codified dance form cum warfare that cracks open to flaunt personal inventiveness.[13]

B-boying can be broken down into three essential categories: toprock, done while standing; power moves, done primarily on the floor; and freezes, poses held for extended periods, usually at the end of a b-boy's turn in the dance circle. Toprock, with its focus on speed and agility, formed the heart of early breaking. Later it was relegated primarily to a dancer's entrance into the circle, becoming a warm-up for the fireworks to follow. As b-boying evolved, dancers who focused on toprock were considered old-fashioned. But a good toprocker was a dancer

with real style. Toprock "require[d] being able to think in three dimensions," said dancer Smily, a.k.a. Danny Dribble, "and the originality to imbue every individual movement with . . . flavor."[14]

Power moves included glides, windmills, spins, and other acrobatics. Over time they became fabulously elaborate. A dancer might do multiple flips, spin on his head, and end in a handstand—anything to impress, and to show up his opponent. B-boys devoted hours to learning and developing new power moves, which became the crux of the form. The best could take a failed power move—a botched head spin, a poorly landed flip—and transform it, on the fly, into something even more spectacular.

Freezes were showstoppers, most frequently used as exclamation points at the end of b-boys'

OPPOSITE: A b-boy in New York's Washington Square Park, 1982.
Leo Vals/Getty Images

LEFT: Children breakdancing in the street in Lawrence, Massachusetts. September, 1984.
AP Photo/Sean Kardon

turns in the dance circle. Sometimes they aimed to humiliate a rival. A b-boy might freeze with his upside-down backside in his competitor's face, holding his nose to tell him he stunk. Other freezes earned respect because of their level of difficulty. Some dancers could freeze while supported only by a shoulder, or by one arm; some could hold unthinkably contorted positions. "You try to put your head on your arm," said a member of the Breakmasters crew, "and your toenails on your ears."[15]

During a battle, a dancer typically entered the circle and did a few steps from each of the categories—toprock, power move, freeze, in that order—with a full set lasting no more than thirty or forty-five seconds. The sequence had a graceful logic. In a b-boy's performance, wrote hip hop scholar Joseph Schloss,

> the toprock is the equivalent of the salutation of a letter. The dancer is addressing the crowd directly, defining his relationship to them, and giving them a sense of what he is about to do. The [power moves are] the body of the letter, in which the dancer explores a variety of themes . . . a kind of story emerges based on the success of each experiment and the order in which the emotions are released. The story is concluded with the freeze . . . a kind of punch line to the story.[16]

Like letter-writers, each b-boy had his own distinctive voice. The dance format may have been predictable, but the point was to personalize each step, to make it truly one's own. Sometimes b-boys, who usually went by catchy pseudonyms, even named themselves after their signature moves: Frosty Freeze, King Uprock.

Continued on page 262

The 1984 film *Breakin'* was a testament to the popularity of b-boying and the individuality it inspires.
© MGM, Photofest

Super Cr3w perform on *America's Best Dance Crew*, 2008. *Chris Polk/ FilmMagic, Getty Images*

The underground b-boy community remained strong throughout the 2000s, but it was an MTV reality competition that put serious b-boys back at center stage. Created by *American Idol* judge Randy Jackson, *America's Best Dance Crew* (2008–2012) pitted crews from across the country against each other in a series of themed battles, with viewers voting to determine who would earn the $100,000 prize. Over the course of its seven seasons, the show introduced America to a new generation of talented crews. While a few of the groups had borderline-gimmicky angles, *America's Best Dance Crew*'s competitors generally wore the b-boy mantle respectfully. "Hip-hop being watered-down can happen with the media, but we do study up on our roots," said Benjamin Chung, a member of the JabbaWockeeZ crew, which won season one. "We realize . . . that this may be some people's only exposure to hip-hop, so we do feel we have a responsibility to portray it correctly."[17] *America's Best Dance Crew* sparked a renewed interest in b-boying, which proved no less television-friendly more than a quarter-century after its first onscreen appearances.

URBAN DANCE
ON THE CONCERT STAGE

Maintaining the spontaneous energy of street dance in a formal setting proved a challenge for choreographers, and efforts to bring urban styles to concert stages frequently produced lukewarm results. Several artists, however, were able to develop hip hop into an eloquent language for dance theater, with Rennie Harris and Doug Elkins foremost among them.

As a child growing up in North Philadelphia, Rennie Harris was first inspired to dance after seeing Don Campbell's group, the Lockers, on *Soul Train*. He started dancing socially, and by his teens was a prominent member of the hip hop scene, performing with Run DMC and the Sugar Hill Gang. Eventually, however, he tired of the commercial world. In 1992 he formed Rennie Harris Puremovement, a professional company with a mission to preserve and promulgate hip hop culture, especially its dance. Harris began choreographing powerful works of dance theater, including *Rome and Jewels* (2000), which told the story of Romeo and Juliet through street dance. The "Caps" faced off against the "Monster Q's"; b-boy battles replaced sword fights. Though Harris deftly conjured the central points of the familiar story, *Rome and Jewels* channeled the spirit of Shakespeare without getting bogged down in plot. Its collage of movement, music, and verbal riffs on the play's indelible language was not always penetrable—"I am tired of understanding everything I watch," Harris wrote in the production's program notes—but it unfolded with an unrelenting force.[18] Harris continues to head Puremovement and is one of the few hip hop choreographers who has created for both classical and modern companies, including Pennsylvania Ballet and Alvin Ailey American Dance Theater.

Rennie Harris performs in *100 Naked Locks*, 2009. *Courtesy Brian Mengini*

Doug Elkins didn't begin dancing until he was nineteen, but quickly became a self-taught b-boy by picking up steps at clubs in New York. Over time Elkins' interests expanded to include not only other urban dance forms—voguing, in particular—but also ballet, modern, and martial arts. From 1988 to 2004 he directed a trailblazing concert group, the Doug Elkins Dance Company. His works explored a unique hybrid style that first married different genres and then turned the result inside-out, creating an erudite mixture of high and low that revealed unlikely similarities between ballet and b-boying, Graham

Doug Elkins' *Throw Like a Girl*, performed by Arthur Aviles Typical Theatre in the Bronx, 2008. *Hiroyuki Ito, Getty Images*

technique and popping. In *Scott, Queen of Marys* (1994), which starred voguing legend Willi Ninja, Elkins somehow made Scottish country dancing and the flamboyant vogue vocabulary look like not-so-distant cousins.

Frustrated with the dance world's limited funding landscape, Elkins left concert dance for a few years after his company folded. In 2006, however, he made a triumphant return to the scene with *Fräulein Maria*, performed by a looser collective, Doug Elkins and Friends. A wickedly witty yet sweet-tempered homage to *The Sound of Music*, the work featured Elkins himself as the Abbess, whose hip hop-tinged solo dance to "Climb Every Mountain" proved strikingly moving.

By the beginning of the twenty-first century, mainstream culture had claimed and transformed much of street dance. But around that time, a new wave of urban dancers started developing their own signature forms.

Out of Los Angeles came clowning and, later, krumping. Developed by performer Tommy the Clown (Thomas Johnson) in Compton in the late 1990s, the upbeat, interactive clowning style was originally intended to entertain kids at birthday parties. As more young people became interested in the form, Johnson realized its potential as an alternative to the gang culture then dominating L.A.'s streets. Some of his mentees went on to create krumping, which, while related aesthetically to clowning, reflected a less optimistic view of the world. Characterized by intense aggression, krumping featured displays of agility and speed designed to intimidate. Arms jabbing, feet stomping, chests popping, krumpers performed with overwhelming urgency, as if possessed. (A disclaimer at the beginning of the 2005 krumping documentary *Rize* announced that none of the film's footage had been sped up, a fact difficult to believe.) Many krumpers saw the style as a way to stay out of trouble, a nonviolent channel for violent feelings.

Jookin'—a relative of other southern forms, including the gangsta walk, buckin', and choppin'—originally developed in Memphis in the 1980s. It experienced a revival beginning around 2010, when a new generation of jookers revitalized the style. Originally a staccato, even bouncy, reflection of the soul-funk rhythms of Memphis's distinctive hip hop music, in its new incarnation, jookin' smoothed out. Innovators added "gliding footwork, as well as . . . popping and waving," wrote critic Marina Harss, "and, finally, the icing on the cake: dancers started using the tips of their sneakers to balance on pointe."[19]

Jookin's pseudo-balletic grace earned mainstream attention first from clips posted on YouTube, and later through musician Janelle Monáe's music video for her 2010 song "Tightrope," which featured several jookers. A

ABOVE: Lil Buck performs with Yo-Yo Ma (background center left), 2013. *Erin Baiano, Associated Press*

few months later, former New York City Ballet dancer Damian Woetzel, noting the jookin'-ballet overlap, asked Lil Buck, one of the breakout stars of "Tightrope," to perform his own take on Anna Pavlova's famous solo "The Dying Swan." Yo-Yo Ma accompanied Buck's extraordinary performance—and a video of the event, with an introduction by director Spike Jonze, quickly racked up more than two million views on YouTube. Buck went on to dance with Madonna at the 2012 Super Bowl halftime show. He also made a name for himself in the concert dance world, performing at the prestigious Vail International Dance Festival (directed by Woetzel), appearing on the cover of *Dance Magazine*, and collaborating with New York City Ballet.

Continued from page 256

B-boy battles could be between individuals, but more commonly two crews faced off. A crew usually culled its dancers from a single neighborhood, and even outside the dance circle, it looked like a family. Older members mentored younger ones; the whole group defended any single member in need. Particularly talented crews achieved a degree of local fame—and sometimes more than that.

Thanks to the caliber of its members, the Rock Steady Crew, founded in 1977, became one of the country's best-known crews. Richie "Crazy Legs" Colon—the dancer credited with inventing the backspin and the windmill—altered the crew formula by recruiting the best b-boys from around the city, rather than just one neighborhood. In the early 1980s the Rock Steady Crew experienced a meteoric rise (with the help, eventually, of some savvy managers). They were invited to perform for the Queen of England, and they became the first b-boys to dance at Carnegie Hall. Though the group appreciated the attention these appearances brought to hip hop dance, some of its members chafed at being presented as talented tricksters. Outsiders, they noticed, tended to ignore or obscure the creative message of hip hop.

Whether insiders liked it or not, the Rock Steady Crew's success was just the beginning of a great wave of publicity for the genre. Soon the *Village Voice* was running front-page articles on b-boys. Other major New York publications, and even *National Geographic*, followed suit.

Breaking owed most of its newfound popularity to several 1980s films. *Flashdance* (1983; see Chapter 9) recruited four of the best-known members of the Rock Steady Crew: Crazy Legs, Ken Swift (Kenneth Gabbert), Frosty Freeze (Wayne Frost), and Mr. Freeze (Marc Lemberger). Though their cameo lasted just seventy-six seconds—they appeared during a back-alley montage set to the classic breaking song "It's Just Begun," by the Jimmy Castor Bunch—it was enough to cement b-boying in the public imagination. The 1983 PBS documentary *Style Wars* took a closer look at the b-boy world, following the Rock Steady Crew's heated rivalry with the Queens-based crew Dynamic Rockers. *Breakin'* (1984), another hip hop breakthrough, starred young rapper Ice-T. Despite its title, *Breakin'* included little actual breaking; most of the dancing was popping or locking. The movie's huge commercial success nonetheless exposed yet more Americans to the world of hip hop.

By 1984 national commercials for Pepsi, Coke, Burger King, and Panasonic had all featured breaking, or at least an imitation of it. The closing ceremonies of that summer's Olympic Games in Los Angeles included a routine by one hundred b-boys. There were "breakdancing" how-to books and numerous instructional VHS tapes. A middle-class housewife living in the suburbs could try out hip hop dance classes at her local Y.

Aspects of the original b-boy ethos were inevitably lost in this translation. A Burger King commercial couldn't help but dilute the importance of breaking's socioeconomic roots, its evolution out of an urban minority's struggle with poverty and alienation. The Rock Steady Crew's early apprehensions regarding breaking's relationship with mainstream culture spread throughout the b-boy community. Yet as more and more young people discovered hip hop culture through television sets and movie screens, as breaking took root in the minds of millions of kids across America, the form achieved a level of ubiquity that ensured its future.

Hip hop's entrance into mainstream culture corresponded with the rise of a format that changed everything: the music video. Launched on August 1, 1981, MTV (originally an abbreviation for "music television") began playing these miniature films around the clock, guided by "video jockeys," or VJs. The kinesthetic appeal of dance, the way it could bring a song to vivid life onscreen, immediately made it a music video staple.

Hip hop formed a cornerstone of MTV's lineup, and as rap artists arrived on the scene, so did b-boys and other street dancers. Eventually music video choreographers began blending the attitude and style of hip hop dance with jazz, gymnastics, and even ballet. The resulting crossbreed, slick and shiny yet still viscerally appealing, proved powerfully seductive.

Michael Jackson, an extraordinary dancer himself, was one of the earliest artists to fully deploy dance in music videos. He became perhaps the greatest force behind the early development of commercial dance. Long a fan of popping and funk boogaloo, Jackson took private lessons from street dancers to master the styles, and he culled many of his backup dancers from that scene. (Oprah Winfrey once asked Jackson where he got his dance moves; he somewhat melodramatically replied, "The children of the ghetto.")[20] Incorporating urban steps into his own smooth, Astaire- and Fosse-inspired vocabulary, he created an inimitable and yet instantly recognizable look. Backed by a chorus of be-zombied dancers in the epic video for "Thriller" (1983), Jackson—who co-choreographed the work—used dance to secure his status as the King of Pop. "He helped turn MTV into DTV," wrote critic Lewis

Michael Jackson in the music video for "Smooth Criminal," part of *Moonwalker*, a 1988 collection of short films released following the album *Bad*. © Warner Home Video, Photofest

Segal, "making television the place where dance films set to new music inspired a generation with their creative power and originality."[21]

Madonna also proved an innovative force in the commercial dance world. In addition to cross-pollinating dance styles, she sometimes appropriated street dance wholesale. Her 1990 hit "Vogue" was inspired by voguing, which she discovered at the New York City club Sound Factory. Its iconic video included several voguers, among them Jose Gutierez and Luis Camacho from the renowned House of Xtravaganza. Fifteen years later, Madonna raided the urban dance scene again, prominently featuring krumpers in her video for "Hung Up."

Hip hop artists themselves harnessed the power of street dance in their music videos. Missy Elliott has made dance the centerpiece of most of her videos, with the stutter-step choreography of "The Rain (Supa Dupa Fly)" (1997) and the breaking of pint-sized (and full-grown) b-boys and -girls in "Work It" (2002) being particular standouts.

In the late 1990s and early 2000s, the commercial dance style pioneered by artists like Jackson seemed to lose some of its freshness. Hundreds of music videos later, choreographers could still crank out entertaining dance sequences, but they felt overproduced. The excitement of the earlier days had dissipated, squeezed by the pressure of the music industry machine, which sought to replicate formulaically whatever had found commercial success. While millions of American teenagers danced along to the videos for Britney Spears's "Oops . . . I Did It Again" and 'N Sync's "Bye Bye Bye" (both 2000), their all-too-glossy choreography was also ripe for parody.

Enter director Spike Jonze, who created several dance-driven videos that subverted the MTV stereotype. Jonze's quirky sensibility, honed during feature films like *Being John Malkovich* (1999), proved the perfect antidote to the overwrought style of most music videos. His film for Fatboy Slim's "Praise You" (1998), rumored to have cost $800, was shot guerilla-style in front of a befuddled crowd outside a Westwood, California, movie theater. Jonze himself starred as Richard Koufey, leader of the fictional Torrance Community Dance Group. He and his ragtag crew of amateurs performed a charmingly homely dance routine, accompanied by an old-school boom box (which was shut off, halfway through the video, by a disgruntled

Madonna with dancers, 1993.
Time and Life Pictures, Getty Images

theater employee). Two years later, Jonze directed actor Christopher Walken in the video for Fatboy Slim's "Weapon of Choice"; he had Walken show off his rusty, high-school-musical-theater dance skills all over the lobby of a Marriott hotel.

Within a few years, however, another seminal work would prove that highly choreographed dance could still be immensely effective in a music video. Beyoncé Knowles' video for "Single Ladies (Put a Ring On It)" (2009) pared away everything but choreography, in fact. Shot in black and white in a bare studio, it featured Beyoncé and two look-alike dancers performing a brilliant, no-holds-barred routine co-created by veteran Frank Gatson and newcomer JaQuel Knight. Gatson and Knight drew heavily from a short 1969 dance by Bob Fosse, "American Breakfast," as seen on *The Ed Sullivan Show*. But the finished product felt decidedly modern. "Single Ladies" eventually earned more than 300 million YouTube views—and set countless Beyoncé fans to flipping their ringless left hands back and forth.

Many of the dancers populating the increasingly sprawling commercial scene, which included television spots and films as well as music videos, came out of a new school of dance training. In the 1970s and early 1980s, most of America's local dance studios taught a little bit of everything—smatterings of ballet, tap, and jazz—without digging intensively into anything. Sometimes cruelly referred to as "Dolly Dinkle" schools by students at more serious ballet academies, these studios provided a great outlet for recreational dancers, but not for most aspiring professionals.

As the sheer number of professional musical theater and commercial dance jobs across the country multiplied, however, more and more high-caliber dancers came through the industry, retired, and, frequently, started teaching. The average dance school's quality increased dramatically as these teachers, with their strong technical skills and diverse experiences, entered the scene. Versatility, they understood, was now expected of professional dancers. Schools began offering not only high-quality ballet, jazz, and tap classes, but also courses in hip hop dance and sometimes ballroom and gymnastics. Over time the best studios began turning out accomplished dancers who, while not always artistically gifted, could handle any technical challenge.

This kind of quantifiably impressive, audition-friendly dancing—with its emphasis on the height of the leg, the number of turns, the airtime in the jump—also lent itself to competitions. Amateur dance competitions became a major industry in the 1990s, attracting thousands of young dancers with their trophies and scholarship prizes. A number of

schools began training specifically for these contests, or spending significant periods of time rehearsing competition routines.

Some of these competitions and competition-oriented studios had less-than-stellar reputations. (The Lifetime reality series *Dance Moms* brought infamy to instructor Abby Lee Miller and her Pittsburgh-based school's competitive team, portrayed, perhaps not entirely honestly, as brutally cutthroat.) The most prestigious competitions, however, held dancers to exceptionally high standards of technique; a title from New York City Dance Alliance, for example, earned a dancer a good deal of respect. Many competition organizations also hosted dance conventions, with classes led by esteemed teachers and choreographers active in the industry. In addition to honing students' technique, these instructors could potentially get them footholds in the professional dance world.

By the mid-2000s, the pool of impressive jack-of-all-trades dancers had deepened considerably. The time was ripe for *So You Think You Can Dance*, a television show that, in asking contestants to perform everything from jazz to ballroom to hip hop, provided the perfect venue for the competition crowd.

Continued on page 270

LEFT: Beyoncé performs "Single Ladies" at a concert in 2011. *Kevin Mazur/WireImage, Getty Images*

BELOW: *So You Think You Can Dance* season-five finalists Kayla Radomski and Kupono Aweau perform "Addiction," an Emmy-winning contemporary routine by Mia Michaels, 2009. *Alberto E. Rodriguez, Getty Images*

In the sleepy summer of 2005, *Dancing with the Stars*—an American version of the BBC show *Strictly Come Dancing*, which had premiered the previous year—began airing on ABC. The premise sounded unlikely: A group of B-list celebrities paired up with professional ballroom champions for a season-long dance-off, with home viewers calling in to determine who stayed and who went each week. Yet the show's strange combination of self-improvement (audiences watched the celebrities' ballroom technique progress week after week) and self-mockery (nearly everyone involved, and particularly sardonic co-host Tom Bergeron, seemed in on the joke) proved immensely appealing. Ratings skyrocketed as America tuned in to watch stars like Pamela Anderson, Marie Osmond, and Lance Bass try out the cha-cha, the waltz, and the jive.

Though mainstream audiences were hooked, the dance community initially reacted with bemusement, and even consternation. Why, they wondered, would anyone want to watch bad dancing? As the show's popularity continued to snowball, however, the prevailing attitude shifted. Eventually well-respected dancers started making guest appearances. New York City Ballet's Tiler Peck, for example, performed a piece choreographed by *So You Think You Can Dance* alum Travis Wall during season ten. And the *Dancing with the Stars* professionals became a highlight for dance lovers. As they returned season after season, ballroom champions such as Karina Smirnoff, Derek Hough, Julianne Hough, Maksim Chmerkovskiy, and Cheryl Burke achieved stardom in their own right. "To some degree [the pros] are responsible for keeping their celebrities on the air," said Bergeron in 2011. "People at home sometimes vote more for the dancer than the star."[22] Later *Dancing with the Stars* added an all-professional troupe, made up of even more remarkable ballroom dancers, which performed special showcase numbers—a boon for ballroom aficionados. Several *So You Think You Can Dance* contestants from the ballroom world joined the *Dancing with the Stars* cast, too, in an unusual form of cross-network synchronicity.

Dancing with the Stars further spurred the growth of ballroom dancing in America, which had been undergoing a resurgence since PBS began airing the annual Ohio Star Ball dance competition in the 1980s. While the form had remained popular with older dancers, in the new millennium young American students began taking up competitive ballroom dance in earnest. The trend proved particularly strong in western states. Utah Valley University became the first higher education institution in the country where undergraduates could major in ballroom dance, and neighboring Brigham Young University began offering a bachelor's degree in dance with a ballroom concentration. This next generation of dancers revitalized ballroom, revealing anew the vibrant, sophisticated form hidden for years beneath layers of greasepaint and self-tanner.

Cheryl Burke and Maurice Greene of *Dancing with the Stars. David Livingston, Getty Images*

Continued from page 267

So You Think You Can Dance, created by *American Idol* producers Simon Fuller and Nigel Lythgoe, premiered on Fox in 2005. After holding auditions at locations around the country, the show trimmed the hopefuls down to twenty finalists, who were then paired up with partners and, week to week, taught routines in various genres, which they performed live during the show. In addition to receiving a cash prize, the winner was crowned America's Favorite—not best—Dancer.

Though the show sometimes pigeonholed its contestants a bit too aggressively (rarely did a so-called "hip hop" finalist have *zero* classical experience), it also showcased an array of specialists. Some serious ballet talent, including former American Ballet Theatre dancer Danny Tidwell and Miami City Ballet alum Alex Wong, found great success on the show, as did several ballroom champions. Niche hip hop dancers—krumpers and, particularly in later seasons, "animators," who drew inspiration from stop-motion animation—earned large fan bases thanks to the series.

So You Think You Can Dance also highlighted an amorphous, ever-evolving, but consistently appealing style, initially known as "lyrical" and later dubbed "contemporary." Usually ballet-based,

contemporary brought together aspects of several other forms, blending classically controlled legwork with the groundedness, floor work, and improvisation of modern and jazz dance. Choreography was frequently rooted in a story, encouraging dancers to express rather than simply perform. Most contestants—especially those from the competition crew—described themselves as contemporary dancers, and some of the show's most memorable routines fell into its contemporary category. Choreographers Mia Michaels and Wade Robson, in particular, constructed contemporary numbers both technically demanding and emotionally resonant—impressive feats, considering the show's two-minute, designed-for-TV dance format. Hip hop duo Tabitha and Napoleon D'umo even crafted "lyrical hip hop" routines, which met contemporary dancers in the middle, adding softer steps and stronger storylines.

So You Think You Can Dance had a profound effect on the larger dance world. Many participants saw it not as a jumpstart to a career, but as a career in itself, at least for a while. At the end of each season, the top ten dancers went on an extended tour, and alums were frequently brought into the *So You Think You Can Dance* family, returning in later seasons as "all-stars" to partner new contestants.

Children do the Dougie in Pittsburgh, 2012. © *Pittsburgh Post-Gazette, ZUMAPRESS.com, Alamy*

Some, like season two finalist Travis Wall, even launched high-profile choreographic careers after making short pieces for the show. The show also helped inspire male dance students, young boys who realized through the series that dance and dancers could, in fact, be cool. And though *So You Think You Can Dance* didn't exactly bridge the gap between the concert and commercial dance worlds, it did expose large television audiences to guest performances by esteemed professional companies, including the Los Angeles Ballet, Cedar Lake Contemporary Ballet, and Alvin Ailey American Dance Theater. "Don't forget, at the end of the day this is Fox broadcasting," Nigel Lythgoe told the *New York Times* in 2008, "and all of a sudden there are the Ailey guys on prime time. I'm really proud of that."[23]

Thanks to the rise of YouTube and its cousins, it's now easier than ever for a dance trend to go viral. MTV may be devoting less and less airtime to music videos, but videos are constantly accessible—and in some cases, exclusively available—on video-sharing sites. In 2013 Billboard announced that YouTube views would even be factored into the calculation of its Hot 100 list. A catchy dance, as much as a catchy melody, can be the "hook" that helps a song reach new heights of popularity.

The list of web-driven dance crazes is enormous and ever-growing. American rapper Soulja Boy (DeAndre Way) started one from the ground up: After debuting his song "Crank Dat (Soulja Boy)" (2007) on the music-based social community Soundclick, he began posting select videos of fans dancing to it on his MySpace page. Within a few weeks the Soulja Boy dance, as sanctioned but not created by Soulja Boy himself, had taken off across the country. In 2010 the group Cali Swag District singlehandedly resuscitated the Dougie, originally popularized by 1980s rapper Doug E. Fresh, by featuring it in the video for their hit single "Teach Me How to Dougie." South Korean pop star Psy (Park Jae-sang) became an international sensation in 2012 when American rapper T-Pain tweeted the video for his song "Gangnam Style," with its captivatingly bizarre "invisible horse dance." Soon Psy was galloping across NBC's *Today Show*, and within a month the daily number of YouTube views generated by "Gangnam Style" had passed the five million mark. Viral web-based dance crazes have also spawned a massive feedback loop: Fans learn the dance, record themselves doing it, and then upload their videos, adding their own voices to the wonderful cacophony that is modern pop culture.

In a way, YouTube's dance audience reflects today's American dance audience as a whole: indiscriminate, sometimes, but also enormous and omnivorous. Americans are passionate consumers—online, on television, in the theater—of dance both high and low.

End Notes

INTRODUCTION

1. As quoted in Kisselgoff, Anna. "Martha Graham Dies at 96; A Revolutionary in Dance." *New York Times*, April 2, 1991. Accessed online at nytimes.com on April 16, 2014.

2. As quoted in Jowitt, Deborah. *Time and the Dancing Image*. New York: W. Morrow, 1988, p. 255.

CHAPTER 1

1. As quoted in Laubin, Reginald and Gladys. *Indian Dances of North America: Their Importance to Indian Life*. Norman; University of Oklahoma Press, 1977. p. 3.

2. As quoted in Laubin and Laubin, p. 81.

3. Highwater, Jamake. *Ritual of the Wind: North American Indian Ceremonies, Music, and Dances*. New York; Viking Press, 1977. p. 64.

4. Laubin and Laubin, p. 290-291.

5. From Collier, John. *American Indian Ceremonial Dances: Navajo, Pueblo, Apache, Zuñi*. New York; Bounty Books (a division of Crown Publishers), 1972. p. 163.

6. Collier, p. 165.

7. Highwater, p. 148.

8. Mason, Bernard S. *Dances and Stories of the American Indian*. New York; The Ronald Press Company, 1944. p. 128.

9. Highwater, p. 172.

10. Axtmann, Ann. "A Diaspora of Native American Dance." Congress on Research in Dance Conference (34th: 2001: New York University). Proceedings, Vol. 2. p. 316.

11. Howard, James Henri. "Pan-Indianism in Native American Dance." *Ethnomusicology*. Ann Arbor; Vol. 27, No. 1, Jan 1983. p. 79.

12. Kavanagh, Thomas W. "Southern Plains Dance: Tradition and Dynamism." As printed in *Native American Dance: Ceremonies and Traditions*. Charlotte Heth, ed. Washington, D.C.; Smithsonian Institution with Starwood Publishing, Inc., 1992. p. 107.

13. Mason, p. 141.

14. Huenemann, Lynn F. "Northern Plains Dance." As printed in *Native American Dance: Ceremonies and Traditions*. p. 134.

15. Highwater, p. 171.

CHAPTER 2

1. Castle, Mr. and Mrs. Vernon. *Modern Dancing*. New York: Harper and Brothers, 1914. p. 43.

2. Franks, A. H. *Social Dance: A Short History*. London: Routledge, Paul and Kegan, 1963. p. 95.

3. Van Winkle Keller, Kate, and Genevieve Shimer. "Playford's 'English Dancing Master' (1651) and Country Dancing in America." p. 61–2 of Needham, Maureen, ed. *I See America Dancing: Selected Readings 1685-2000*. Chicago: University of Illinois Press, 2002.

4. "A History of Social Dance in America: Opposition." American Antiquarian Society Online Exhibitions. www.americanantiquarian.org/Exhibitions/Dance/opposition.htm. Accessed July 21, 2013.

5. Wagner, Ann Louise. *Adversaries of Dance: From the Puritans to the Present*. Chicago: University of Illinois Press, 1997. p. 48.

6. As quoted in Nevell, Richard. *A Time to Dance: American Country Dancing from Hornpipe to Hot Hash*. New York: St. Martin's Press, 1977. p. 30.

7. Andrews, E. D. "The Dance in Shaker Ritual." *Chronicles of the American Dance*. Paul Magriel, ed. New York: Henry Holt and Company, 1948, p. 10.

8. As quoted in Needham, p. 109.

9. Wallace, Carol McD. "Dreams of Flight." p. 25-26 of *Dance: A Very Social History*. New York: The Metropolitan Museum of Art, and Rizzoli International Publications, Inc., 1986.

10. Nevell, p. 41

11. Hazzard-Gordon, Katrina. *Jookin': The Rise of Social Dance Formations in African-American Culture*. Philadelphia: Temple University Press, 1990. p. 18.

12. Giordano, Ralph G. *Social Dancing in America: A History and Reference*. Westport, CT: Greenwood Press, 2007. Vol. 1. p. 149.

13. As printed in Hazzard-Gordon, p. 33.

14. As printed in Giordano, Vol. 1, p. 151.

15. De Mille, Agnes. *America Dances*. New York: Macmillan Publishing Co., 1980, p. 10.

16. As printed in Needham, p. 116.

17. As printed in Giordano, Vol. 1, pp. 288–289.

18. Hazzard-Gordon, p. 83.

19. Castle, Mr. and Mrs. Vernon. *Modern Dancing*. New York: Harper and Brothers, 1914. p. 18.

20. The Castles, p. 18–19.

21. Some states have since reversed the ban.

22. Giordano, Vol. 2, p. 63.

23. Stearns, Marshall Winslow and Jean. *Jazz Dance: The Story of American Vernacular Dance*. New York : Da Capo Press, 1994. p. 328.

24. As quoted in Giordano, Vol. 2, p. 87.

25. Martin, John. "The GI Makes With the Hot Foot." *New York Times Magazine*, January 9, 1944. p. SM14.

26. Driver, Ian. *A Century of Dance: A Hundred Years of Musical Movement, from Waltz to Hip Hop*. London: Octopus Publishing Group Limited, 2000. p. 89.

27. *New York Times*, February 23, 1957, p. 12.

28. As printed in Giordano, Vol. 2, p. 142.

29. Wolfe, Tom. "The Peppermint Lounge Revisited." *The Kandy-Kolored Tangerine-Flake Streamline Baby*. New York: Bantam Books, 1999. p. 53.

30. Driver, p. 193.

31. From "The Twist: Brave New Whirl" (1962) as printed in Needham, p.123.

32. Jones, Alan, and Jussi Kantonen. *Saturday Night Forever: The Story of Disco*. Chicago: A Capella Books, 2000. p. 35.

CHAPTER 3

1. London: Chapman & Hall, Ltd., 1913. Accessed online at gutenberg.org/files/675/675-h/675-h.htm on August 4, 2013.

2. Sommer, Sally R. "Tap Dance." *The International Encyclopedia of Dance*. New York: Oxford University Press USA, 2004. Accessed online at oxfordreference.com on August 16, 2013.

3. As quoted in Emery, Lynne Fauley. *Black Dance: From 1619 to Today*. Princeton, NJ: Princeton Book Co., 1988. p. 181.

4. As quoted in Stearns, Marshall Winslow and Jean. *Jazz Dance: The Story of American Vernacular Dance*. New York: Da Capo Press, 1994. p. 45.

5. Emery, p. 185–6.

6. Nash, Barbara. *Tap Dance*. Dubuque, Iowa: W. C. Brown Co., 1969. p. 5.

7. Frank, Rusty E. *Tap! The Greatest Tap Dance Stars and Their Stories, 1900–1955*. New York: Da Capo Press, 1994.

8. *Jazz Dance*, p. 191.

9. Laurie, Joe, Jr. *Vaudeville*. New York: Henry Holt & Co., 1953. pp. 56, 203.

10. Stearns, p. 80.

11. Stearns, p. 87.

12. Frank, p. 53.

13. Driver, Ian. *A Century of Dance: A Hundred Years of Musical Movement, from Waltz to Hip Hop*. London: Octopus Publishing Group Limited, 2000. p. 102.

14. Stearns, pp. 174–175.

15. Stearns, p. 176.

16. Emery, p. 213.

17. Stearns, p. 133, 137.

18. Stearns, p. 181.

19. As quoted in Emery, p. 233.

20. As quoted in Stearns, p. 188.

21. As quoted in Stearns, p. 158.

22. Stearns, p. 285.

23. As quoted in Stearns, p. 307.

24. Frank, p. 155.

25. As quoted in Frank, p. 65.

26. De Mille, Agnes. *America Dances*. New York: Macmillan Publishers, 1980. p. 86.

27. Driver, p. 99.

28. Rees, Heather. *Tap Dancing: Rhythm in Their Feet*. Ramsbury: Crowcod, 2003. p. 24-25.

29. As quoted by Weber, Bruce. "Jeni LeGon, Singer and Solo Tap-Dancer, Dies at 96." *New York Times*, December 16, 2012. p. A33.

30. Driver, p. 106.

31. Rees, p. 22.

32. As quoted in Stearns, p. 220.

33. Stearns, p. 221.

34. *America Dances*, p. 89.

35. *America Dances*, p. 90.

36. Valis Hill, Constance. *Tap Dancing America: A Cultural History*. New York: Oxford University Press, 2010. p. 169.

37. *Tap Dancing America*, p. 169.

38. As quoted in Valis Hill, p. 237.

39. As quoted in Valis Hill p. 233.

40. As quoted in Valis Hill, p. 236.

41. As quoted in Driver, p. 115.

42. As quoted in Valis Hill, p. 307.

43. As quoted in Driver, p. 117.

44. *Tap Dancing America*, p. 310.

45. As quoted in Valis Hill, p. 316.

46. As quoted in Valis Hill, p. 318.

47. As quoted in Macel, Emily. "The Fast and the Furious." *Dance Magazine*, May 2008. Accessed online at dancemagazine.com.

CHAPTER 4

1. As quoted in Anderson, Janet. *Modern Dance*. New York: Chelsea House, 2010. p. 25

2. Reynolds, Nancy, and Malcom McCormick. *No Fixed Points: Dance in the Twentieth Century*. New Haven and London: Yale University Press, 2003. p. 4.

3. Reynolds and McCormick, p. 5.

4. Reynolds and McCormick, p. 5.

5. Anderson, p. 13.

6. Reynolds and McCormick, p. 5.

7. As quoted in Reynolds and McCormick, p. 8.

8. As quoted in Anderson, p. 17.

9. De Mille, Agnes. *America Dances*. New York: Macmillan Publishing Co., 1980. p. 43.

10. Maynard, Olga. *American Modern Dancers: The Pioneers*. Boston: Little, Brown, 1965. p. 55.

11. As quoted in Ruyter, Nancy Lee Chalfa. *Reformers and Visionaries: The Americanization of the Art of Dance*. New York: Dance Horizons, 1979. pp. 34–5.

12. Ruyter, p. 37. (It should be noted, however, that Duncan never tried to do "Greek dancing," despite the persistence of that claim.)

13. De Mille, p. 45.

14. As quoted in Reynolds and McCormick, p. 14.

15. Ruyter, p. 57.

16. Sherman, Jane. *The Drama of Denishawn Dance*. New York: M. Mathesius, 2005. p. 3.

17. St. Denis, Ruth. *An Unfinished Life*. Brooklyn: Dance Horizons, 1969. p. 9.

18. Reynolds and McCormick, p. 23.

19. As quoted in Ruyter, p. 63.

20. As quoted in Ruyter, p. 67.

21. Shawn, Ted. *Ruth St. Denis, Pioneer and Prophet*. San Francisco: J. H. Nash, 1920. Vol. I. p. 34.

22. Anderson, p. 30.

23. As quoted in Sherman, Jane. *The Drama of Denishawn Dance*. New York: M. Mathesius, 2005. p. 5.

24. As quoted in Reynolds and McCormick, p. 29.

25. Reynolds and McCormick, p. 25.

26. Maynard, p. 92.

27. Rogisin, Elinor. *The Dance Makers: Conversations with American Choreographers*. New York: Walker, 1980. p. 4.

28. Maynard, p. 106.

29. As quoted in Maynard, p. 106.

30. Anderson, p. 40.

31. Maynard, p. 116.

32. As quoted in Anderson, p. 43.

33. From *Blood Memory: An Autobiography*. New York and London: Doubleday, 1991. p. 117.

34. From "The Dance: Native Talent." *New York Times*, November 19, 1933. p. X2.

35. *Blood Memory*, p. 114.

36. As quoted in Kisselgoff, Anna. "Martha Graham Dies at 96; A Revolutionary in Dance." *New York Times*, April 2, 1991. Accessed online at nytimes.com on October 14, 2013.

37. Maynard, p. 131.

38. Reynolds and McCormick, p. 162.

39. Reynolds and McCormick, p. 166.

40. Anderson, p. 50.

41. Maynard, p. 160.

42. As quoted in Anderson, p. 48.

43. Reynolds and McCormick, p. 168.

CHAPTER 5

1. As quoted in Teachout, Terry. *All in the Dances: A Brief Life of George Balanchine*. Harcourt, Inc.: Orlando, 2004. p. 73.

2. As quoted in Homans, Jennifer. *Apollo's Angels: A History of Ballet*. New York: Random House, 2010. p. 470.

3. Homans, p. 470.

4. Reynolds, Nancy, and Malcom McCormick. *No Fixed Points: Dance in the Twentieth Century*. New Haven and London: Yale University Press, 2003. p. 109.

5. From *Dance to the Piper*. Boston: Little, Brown, 1952. p. 45.

6. As quoted in Maynard, Olga. *The American Ballet*. Philadelphia: Macrae Smith Co., 1959. p. 30.

7. Maynard, p. 33.

8. Reynolds and McCormick, p. 117.

9. From *Balanchine's Complete Stories of the Great Ballets*. Francis Mason, ed. New York: Doubleday, 1954. p. 22.

10. From Kirstein's *Thirty Years: The New York City Ballet*. New York: Knopf, 1978. pp. 26–7.

11. Kirstein, p. 33.

12. As quoted in Jowitt, Deborah. *Time and the Dancing Image*. New York: W. Morrow, 1988. p. 255.

13. Jowitt, p. 256.

14. Kirstein, p. 84.

15. As quoted in Reynolds and McCormick, p. 282.

16. From "It's a Wise Child," *New Yorker*, June 9, 1975. (Croce was speaking of Robbins' return to this style in the 1975 *Ma Mère l'Oye*.) As printed in *Afterimages*. New York: Alfred A. Knopf, 1977. p. 155.

17. Payne, Charles. *American Ballet Theatre*. New York: A. A. Knopf, 1977. p. 208.

18. From "A Briefing in American Ballet." As printed in *Looking at the Dance*. New York: Horizon Press, 1968. p. 403.

19. As quoted in Reynolds and McCormick, p. 310.

20. Teachout, p. 91.

21. Homans, p. 467.

22. Homans, p. 454.

23. Reynolds and McCormick, p. 317.

24. From "Dreams that Money Can Buy," January 1970. As printed in *Afterimages*, p. 281.

25. Reynolds and McCormick, p. 472.

26. From "Esprit de Joie," April 7, 1970. As printed in *At the Vanishing Point: A Critic Looks at Dance*. Saturday Review Press, 1972. p. 73.

27. From "The Two Trockaderos," *New Yorker*, October 14, 1974. As printed in *Afterimages*, p. 78.

28. From "The Two Trockaderos," as printed in *Afterimages*, p. 79.

29. Homans, p. 498.

30. From "Dances at a Gathering," nycballet.com. Accessed on November 5, 2013.

31. As quoted in Reynolds and McCormick, p. 534.

32. From "Joffrey Jazz," *New Yorker*, October 29, 1973. As printed in *Afterimages*, p. 14.

33. Jowitt, p. 274.

CHAPTER 6

1. As quoted in Vaughan, David. *Merce Cunningham: Fifty Years*. New York: Aperture, 1997. p. 10.

2. From *The Borzoi Book of Modern Dance*. New York: Dance Horizons, 1969. p. 214.

3. As quoted in Jewish Women's Archive. "Women of Valor: Anna Sokolow." Accessed at jwa.org/womenofvalor/sokolow on January 10, 2014.

4. From "Study in Despair; Anna Sokolow's 'Rooms' Has Premiere at ANTA Theatre to Score by Kenyon." *New York Times*, May 16, 1955. p. 26.

5. From "Lang: Speaking for Herself." *Dance Magazine*, September 1974. p. 53.

6. Reynolds, Nancy, and Malcolm McCormick. *No Fixed Points: Dance in the Twentieth Century*. New Haven and London: Yale University Press, 2003. p. 372.

7. From "Harmony's Fervent Apostle," *Village Voice*, September 23–29, 1981. As printed in *The Dance in Mind*. Boston: David Godine, 1985. p. 206.

8. Lloyd, *Borzoi Book*, p. 293.

9. As quoted in Lloyd, p. 300.

10. As quoted in Lloyd, p. 240.

11. Reynolds and McCormick, p. 327.

12. From *An Unfinished Memoir*, 1958. As printed in Gottlieb, Robert, ed. *Reading Dance: A Gathering of Memoirs, Reportage, Criticism, Profiles, Interviews, and Some Uncategorizable Events*. New York: Pantheon Books, 2008. p. 646

13. Reynolds and McCormick, p. 330.

14. Jowitt, Deborah. "Man, the Marvelous Mechanism." *Village Voice*, October 19, 1982. As printed in *Dance in Mind*, p. 203.

15. From "Dance: Semantics: New Abstract Conceptions Qualify and Vitalize Modern Artforms." *New York Times*, August 18, 1957. p. X12.

16. Jowitt, "Man, the Marvelous Mechanism," as printed in *Dance in Mind*, p. 199.

17. Reynolds and McCormick, p. 377.

18. Warren, Larry. *Lester Horton: Modern Dance Pioneer*. M. Dekker, 1977. p. 66.

19. Perron, Wendy. "Katherine Dunham: One-Woman Revolution." *Dance Magazine*, August 2000. As printed in *Through the Eyes of a Dancer*. Middletown, CT: Wesleyan University Press, 2013. p. 147.

20. Lloyd, p. 245.

21. Perron, "Katherine Dunham: One-Woman Revolution," as printed in *Through the Eyes of a Dancer*, p. 150.

22. From "The Dance: Five Artists: Second Annual Joint Recital Project of the Y.M.H.A." February 21, 1943. p. X5.

23. As quoted in "Primus, Pearl." *The International Encyclopedia of Dance*. Selma Jeanne Cohen, ed. Oxford University Press, 1998. Accessed online at oxfordreference.com on January 3, 2014.

24. As quoted in Reynolds and McCormick, p. 346.

25. Reynolds and McCormick, p. 348.

26. As quoted in Lewis-Ferguson, Julinda. *Alvin Ailey Jr.: A Life in Dance*. New York: Walker and Company, 1994. p. 1.

27. As quoted in Cohn, Ellen. "Alvin Ailey, Arsonist: Modern Dance Is Getting Hot." *New York Times Magazine*, April 29, 1973. p. 286.

28. From *At the Vanishing Point*. New York: Saturday Review Press, 1972. p. 161.

29. As quoted in Vaughan, David. *Merce Cunningham: Fifty Years*. New York: Aperture, 1997. p. 17.

30. As quoted in Vaughan, p. 29.

31. From "Elegance in Isolation," as printed in *Looking at the Dance*. New York: Popular Library. 1968. pp. 303–304.

32. As quoted in Vaughan, p. 35.

33. Vaughan, p. 58.

34. From "Pale Horse, Pale Rider," *New Dance Review*, 1994. As printed in *Reading Dance*, p. 483.

35. As quoted in Vaughan, p. 67.

36. From "Zen and the Art of Dance," *Village Voice*, January 17, 1977. As printed in *The Dance in Mind*, p. 30.

37. Reynolds and McCormick, p. 356.

38. From "Twos and Threes." *New Yorker*, May 4, 2009. p. 77.

39. As quoted in Taylor, Paul. *Private Domain*. New York: Alfred A. Knopf, 1987.

40. Though the score simply instructs the performer(s) not to play their instruments for four minutes and thirty-three seconds, Cage insisted it wasn't actually "silent"; the piece consists of the incidental sounds the listener hears as it is performed.

41. From *Dancers, Buildings, and People in the Streets*. New York: Horizon Press Publishers, 1965. p. 225.

42. From "Paul Taylor," from the program for the Paul Taylor Dance Company's fiftieth anniversary, October 14, 2004. As printed in *Reading Dance*, p. 1195.

43. *Private Domain*. p. 306.

44. Jowitt, "A Fishy Conversation," as printed in *The Dance in Mind*, pp. 49–50.

45. As quoted in Reynolds and McCormick, p. 388.

CHAPTER 7

1. "Some Retrospective Notes on a Dance for 10 People and 12 Mattresses Called 'Parts of Some Sextets,' Performed at the Wadsworth Atheneum, Hartford, Connecticut, and Judson Memorial Church, New York, in March 1965." *Tulane Drama Review 10*, Winter 1965. p. 168.

2. From *Push Comes to Shove: An Autobiography*. New York: Bantam Books, 1992. p. 89.

3. Dunn as quoted in Banes, Sally. *Democracy's Body*. Ann Arbor, MI: UNI Research Press, 1983. p. 5.

4. Reynolds, Nancy and Malcom McCormick. *No Fixed Points: Dance in the Twentieth Century*. New Haven and London: Yale University Press, 2003. p. 399.

5. Banes, Sally. *Terpsichore in Sneakers: Post-Modern Dance*. Middletown, CT: Wesleyan University Press, 1987. p. xix.

6. From "Judson concerts #3, #4," *Village Voice*, February 28, 1963.

7. *Terpsichore in Sneakers*, p. xxiv.

8. As quoted in Jowitt, Deborah. *The Dance in Mind*. Boston: David Godine, 1985. pp. 309-10.

9. From *The Dance in Mind*, p. 324.

10. As quoted in *Terpsichore in Sneakers*, p. 24.

11. *Terpsichore in Sneakers*, p. 28.

12. As quoted in Reynolds and McCormick, p. 404.

13. *Terpsichore in Sneakers*, p. 44.

14. From *Time and the Dancing Image*. New York: W. Morrow, 1988. p. 307.

15. *Terpsichore in Sneakers*, p. xix-xx.

16. *Terpsichore in Sneakers*, p. 101.

17. Reynolds and McCormick, p. 412.

18. *Terpsichore in Sneakers*, p. 108.

19. As quoted in *Terpsichore in Sneakers*, p. 133.

20. As quoted in Riding, Alan. "A Star Everywhere Else, a Stranger at Home." *New York Times*, October 8, 2000. Accessed online at nytimes.com on January 31, 2014.

21. Reynolds and McCormick, p. 417.

22. As quoted in *The Dance in Mind*, p. 69.

23. As quoted in *Terpsichore in Sneakers*, p. 81.

24. As quoted in *Terpsichore in Sneakers*, p. 119.

25. *Terpsichore in Sneakers*, p. 120.

26. From "Trisha Brown on Tour," *Dancing Times 86*, no. 1028, May 1996. As printed in *Through the Eyes of a Dancer*. Middletown, CT: Wesleyan University Press, 2013. p. 106.

27. As quoted in *Terpsichore in Sneakers*, p. 150.

28. From "Dancing a Song," *Village Voice*, May 20-28, 1981. As printed in *The Dance in Mind*, p. 96.

29. *Terpsichore in Sneakers*, p. 156.

30. *Terpsichore in Sneakers*, p. 173.

31. *Terpsichore in Sneakers*, p. 188.

32. Reynolds and McCormick, p. 616.

33. *Terpsichore in Sneakers*, p. 208.

34. *Terpsichore in Sneakers*, p. 53.

35. *Terpsichore in Sneakers*, p. 209.

36. From "People Improvisation: Grand Union." *Soho Weekly News*, May 6, 1976. As printed in *Through the Eyes of a Dancer*, p. 25.

37. *Push Comes to Shove*, p. 89.

38. As quoted in Reynolds and McCormick, p. 421.

39. Rogosin, Elinor. *The Dance Makers: Conversations with American Choreographers*. New York, 1980. pp. 136 and 147.

40. From *The Dance in Mind*, p. 167.

41. From "Premiere by Lar Lubovitch." *New York Times*, May 9, 1985. Accessed online at nytimes.com on January 25, 2014.

42. From *Time and the Dancing Image*, p. 63.

43. From "Not Ballet, Not Acrobatics, But Pilobolus!" *New York Times*, November 20, 1977. p. D1.

44. Reynolds and McCormick, p. 613.

45. From "Discussing the Undiscussable." *New Yorker*, December 26, 1994. p. 54.

46. Reynolds and McCormick, p. 621.

47. As quoted in Acocella, Joan. *Mark Morris*. New York: The Noonday Press, 1993. p. 116.

48. As quoted in Acocella, p. 64.

49. As quoted in Acocella, p. 252.

50. Acocella, p. 51.

51. Acocella, p. 65.

52. Morris as quoted in Acocella, p. 257.

53. Acocella, p. 201.

CHAPTER 8

1. As quoted by Gerald Siegmund in "The Space of Memory: William Forsythe's Ballets." *William Forsythe and the Practice of Choreography: It Starts from Any Point*. Steven Spier, ed. New York: Routledge, 2011. p. 128.

2. Jowitt, Deborah. *The Dance in Mind*. Boston: David Godine, 1985. pp. 198 and 231.

3. Jowitt, p. 197.

4. From *Push Comes to Shove: An Autobiography*. New York: Bantam Books, 1992. p. 177.

5. Reynolds, Nancy, and Malcom McCormick. *No Fixed Points: Dance in the Twentieth Century*. New Haven and London: Yale University Press, 2003. p. 440.

6. Siegmund in *William Forsythe and the Practice of Choreography*. p. 128.

7. As quoted by Diane Solway in "Is It Dance? Maybe. Political? Sure." *New York Times*, February 18, 2007. Accessed online at nytimes.com.

8. As quoted in Roy, Sanjay. "Step-by-step guide to dance: William Forsythe." *The Guardian*, October 6, 2008. Accessed online at theguardian.com.

9. As quoted in Sulcas, Roslyn. "Watching the Ballett Frankfurt, 1988–2009." *William Forsythe and the Practice of Choreography*, p. 15.

10. From "Closed Circuits." *New Yorker*, January 30, 1984. p. 84.

11. King as quoted in Reynolds and McCormick, p. 478.

12. Anawalt, Sasha. *The Joffrey Ballet: Robert Joffrey and the Making of an American Dance Company*. New York: Scribner, 1996. p. 344.

13. From "Robert Joffrey Breathes Ballet." *New York Times*, March 3, 1985. Accessed online at nytimes.com.

14. From "Americans from Abroad." *New Yorker*, December 5, 1983. As printed in *Sight Lines*. New York: Knopf, 1987. p. 149.

15. Fraser, John. *Private View: Inside Baryshnikov's American Ballet Theatre*. New York: Bantam Books, 1988. p. 61.

16. As quoted in Fraser, p. 63.

17. From "The Legacy," *New Yorker*, May 23, 1983. As printed in *Sight Lines*, p. 123.

18. Kisselgoff, Anna. "Baryshnikov Leaving Ballet Theater in '90." *New York Times*, June 22, 1989. Accessed online at nytimes.com.

19. Reynolds and McCormick, p. 539.

20. Croce, Arlene. "Signs and Portents." *New Yorker*, July 18, 1983. As printed in *Sight Lines*, p. 143.

21. Reynolds and McCormick, p. 558.

CHAPTER 9

1. As quoted in Conrad, Christine. *Jerome Robbins: That Broadway Man, That Ballet Man*. London: Booth-Clibborn Editions, 2000. p. 151.

2. As quoted in Lewis, Emory. "Helen Tamiris: Plain and Fancy." *Dance Magazine*, June 1955. p. 23.

3. Ewen, David. *The Story of America's Musical Theater*. Philadelphia: Chilton Book Co., 1968. p. 8.

4. Ewen, p. 58.

5. As quoted in Smith, Cecil. *Musical Comedy in America*. New York: Theatre Arts Books, 1981. p. 109.

6. Reynolds, Nancy, and Malcolm McCormick. *No Fixed Points: Dance in the Twentieth Century*. New Haven and London: Yale University Press, 2003. p. 683.

7. Ewen, p. 68.

8. "Numbers for Our Revues: Raising the Standard of the Specialties in Broadway Attractions." October 18, 1931. p. 110.

9. As quoted in Taper, Bernard. *Balanchine: A Biography*. Berkeley/London: University of California Press, 1996. p. 183.

10. As quoted in Ewen, p. 181.

11. *America Dances*. New York: Macmillan, 1980. p. 188.

12. *The Borzoi Book of Modern Dance*. New York: Dance Horizons, 1969. p. 333.

13. "The New Play." *New York Times*, March 14, 1947. p. 28.

14. "Jack Cole: 'Magdalena,' the Roxy and An Artist of Gifts." *New York Times*, November 7, 1948. p. X6.

15. Reynolds and McCormick, p. 697.

16. Smith, p. 235.

17. As quoted in Conrad, p. 205.

18. "From Jerome Robbins, 20 Years of Broadway the Way It Was." February 27, 1989. Accessed online at nytimes.com.

19. As quoted in Jamison, Barbara. "Kidd from Brooklyn." *New York Times Magazine*, June 13, 1954. p. 42.

20. *Musical Comedy in America*. p. 339.

21. *Fosse*. Boston/New York: Eamon Dolan/Houghton Mifflin Harcourt, 2013. p. 95.

22. As quoted in Wasson, *Fosse*, p. 207.

23. "A Chorus Line." *New York Times*, May 22, 1975. Accessed online at nytimes.com.

24. "In a Top 40 State Of Mind." *New York Times*, October 25, 2002. Accessed online at nytimes.com.

25. *America Dances*, p. 199.

26. Reynolds and McCormick, p. 721.

27. *Gotta Sing, Gotta Dance: A History of Film Musicals*. London/New York: Hamlyn, 1970. p. 279.

28. As quoted in Kobal. *Gotta Sing, Gotta Dance*, p. 298.

29. Reynolds and McCormick, p. 737.

CHAPTER 10

1. As quoted in Schloss, Joseph Glenn. *Foundation: B-Boys, B-Girls, and Hip-Hop Culture in New York*. Oxford/New York: Oxford University Press, 2009. p. 68.

2. "To the Beat Y'all: Breaking Is Hard to Do." *Village Voice*, April 10, 1981. As printed in *Writing Dancing in the Age of Postmodernism*. Hanover: University Press of New England, 1994. p. 121.

3. As quoted in Schloss, p. 125.

4. "Breakdancing: A Reporter's Story." *Folklife Annual*, 1986. As printed in *Writing Dancing*, p. 132.

5. Guzman-Sanchez, Thomas. *Underground Dance Masters: Final History of A Forgotten Era*. Santa Barbara, CA: Praeger, 2012. pp. 10–15, 25.

6. As quoted in Guzman-Sanchez, p. 34.

7. Rajakumar, Mohanalakshmi. *Hip Hop Dance*. Santa Barbara, CA: Greenwood, 2012. p. xv.

8. Rajakumar, p. xxi.

9. As quoted in Banes, "To the Beat Y'all," *Village Voice*. As printed in *Writing Dancing*, p. 123.

10. Rajakumar, p. xxxviii.

11. Schloss, p. 18.

12. As quoted in Schloss, p. 59.

13. "To the Beat Y'all," *Village Voice*. As printed in *Writing Dancing*, p. 122.

14. As quoted in Rajakumar, p. 19.

15. As quoted in Banes, Sally. "Breaking." *Fresh: Hip Hop Don't Stop*. Co-authored with Nelson George, Susan Flinker, and Patty Romanowski. New York: Random House/Sarah Lazin, 1985. As printed in *Writing Dancing*, p. 147.

16. *Foundation*, p. 87.

17. As quoted in Bloom, Julie. "Street Moves, in the TV Room." *The New York Times*, June 8, 2008. Accessed online at nytimes.com.

18. As quoted in Zimmer, Elizabeth. "Fusing Shakespeare, Hip-hop Dance: Rennie Harris' 'Rome And Jewels' Premieres Here Before Embarking On A World Tour." *The Philadelphia Inquirer*, June 16, 2000. Accessed online at philly.com.

19. "Mesmerizing Moves." *Dance Magazine*, August 2013. p. 26.

20. As quoted in Guzman-Sanchez, p. 122.

21. "Why Michael Jackson danced like no one else." Culture Monster blog, *Los Angeles Times*. June 26, 2009. Accessed at latimesblogs.com.

22. As quoted in Barnes, Brooks. "Realignment of Star Power." *New York Times*, September 25, 2011. Accessed online at nytimes.com.

23. La Rocco, Claudia. "Yes, They All Do Think They Can Dance." November 16, 2008. Accessed online at nytimes.com.

Bibliography

BOOKS

Acocella, Joan. *Mark Morris*. New York: The Noonday Press, 1993.

Anawait, Sasha. *The Joffrey Ballet: Robert Joffrey and the Making of an American Dance Company*. New York: Scribner, 1996.

Anderson, Janet. *Modern Dance*. New York: Chelsea House, 2010.

Balanchine, George. *Balanchine's Complete Stories of the Great Ballets*. Francis Mason, ed. New York: Doubleday, 1954.

Balliett, Whitney. *Such Sweet Thunder: Forty-Nine Pieces on Jazz*. Indianapolis: Bobbs-Merrill Co., 1966.

Banes, Sally. *Democracy's Body*. Ann Arbor, MI: UNI Research Press, 1983.

_____. *Terpsichore in Sneakers: Post-Modern Dance*. Middletown, CT: Wesleyan University Press, 1987.

_____. *Writing Dancing in the Age of Postmodernism*. Hanover, NH: University Press of New England, 1994.

Barrère, Dorothy B., Mary Kawena Pukui and Marion Kelly. *Hula: Historical Perspectives*. Honolulu: Department of Anthropology, Bernice Pauahi Bishop Museum, 1980.

Bischoff, Eugene H. *American Indian Dances: Cut and Color*. Albuquerque: Eukabi Pub, 1952.

Bland, Alexander. *A History of Ballet and Dance in the Western World*. New York: Praeger Publishers, 1976.

Bordman, Gerald Martin. *American Musical Theatre: A Chronicle*. New York: Oxford University Press, 2001.

Brown, Carolyn. *Chance and Circumstance: Twenty Years with Cage and Cunningham*. New York: Alfred A. Knopf, 2007.

Castle, Mr. and Mrs. Vernon. *Modern Dancing*. New York: Harper and Brothers, 1914.

Chang, Jeff. *Can't Stop Won't Stop: A History of the Hip-Hop Generation*. New York: St. Martin's Press, 2005.

Chujoy, Anatole. *The New York City Ballet*. New York: Alfred A. Knopf, 1953.

Cobb, William Jelani. *To the Break of Dawn: A Freestyle on the Hip Hop Aesthetic*. New York: New York University Press, 2007.

Collier, John. *American Indian Ceremonial Dances: Navajo, Pueblo, Apache, Zuni*. New York: Bounty Books (a division of Crown Publishers), 1972. (First published in 1949 under title: *Patterns and Ceremonials of the Indians of the Southwest*.)

Conrad, Christine. *Jerome Robbins: That Broadway Man, That Ballet Man*. London: Booth-Clibborn Editions, 2000.

Croce, Arlene. *Afterimages*. New York: Alfred A. Knopf, 1977.

_____. *Sight Lines*. New York: Alfred A. Knopf, 1987.

Current, Richard Nelson. *Loie Fuller: Goddess of Light*. Boston: Northeastern University Press, 1997.

De Mille, Agnes. *America Dances*. New York: Macmillan Publishing Co., 1980.

_____. *Dance to the Piper*. Boston: Little, Brown, 1952.

Denby, Edwin. *Dancers, Buildings, and People in the Streets*. New York: Horizon Press Publishers, 1965.

_____. *Looking at the Dance*. New York: Horizon Press, 1968.

Dickens, Charles. *American Notes*. London: Chapman & Hall, Ltd., 1913. Accessed online at www.gutenberg.org/files/675/675-h/675-h.htm on August 4, 2013.

Driver, Ian. *A Century of Dance: A Hundred Years of Musical Movement, from Waltz to Hip Hop*. London: Octopus Publishing Group Limited, 2000.

Duncan, Isadora. *The Art of the Dance*. Sheldon Cheney, ed. Theatre Arts Books, 1928.

_____. *My Life*. New York: London: Liveright, 1995. (First published in 1927 by Boni & Liveright, Inc.)

Dunning, Jennifer. *Alvin Ailey: A Life in Dance*. Reading, MA: Addison-Wesley, 1996.

Emery, Lynne Fauley. *Black Dance: From 1619 to Today*. Princeton, NJ: Princeton Book Co., 1988.

Engel, Lehman. *The American Musical Theater*. New York: Macmillan, 1975.

Evans, Bessie and May G. *American Indian Dance Steps*. New York: Hacker Art Books, 1975. (Reprint of the 1931 ed. published by A. S. Barnes, New York.)

Ewen, David. *The Story of America's Musical Theater*. Philadelphia: Chilton Book Co., 1968.

Fitzgerald, Tamsin. *Hip Hop and Urban Dance*. Chicago: Heinemann Library/Pearson Inc., 2010.

Frank, Rusty E. *Tap! The Greatest Tap Dance Stars and Their Stories, 1900–1955*. New York: Da Capo Press, 1994.

Franks, A. H. *Social Dance: A Short History*. London: Routledge, Paul and Kegan, 1963.

Fraser, John. *Private View: Inside Baryshnikov's American Ballet Theatre*. New York: Bantam Books, 1988.

García-Márquez, Vicente. *The Ballets Russes: Colonel de Basil's Ballets Russes de Monte Carlo, 1932–1952*. New York: Alfred A. Knopf, 1990.

Gilbert, Douglas. *American Vaudeville: Its Life and Times*. New York: Dover Publications, 1963.

Gilvey, John Anthony. *Before the Parade Passes By: Gower Champion and the Glorious American Musical*. New York: St. Martin's Press, 2005.

Giordano, Ralph G. *Social Dancing in America: A History and Reference*. Westport, CT: Greenwood Press, 2007. Vols. 1 and 2.

Goodwin, Andrew. *Dancing in the Distraction Factory: Music Television and Popular Culture*. Minneapolis: University of Minnesota Press, 1992.

Gottfried, Martin. *Broadway Musicals*. New York: H. N. Abrams, 1979.

_____. *More Broadway Musicals Since 1980*. New York: H. N. Abrams, 1991.

Graham, Martha. *Blood Memory: An Autobiography*. New York and London: Doubleday, 1991.

Guzman-Sanchez, Thomas. *Underground Dance Masters: Final History of a Forgotten Era*. Santa Barbara, CA: Praeger, 2012.

Hazzard-Gordon, Katrina. *Jookin': The Rise of Social Dance Formations in African-American Culture*. Philadelphia: Temple University Press, 1990.

Heth, Charlotte, ed. *Native American Dance: Ceremonies and Traditions*. Washington, D.C.: Smithsonian Institution with Starwood Publishing, Inc., 1992.

Highwater, Jamake. *Ritual of the Wind: North American Indian Ceremonies, Music, and Dances*. New York: Viking Press, 1977.

Homans, Jennifer. *Apollo's Angels: A History of Ballet*. New York: Random House, 2010.

Johnston, Jill. *Marmalade Me*. New York: Dutton, 1971.

Jones, Alan, and Jussi Kantonen. *Saturday Night Forever: The Story of Disco*. Chicago: A Capella Books, 2000.

Jowitt, Deborah. *The Dance in Mind*. Boston: David Godine, 1985.

_____. *Time and the Dancing Image*. New York: William Morrow, 1988.

Kirstein, Lincoln. *Thirty Years: The New York City Ballet*. New York: Alfred A. Knopf, 1978.

Kobal, John. *Gotta Sing, Gotta Dance: A History of Film Musicals*. London and New York: Hamlyn, 1970.

Laubin, Reginald, and Gladys. *Indian Dances of North America: Their Importance to Indian Life*. Norman: University of Oklahoma Press, 1977.

Laurie, Joe Jr. *Vaudeville*. New York: Henry Holt & Co., 1953.

Lewis-Ferguson, Julinda. *Alvin Ailey, Jr.: A Life in Dance*. New York: Walker and Company, 1994.

Lloyd, Margaret. *The Borzoi Book of Modern Dance*. New York: Dance Horizons, 1969.

Lukens, Robert L., and Robert W. Miller. *Hula: Dance of the Islands*. Honolulu: Hawaiian School of Hula Dancing, 1935.

Magriel, Paul, ed. *Chronicles of the American Dance*. New York: Henry Holt and Company, 1948.

Mason, Bernard S. *Dances and Stories of the American Indian*. New York: The Ronald Press Company, 1944.

Maurer, Tracy. *Tap Dancing: Let's Dance*. Vero Beach, FL: Rourke Press, 1997.

Maynard, Olga. *The American Ballet*. Philadelphia: Macrae Smith Co., 1959.

_____. *American Modern Dancers: The Pioneers*. Boston: Little, Brown, 1965.

McDonagh, Don. *The Rise and Fall and Rise of Modern Dance*. Pennington, NJ: A Cappella Books, 1990. (First published in 1970 by Outerbridge.)

Nash, Barbara. *Tap Dance*. Dubuque, IA: W. C. Brown Co., 1969.

Needham, Maureen, ed. *I See America Dancing: Selected Readings 1685–2000*. Chicago: University of Illinois Press, 2002.

Nevell, Richard. *A Time to Dance: American Country Dancing from Hornpipe to Hot Hash*. New York: St. Martin's Press, 1977.

Osterreich, Shelley Anne. *The American Indian Ghost Dance, 1870 and 1890: An Annotated Bibliography*. New York: Greenwood Press, 1991.

Payne, Charles. *American Ballet Theatre*. New York: Alfred A. Knopf, 1977.

Perron, Wendy. *Through the Eyes of a Dancer*. Middletown, CT: Wesleyan University Press, 2013.

Rajakumar, Mohanalakshmi. *Hip Hop Dance*. Santa Barbara, CA: Greenwood Press, 2012.

Rees, Heather. *Tap Dancing: Rhythm in Their Feet*. Ramsbury, UK: The Crowood Press, 2003.

Reynolds, Nancy, and Malcom McCormick. *No Fixed Points: Dance in the Twentieth Century*. New Haven, CT: Yale University Press, 2003.

Reynolds, Simon. *Bring the Noise: 20 Years of Writing About Hip Rock and Hip Hop*. Berkeley, CA: Soft Skull Press, 2011.

Rogosin, Elinor. *The Dance Makers: Conversations with American Choreographers*. New York: Walker, 1980.

Roseman, Janet Lynn. *Dance Masters: Interviews with Legends of Dance*. New York: Routledge, 2001.

Ruyter, Nancy Lee Chalfa. *Reformers and Visionaries: The Americanization of the Art of Dance*. New York: Dance Horizons, 1979.

Schloss, Joseph Glenn. *Foundation: B-Boys, B-Girls, and Hip-Hop Culture in New York*. New York: Oxford University Press, 2009.

Schlundt, Christina L. *Dance in the Musical Theatre: Jerome Robbins and His Peers, 1934–1965: A Guide*. New York: Garland Publishing, Inc., 1989.

Shawn, Ted. *Ruth St. Denis, Pioneer and Prophet*. San Francisco: J. H. Nash, 1920.

Sherman, Jane. *The Drama of Denishawn Dance*. New York: M. Mathesius, 2005.

Siegel, Marcia B. *At the Vanishing Point: A Critic Looks at Dance*. New York: Saturday Review Press, 1972.

Smith, Cecil. *Musical Comedy in America*. New York: Theatre Arts Books, 1981.

Smith, Karen Lynn. *Popular Dance: From Ballroom to Hip-Hop*. New York: Chelsea House Publishers, 2010.

Sorrell, Walter, ed. *The Dance Has Many Faces*. 3d ed. Pennington, NJ: A Cappella Books, 1992.

Spier, Steven, ed. *William Forsythe and the Practice of Choreography: It Starts from Any Point*. New York: Routledge, 2011.

Squires, John L., and Robert E. McLean. *American Indian Dances: Steps, Rhythms, Costumes and Interpretation*. New York: Ronald Press Company, 1963.

Stearns, Marshall Winslow and Jean. *Jazz Dance: The Story of American Vernacular Dance*. New York: Da Capo Press, 1994.

St. Denis, Ruth. *An Unfinished Life*. New York: Dance Horizons, 1969.

Stephenson, Richard M., and Joseph Iaccarino. *The Complete Book of Ballroom Dancing*. New York: Doubleday, 1992.

Taper, Bernard. *Balanchine: A Biography*. Berkeley, CA: University of California Press, 1996.

Taylor, Paul. *Private Domain*. New York: Alfred A. Knopf, 1987.

Teachout, Terry. *All in the Dances: A Brief Life of George Balanchine*. New York: Harcourt, Inc., 2004.

Tharp, Twyla. *Push Comes to Shove: An Autobiography*. New York: Bantam Books, 1992.

Valis Hill, Constance. *Tap Dancing America: A Cultural History*. New York: Oxford University Press, 2010.

Vaughan, David. *Merce Cunningham: Fifty Years*. New York: Aperture, 1997.

Wagner, Ann Louise. *Adversaries of Dance: From the Puritans to the Present*. Chicago: University of Illinois Press, 1997.

Wallace, Carol McD., Don McDonagh, Jean L. Druesedow, Laurence Libin, and Constance Old. *Dance: A Very Social History*. New York: The Metropolitan Museum of Art and Rizzoli International Publications, Inc., 1986.

Warren, Larry. *Lester Horton: Modern Dance Pioneer*. Princeton, NJ: Dance Horizons/Princeton Book Co., 1991.

Wasson, Sam. *Fosse*. Boston and New York: Eamon Dolan and Houghton Mifflin Harcourt, 2013.

ARTICLES

Acocella, Joan. "Twos and Threes." *New Yorker*, May 4, 2009, p. 77.

Atkinson, Brooks. "The New Play." *New York Times*, March 14, 1947, p. 28.

Axtmann, Ann. "A Diaspora of Native American Dance." *Congress on Research in Dance Conference* (34th: 2001: New York University). Proceedings, vol. 2, pp. 312–319.

Barnes, Brooks. "Realignment of Star Power." *New York Times*, September 25, 2011. Accessed online at nytimes.com.

Barnes, Clive. "A Chorus Line." *New York Times*, May 22, 1975. Accessed online at nytimes.com.

Bloom, Julie. "Street Moves, in the TV Room." *New York Times*, June 8, 2008. Accessed online at nytimes.com.

Bracker, Milton. "Experts Propose Study of 'Craze': Liken it to Medieval Lunacy, 'Contagious Dance Furies' and Bite of Tarantula." *New York Times*, February 23, 1957, p. 12.

Brantley, Ben. "In a Top 40 State Of Mind." *New York Times*, October 25, 2002. Accessed online at nytimes.com.

Cohn, Ellen. "Alvin Ailey, Arsonist: Modern Dance Is Getting Hot." *New York Times Magazine*, April 29, 1973, p. 286.

Croce, Arlene. "Closed Circuits." *New Yorker*, January 30, 1984, pp. 84–87.

———. "Discussing the Undiscussable." *New Yorker*, December 26, 1994, p. 54.

Dunning, Jennifer. "Alvin Ailey, a Leading Figure In Modern Dance, Dies at 58." *New York Times*, December 2, 1989. Obituaries. Accessed online at nytimes.com.

———. "Premiere by Lar Lubovitch." *New York Times*, May 9, 1985. Accessed online at nytimes.com.

———. "Robert Joffrey Breathes Ballet." *New York Times*, March 3, 1985. Accessed online at nytimes.com.

Granert, Ruth E. "Alwin Nikolais's Total Theater." *Dance Magazine*, December 1979, pp. 56–69.

Harss, Marina. "Mesmerizing Moves." *Dance Magazine*, August 2013, pp. 26–30.

Howard, James Henri. "Pan-Indianism in Native American Dance." *Ethnomusicology*. Ann Arbor, MI: v. 27, no. 1, January 1983, pp. 71–82.

Jamison, Barbara. "Kidd from Brooklyn." *New York Times Magazine*, June 13, 1954, p. 42.

Johnston, Jill. "Judson concerts #3, #4." *Village Voice*, February 28, 1963.

Kaufman, Sarah. "Obituary for Modernist Choreographer Merce Cunningham." *Washington Post*, July 28, 2009. Accessed online at washingtonpost.com.

Kisselgoff, Anna. "Baryshnikov Leaving Ballet Theater in '90." *New York Times*, June 22, 1989. Accessed online at nytimes.com.

———. "Martha Graham Dies at 96; A Revolutionary in Dance." *New York Times*, April 2, 1991. Accessed online at nytimes.com.

Lang, Pearl. "Lang: Speaking for Herself." *Dance Magazine*, September 1974, pp. 50–53.

La Rocco, Claudia. "Yes, They All Do Think They Can Dance." *New York Times*, November 16, 2008. Accessed online at nytimes.com.

Lewis, Emory. "Helen Tamiris: Plain and Fancy." *Dance Magazine*, June 1955, pp. 21–23, 68, 74–79.

Macel, Emily. "The Fast and the Furious." *Dance Magazine*, May 2008. Accessed online at dancemagazine.com.

Martin, John. "The Dance: Native Talent." *New York Times*, November 19, 1933, p. X2.

———. "The GI Makes With the Hot Foot." *New York Times Magazine*, January 9, 1944, p. SM14.

———. "Jack Cole: 'Magdalena,' the Roxy and An Artist of Gifts." *New York Times*, November 7, 1948, p. X6.

———. "Numbers for Our Revues: Raising the Standard of the Specialties in Broadway Attractions." *New York Times*, October 18, 1931, p. 110.

———. "Study in Despair; Anna Sokolow's 'Rooms' Has Premiere at ANTA Theatre to Score by Kenyon." *New York Times*, May 16, 1955, p. 26

McGuire, Mabelle B., and Ellen W. Jacobs. "Hula." *Dance Magazine*, December 1969, pp. 59–61, 82.

McNamara, Maggie. "Bending Reality." *Dance Spirit*, March 2014, pp. 64–67.

Nikolais, Alwin. "Dance: Semantics." *New York Times*, August 18, 1957, p. X12.

Orts, Neil Ellis. "Louis Horst." *Dance Teacher*, February 2010. Accessed online at dance-teacher.com.

Rainer, Yvonne. "Some Retrospective Notes on a Dance for 10 People and 12 Mattresses Called 'Parts of Some Sextets,' Performed at the Wadsworth Atheneum, Hartford, Connecticut, and Judson Memorial Church, New York, in March 1965," *Tulane Drama Review* 10 (T-30, Winter 1965), p. 168.

Rich, Frank. "From Jerome Robbins, 20 Years of Broadway the Way It Was." *New York Times*, February 27, 1989. Accessed online at nytimes.com.

Riding, Alan. "A Star Everywhere Else, a Stranger at Home." *New York Times*, October 8, 2000. Accessed online at nytimes.com.

Roy, Sanjay. "Step-by-Step Guide to Dance: American Ballet Theatre." *The Guardian*, March 17, 2009. Accessed online at theguardian.com.

———. "Step-by-Step Guide to Dance: William Forsythe." *The Guardian*, October 6, 2008. Accessed online at theguardian.com.

Segal, Lewis. "Why Michael Jackson Danced Like No One Else." Culture Monster blog, *Los Angeles Times*, June 26, 2009. Accessed at latimesblogs.com.

Sherman, Jane. "The American Indian Imagery of Ted Shawn." *Dance Chronicle*. Vol. 12, No. 3 (1989), pp. 366–382.

Solway, Diane. "Is It Dance? Maybe. Political? Sure." *New York Times*, February 18, 2007. Accessed online at nytimes.com.

Sommer, Sally R. "Tap Dance." *The International Encyclopedia of Dance*. New York: Oxford University Press, 2004. Accessed online at oxfordreference.com.

Stillman, Amy Kuʻuleialoha. "Hula." *The International Encyclopedia of Dance*. New York: Oxford University Press, 2004. Accessed online at oxfordreference.com.

Sulcas, Roslyn. "Follow Every Rainbow, Search High and Low." *New York Times*, December 14, 2009. Accessed online at nytimes.com.

Todd, Arthur. "Four Centuries of American Dance: Dance of the American Indian." *Dance Magazine*, September 1949, pp. 18–19, 30–31.

Valis Hill, Constance. "Tap Dance in America: A Very Short History." 2002. Accessed online at nypl.org.

Weber, Bruce. "Jeni LeGon, Singer and Solo Tap-Dancer, Dies at 96." *New York Times*, December 16, 2012, p. A33.

Wein Shiovitz, Brynn. "It's About Time: Mastering The Time Step." *Dance Spirit*, April 2010. Accessed online at dancespirit.com.

Willis, Cheryl M. "Tap Dance: Manifestation of the African Aesthetic." From *African Dance*, edited by Kariamu Welsh Asante. Trenton, NJ: Africa World Press, 1996, pp. 145–159.

Wolfe, Tom. "The Peppermint Lounge Revisited." In *The Kandy-Kolored Tangerine-Flake Streamline Baby*. New York: Bantam Books, 1999. pp. 51–56.

Zimmer, Elizabeth. "Fusing Shakespeare, Hip-hop Dance: Rennie Harris' 'Rome And Jewels' Premieres Here Before Embarking On A World Tour." *Philadelphia Inquirer*, June 16, 2000. Accessed online at philly.com.

Acknowledgments

As a journalist, not a historian, it was with great anxiety that I began working on a book covering such a massive swath of dance history—history that means so much to dance's artists and enthusiasts. I'm deeply indebted to my editor, Grace Labatt, who convinced me I could do this, talked me off several ledges along the way, and provided gentle, kind, discerning guidance.

The New York Public Library for the Performing Arts became my second home as I wrote. Without its wonderful staff, particularly the specialists of the Jerome Robbins Dance Division, I would have researched in circles. I spent so many happy afternoons on the library's third floor perusing their recommendations.

To the past and present editors of *Dance Spirit*, *Pointe*, and *Dance Magazine*: It's been a heck of a lot of fun working alongside you. I'm constantly impressed by, and grateful for, the fantastic depths of your dance nerdiness. Thanks to Kina Poon, Alison Feller, Katie Rolnick, Jenny Dalzell, Rachel Zar, and Michael Bailey for not only tolerating book-related crankiness but also cheering me on (and up) during this process. Thanks also to my other New York cheerleaders, Katie Drabble, Courtney Mee, and Meghan Muntean, who've rooted for my dance writing from the beginning.

I grew up idolizing Wendy Perron and her keen, incisive essays and criticism. So my eighteen-year-old self would have a conniption upon reading this next sentence: Without Wendy's knowledge and support, Chapter 7 in particular would have been a daunting uphill climb. (Please go buy a copy of her lovely book, *Through the Eyes of a Dancer*.)

Alicia Graf Mack humbles me. Another longtime idol, she is not only one of the world's most extraordinary dancers, but also a writer of elegance and vivacity. It's an honor to have her words, her thoughtful perspective on a world she knows from the inside out, open this history.

To the dance teachers who unlocked ballet for me, especially Kathryn Anderson, Chip Morris, and Elaine Bauer: Thank you for the introduction to a field so rich, so all-consuming, so transcendent. A perpetual know-it-all, I couldn't have been the easiest student, but you recognized and nurtured what has become my life's defining passion. I'm grateful, too, to the writers and professors who helped me translate that passion into words, especially Katie Roiphe, Susie Linfield, and William C. Jordan.

The stories I tell about my "Disney" family tend to raise eyebrows. But they're all true. (The one about group sing-alongs on long car rides? That still happens.) I loved growing up in a house full of music, and I'm continually inspired by the talents of my brothers, John and Jeffrey, and my parents. Mom and Dad—I don't know how you made it through all those ballet performances, not to mention hours upon hours of dance videos, but thank you for always watching "with quiet courage." You're also two of the best editors a writer could ask for. From the beginning you've helped bring my frequently blurry thoughts into focus, pushing me to look closer, think harder, be better.

Finally, to my "silent partner": I won't embarrass you. Thank you for everything.

About the Author

Margaret Fuhrer, editor in chief of *Dance Spirit* magazine and former editor at *Dance Magazine* and *Pointe*, is an arts writer living in New York City. A longtime dancer and choreographer, she has a bachelor's degree in history from Princeton University and a master's degree in journalism from New York University.

Index